FORENSIC FILES NOW
Inside 40 Unforgettable True Crime Cases

REBECCA REISNER

D1319283

Prometheus Books

Essex, Connecticut

An imprint of Globe Pequot, the trade division of The Rowman & Littlefield Publishing Group, Inc.
4501 Forbes Blvd., Ste. 200
Lanham, MD 20706
www.rowman.com

Distributed by NATIONAL BOOK NETWORK

British Library Cataloguing in Publication Information Available

Library of Congress Cataloging-in-Publication Data
Names: Reisner, Rebecca, 1963– author.
Title: Forensic files now : inside 40 unforgettable true crime cases / Rebecca Reisner.
Description: Lanham : Prometheus, [2022] | Summary: "In Forensic Files Now, author Rebecca Reisner shares her own gripping retellings of 40 favorite cases profiled on the hit TV show along with fascinating updates adapted from her popular blog, ForensicFilesNow.com, and a Foreword by Forensic Files creator Paul Dowling"—Provided by publisher.
Identifiers: LCCN 2022011971 (print) | LCCN 2022011972 (ebook) | ISBN 9781633888289 (paperback) | ISBN 9781633888296 (epub)
Subjects: LCSH: Forensic sciences—Case studies. | Criminal investigation—Case studies. | Murder—Case studies.
Classification: LCC HV8079.H6 R45 2022 (print) | LCC HV8079.H6 (ebook) | DDC 363.25/9523—dc23/eng/20220419
LC record available at https://lccn.loc.gov/2022011971
LC ebook record available at https://lccn.loc.gov/2022011972

For Estelle S. Reisner and in memory of Gerald S. Reisner

Contents

Foreword

Paul Dowling

As the creator of *Forensic Files*, I'm often asked why the program has enjoyed such global success for 25 years. The truth is, I really don't know. It was the first forensic crime series, so that helped. We had great cases, storytelling, production . . . but so do a lot of other programs. I tell my kids: timing. We were at the right place at the right time.

Forensic Files was, from the start, a different kind of a true-crime series. For one, we made it a half hour rather than an hour, so the story moves along quickly. We avoided the teases before and recaps after commercial breaks . . . they waste valuable storytelling time. We produced original music to add to the drama. And the choice of Peter Thomas as the original narrator, with his "around the campfire" delivery, certainly added the special sauce.

The goal was to make *Forensic Files* as mysterious and riveting as a great crime movie. For example, when we interviewed a killer in prison, we took him or her out of prison garb to avoid giving the ending away. When we re-created scenes, we took extra care to duplicate everything from the original crime: crashes, sinkings, firearms, explosives, even animals. All had to match what really happened, and it had to be done safely. We had zero accidents in more than 400 episodes.

At the heart of any true-crime series are the cases that are covered. Are there real mysteries? In the case of *Forensic Files*, how is science involved in the investigations? Our mantra was "How did science catch the bad guy?"

Looking back over the past 25 years, I knew we made a great television program. What no one could have known is the impact *Forensic Files* had. Criminalistics became a career choice and part of school curriculums all over the world. Forensic scientists became celebrities, cases became famous, and social media exploded. Viewer groups discussed their favorite episodes and hated criminals, and fans bragged of watching episodes multiple times.

Forensic Files has been truly unprecedented in television history. For its 25 über-successful years on the air, it has achieved global popularity, been lauded for its trendsetting production and storytelling style, and has lifted up science and law enforcement by making sure certain people know they're "not gonna get away with it."

Rebecca's book takes a deep dive into *Forensic Files* and even more so into the hearts and minds of the viewers who love it. As Peter Thomas says, "Thanks for watching *Forensic Files*."

Introduction

Opening Statement from the Book Author

Why has *Forensic Files* had a hold on me since it debuted in 1996? I've watched some of my favorite episodes upward of 10 times.

I've always enjoyed true crime, but I have only a marginal interest in things like mitochondrial DNA and medium-velocity blood splatter—the scientific content that made *Forensic Files* famous.

The first reason is structure. The writers and editors tell the story in a compact way so it never gets tiresome.

And *Forensic Files'* writing is unpretentious. Sure, the scripts toss around "succinylcholine" and "mass spectrometry," but that's only because they're vital to the story. Otherwise, you'll hear words we can all understand.

As Paul Dowling once recounted to me: "A screenwriter had me look at a script, and I said, 'What does this word mean? I have two college degrees and I don't know.' If you were at a picnic or dinner party and someone used that word, how would it make you feel?" (I went back and changed "matricide" to "murder" in my very first blog post.)

Next, it fascinates me that people who look and act like typical PTA-attending moms and dads—the kind of folks who would feel guilty about grabbing the last cupcake in the office break room—can dial down their consciences enough to murder their spouses and make their own children half orphans.

I guess the series's number one attraction is the biographical element of the stories. The late narrator Peter Thomas told the show's tales compassionately without exploiting the victims or manipulating viewers' emotions.

But what about what happens after the closing guitar chords? The sentence-long epilogues that the producers started adding to the final credits are great, but I want more. I need more.

Why did Ron Gillette, who murdered his wife by pressing her face into a plastic bag, get out of jail after only 15 years?

How did neighbors react when they discovered that wealthy, retired factory owner Howard Elkins beat his pregnant girlfriend to death and stored her body in a barrel under his house for 30 years?

What ever happened to 12-year-old Collier Boyle, who testified against his father, Jack Boyle, MD, for killing his mother?

For each chapter of this book, I've taken posts and added something new: an interview that fills in the blanks or gives additional perspectives or "updates the updates" since I first wrote about the cases for my blog starting in 2016.

Please come along with me for our own investigation.

Anthony Pignataro

Bad Plastic Surgeon

And Even Worse Husband

Forensic Files *episode "Bad Medicine"*

The *Forensic Files* episode about Dr. Anthony Pignataro isn't in heavy rotation on TV, so you may not have caught it multiple times.

But really, all one needs is a single viewing to remember it forever. "Bad Medicine" tells of how a cosmetic surgeon accidentally kills a patient, then deliberately poisons his wife.

And here's the part that's pretty much impossible to forget.

Years before his crimes, Anthony Pignataro made a name for himself as the inventor of the snap-on toupee, which attaches to a man's head via bolts surgically implanted in the skull.

Pignataro started losing his hair at age 23 and was his own first customer.

I'm not sure whether it was due to the hairpiece, but Pignataro thought an awful lot of himself. Once he opened his own plastic surgery facility, he didn't see the need to hire an anesthesiologist or a qualified nurse to help him.

For Pignataro, those deficiencies eventually led to prison time and the loss of his livelihood. For this chapter, I looked into what Pignataro, who was released in 2013, is doing today.

But first, here's a recap of the episode, along with other information culled from internet research as well as Ann Rule's book about the case, *Last Dance, Last Chance* (2003).

Deborah Rago was born into a financially strained family in Williamsville, New York, in 1957.

In 1978, when Debbie was working as a pharmacy technician, she met Lehigh University student Anthony Pignataro, whom Rule described as almost six feet tall with classic, balanced features. The guy also possessed some charm. "He had an easy way of talking, very smooth," recalls investigative reporter Charlie Specht, who later covered Pignataro's case for the Buffalo station WKBW.

One night, Debbie and Anthony fell in love on the dance floor to the Donna Summer hit "Last Dance."

Anthony was the son of Ralph Pignataro, a respected surgeon in Buffalo, New York. He wanted to follow his father into the profession. The mainland U.S. medical schools Anthony applied to rejected him, so he enrolled at the San Juan Bautista School of Medicine in Puerto Rico.

Debbie waited for him to finish, and they finally married in 1985. Within the first year, a concerned party tipped her off that Anthony was cheating on her.

She took her father's advice to "forgive once" and decided that Anthony deserved another chance.

The professionals at the hospitals where the young surgeon worked, on the other hand, didn't think the guy merited any chance as a physician.

They figured out pretty quickly that the arrogant doctor in their midst had some scary gaps in his knowledge.

But incompetent people rarely get kicked out of their fields right away.

Pignataro eventually opened his own plastic surgery practice in the Buffalo suburb of West Seneca, New York.

He made a fortune doing breast implants and other cosmetic procedures. To widen his profit margin, Pignataro skimped on overhead costs. He hired a licensed practical nurse (instead of a registered nurse) and a high school student to assist him during procedures.

The Pignataros had a son and daughter by this time and lived in a big house in West Seneca. Anthony and his toupee cruised around in a red Lamborghini.

Meanwhile, he made some bad surgical mistakes. After he performed an abdominoplasty on a patient named Terri LaMarti and sent her home, she had, as she said, blood "pooling at my feet" and felt excruciating pain, but Pignataro angrily yelled at her and her husband when they complained, according to her interviews with WKBW and the Oxygen Network. She ended up going to the emergency room and ultimately needing 13 more surgeries to fix the damage Pignataro caused, according to WKBW.

But back in those pre-Yelp days, word didn't get around fast enough, and the practice continued to thrive until tragedy struck.

In 1996, a 26-year-old mother of two from Depew, New York, stopped breathing during a breast augmentation operation. Pignataro's facility didn't have a ventilator, and Sarah Smith died.

The investigation that followed laid bare Anthony Pignataro's incompetence for all the world to see.

It turned out that he wasn't a board-certified plastic surgeon or even a qualified plastic surgeon. He hadn't administered Sarah Smith's anesthetic properly. The New York state health board ended up charging him with 30 counts of professional misconduct.

Anthony pleaded guilty to criminally negligent homicide and received six months in jail, a $5,000 fine, and community service. He lost his medical license. Judge Ronald H. Tills noted that Pignataro would "never practice medicine again—anywhere in the world."

And there wasn't any fancy legal footwork to delay jail time. The judge had Pignataro taken directly from the courtroom to a prison cell, while Debbie Pignataro "sobbed in the back row," according to a 1998 Associated Press story.

After his release, Anthony had trouble finding another job, but Debbie stood by him. His well-to-do mother, Lena Pignataro, helped out the family financially.

Anthony had another affair, and Debbie took him back again.

But soon, emotional anguish was the least of her problems. In 1999, Debbie started feeling ill with nausea and numbness of the limbs. She had severe pain elsewhere. The symptoms came and went. When they were bad, she had to stay in bed.

Debbie began having memory loss and needed to use a wheelchair at times.

Anthony told her the answer was to have her gallbladder removed, but her doctors vetoed that plan; they said surgery would kill her in her weakened state.

Finally, one of her doctors did a hair test and found Debbie had consumed 29,580 milligrams of arsenic.

Anthony suggested that the family of Sarah Smith, the patient who died, was poisoning Debbie to punish him. But the arsenic was traced to some ant insecticide the good doctor had purchased himself.

He was sneaking arsenic into his wife's food, investigators determined.

The prosecution found evidence suggesting that Anthony hoped the arsenic poisoning would cause Debbie to die during surgery so that the medical establishment would see that it was normal for operations to kill people sometimes—and he would thus be absolved for Sarah Smith's death.

Anthony Pignataro ended up pleading guilty to charges related to the arsenic poisoning. Judge Mario J. Rossetti labeled the former surgeon's life "a charade of misrepresentation," called him self-centered and manipulative, and said he showed "disrespect for the value of human life," as reported in *Last Dance, Last Chance*.

Rossetti gave him 15 years.

Despite his guilty plea, Anthony at various times claimed that Debbie Pignataro poisoned herself in a suicide bid, an idea ridiculed by Erie County district attorney Frank Sedita.

Debbie, who appeared on *Forensic Files*, remarked without bitterness that she would never harm herself and that her ex-husband should be forced to ingest arsenic himself.

She has also stated that her former spouse will never take responsibility for attempting to kill her.

But universal disdain and a second stint behind razor wire couldn't crush Pignataro's ego. Not long after his release in 2013, he returned to the Buffalo area, changed his name to Tony Haute, and opened a business called Tony Haute Cosmetique LLC.

The company sold a line of skin-care creams formulated from "one's own DNA-derived plasma." His website referred to him as a doctor.

The Erie County district attorney subsequently opened a criminal investigation into Pignataro's new venture, and the ex-convict ended up taking down his website, according to a WKBW story by Charlie Specht in 2017.

"He basically said, 'I had no idea—I'm just trying to sell some cosmetics and if you can find it's illegal, I'll stop,'" Specht, who now is an investigative journalist for the *Buffalo News*, told me in an interview. "But that's not the way you do it—you get approval first."

Pignataro responded to WKBW's report by stating that he changed his name in an effort to make a new start. He apologized to his ex-wife and the Smith family, although he didn't make any specific admissions about his guilt. Pignataro also said that he worked as a delivery driver.

But as of February 2018, Pignataro's e-tail skin care site was back up and included an imitation version of the classic medical logo of two serpents wrapped around a staff. The site was down again as of July 2018. Next, Pignataro went to Florida, where he was advertising himself as a caregiver for geriatric patients. (Thanks to readers Sean K., Rosemarie, and LC, who originally wrote into my blog with tips.)

As for Debbie Pignataro, *Forensic Files* stated that much of the damage to Debbie's health is irreversible and showed her in a wheelchair, but a recent report from a West Seneca–area source says that her mobility appears to have improved and she can walk unassisted.

Her son, Ralph, grew up to be a lawyer, and Debbie finds it frustrating that "every time his name comes up, his father's name comes up," says Specht. "Debbie's son is a nice guy."

Meanwhile, Debbie's former husband will probably reinvent himself as something or other a few more times, but let's hope that the only person he ever incapacitates is himself.

Armed with the knowledge of Barbara's track record, investigators began to dig deeper. A reenactment of the shooting revealed inconsistencies in Barbara's story.

And fortunately, a tantalizing piece of evidence came to light, and it backed up Jolynn's claims.

A student cleaning out a locker at Durham High came across an audiocassette that Russ had recorded on January 29, 1988—just three days before his own death.

In a voice from the grave, Russ Stager explained that Barbara had been cheating on him (by this time, she had apparently broken free of any sexual inhibitions of her youth), and he suspected Barbara's previous husband's death was no accident. Plus, Barbara's behavior had been suspect. Russ recounted that, on two occasions, Barbara woke him up during the night to offer him some pills to help him sleep.

On a prior occasion, Russ had told Jolynn that if anything awful happened to him, Barbara probably did it.

After a thorough investigation of the forensics, police theorized that Russ's pistol was actually kept in a drawer—he belonged to the army reserves and knew better than to leave a gun under a pillow. He also didn't keep his gun loaded.

Ballistic tests showed that pulling the trigger on that particular .25-caliber model would require four pounds of pressure, way too much to have occurred accidentally as Barbara contended.

Plus, there were the finances. "I told [investigator] Ricky Buchanan that I want to see all her bank records and know everything about her, every dollar she's spent," Eric Evenson told me during an interview. "I also asked the victim's mother to tell me everything about this person. I got to know Barbara through others—I needed to know what was on her mind."

It turned out that Barbara's boss at the radio station had actually called Doubleday to verify her story about the $100,000—and found out the publishing company had never heard of her book, according to Evenson.

Meanwhile, friends and neighbors of the couple were "astonished" when the authorities arrested the seemingly ideal wife and mother in their midst, according to a Knight Ridder account.

The Stagers' church held a fund-raiser to pay Barbara's bail.

The prosecution, however, had a strong case—contending that Barbara sneaked the gun out of the drawer, loaded it, shot Russ, and lay a shell casing near his pillow before calling 911.

Barbara was in a hurry to rid herself of Russ because she wanted his $170,000 life insurance payout fast, investigators believed. Apparently, the lower-budget lifestyle the couple had adopted was cramping her style.

In May 1989, after a highly publicized trial during which the prosecution called 83 witnesses to the stand, a jury deliberated less than an hour before convicting Barbara Stager of murder.

She received a death sentence. The state set the execution date for just two months later. They like to do things speedily in North Carolina—or at least try.

But the state supreme court later voided that death sentence over a technicality. At the 1993 resentencing trial, Barbara's younger son, Jason Stager, testified that he felt his mother was innocent.

This time, she got a life sentence, which allowed for the possibility of parole. (North Carolina lawmakers revoked parole eligibility for lifers the following year, but Barbara was grandfathered in.)

Sources vary as to the reason the authorities decided not to try Barbara for Larry Ford's death. Either they thought it unnecessary under the original death sentence or they didn't have enough evidence.

Today, Barbara Stager is safely tucked away in the North Carolina Correctional Institution for Women in Raleigh. To make sure she stays there, Eric Evenson and Russ Stager's mother—now in her 90s—have attended four in-person and two remote parole hearings to urge the board to keep Barbara locked up.

Barbara's behavior while incarcerated hasn't helped her cause, according to her record with the North Carolina Department of Public Safety.

She disobeyed orders in 1989. In 1994, she attempted an unspecified "Class C offense," a category including such misdeeds as failing to show up for work or fighting with other inmates. She disobeyed orders again in 2017.

As for what happened to Barbara Stager's sons after her imprisonment, the younger one went to live with an uncle, and the other was old enough to get by on his own.

Russ Stager's first wife, Jolynn Snow, married again, to a kitchen remodeler, and she helps run his business, according to the Raleigh *News & Observer*.

In addition to being the subject of many true-crime shows, Barbara Stager's crime inspired a made-for-TV dramatization of the book *Before He Wakes*. It got so-so reviews, but it stars Jaclyn Smith—that's right, one of the original Charlie's Angels—as the character based on Barbara Stager.

CHAPTER 3

Betty Lee

Death of a Damsel in Distress

ROBERT FRY MURDERS A MOTHER OF FIVE
Forensic Files *episode "Four on the Floor"*

A combination of bad companions and bad luck led a woman named Betty Lee to a horrible end on a spring night near Farmington, New Mexico.

A divorced mother of five, Betty was taking a break and enjoying some drinks with a couple of girlfriends.

But her so-called friends ditched her, and she accepted a ride home with a stranger who seemed kindhearted, but wasn't.

For this chapter, I looked around for an explanation for why Betty's girlfriends abandoned her that night and where the killer, Robert Fry, and his accomplice, Leslie Engh, are today.

But first, here's a recap of "Four on the Floor," along with additional information from internet research.

Robert Fry, 26, was cruising around in his Ford Aspire near a bar called the Turnaround on June 6, 2000.

Forensic Files gives Fry's occupation as construction worker, but a newspaper account describes him as a "marginally employed Navy veteran" who served in Guam, then worked on and off as a bouncer, security guard, and driver.

In his spare time, Fry enjoyed playing Dungeons & Dragons and collecting knives.

Neither Betty Lee nor the authorities knew it, but the hot-tempered, beer-swilling Fry was a serial killer. He had already committed three murders and allegedly liked to prey on Native Americans.

Betty, a Diné College nursing student from Shiprock, New Mexico, belonged to the Navajo Nation. Her hobbies were gardening and herb gathering.

She and two other women went to the Turnaround together, but her friends met two men there and decided to go to a motel together, leaving Betty without a ride home.

She tried to call her brother from a pay phone but couldn't reach him and broke down in tears.

Bobby Fry pulled up beside the 36-year-old Betty, said that he hated "to see a woman cry," and offered a ride.

Fry, who had his young buddy Leslie Engh in the car, drove Betty to a remote dirt road in Farmington, saying he had to stop to relieve himself.

The powerful six-foot, one-inch Fry then dragged Betty out of the car and attempted to rape her. When she resisted, he stabbed her in the chest. She fled on foot, but Fry caught up and killed her with a sledge-hammer.

Engh helped Fry conceal her body in some bushes. They threw her clothes in a ravine.

But there was no quick getaway for those two. The Ford Aspire got stuck in some soft sand as they tried to reach the highway. Around 4 a.m., Fry called his parents for help. They showed up, but their pickup truck was paralyzed in the sand, too, as was the first tow truck they summoned, according to *Forensic Files*.

Finally, Bloomfield Towing owner Charlie Bergin answered a call and pulled all three vehicles free. They went their separate ways.

The *Albuquerque Journal*, however, gives a slightly different version of events.

Although the ending is consistent with the *Forensic Files* account—three vehicles were immobilized in the sand and Bergin freed them all—the newspaper reported that, when Gloria and James Fry initially came on the scene, they didn't get stuck.

Instead, they left their son's sedan there and gave him a ride home, where he "changed clothes and cleaned up." They also dropped Engh at his place. The Frys' truck got stuck when they returned to the scene to tow the Ford Aspire, according to the *Albuquerque Journal* story.

Bergin probably had no idea that a homicide had taken place near the scene, but one has to wonder about Robert Fry's parents.

The next day, an electrical-line inspector found Betty's body after following a trail of blood (he suspected someone had poached a deer) off the road.

Police recovered a cell phone Charlie Bergin had discarded at the scene. He and his wife had argued on the phone, and he threw it away in a fit of anger, according to *Forensic Files*.

Bergin identified Fry and Engh as the men who summoned for help.

Investigators tracked shoe prints at the murder scene to footwear found during searches of Fry's and Engh's homes. Both sets of shoes had Betty Lee's blood on them.

A bloodstain on Fry's T-shirt suggested that he was the one who hit Betty with the sledgehammer.

Fry stayed quiet after the authorities detained him.

Engh, who was only 22 years old and looked like a baby chicken, cracked and told detectives everything, then testified against Fry.

In April 2002, a jury convicted Fry of kidnapping, attempted criminal sexual penetration, and second-degree murder.

Fry apologized to the more than 20 of Betty Lee's relatives present in the courtroom and asked the jury to spare his life for the sake of his parents, the *Albuquerque Journal* reported.

But the jury delivered a death sentence, which is not a common decision in New Mexico.

Engh got 40 years.

But wait—there's more. Betty Lee's homicide led to new investigations that ultimately revealed that Robert Fry killed Joseph Fleming, 24, and Matthew Trecker, 18, back in 1996. The murders took place in a shop called the Eclectic. Fry had sneaked away with some expensive knives and swords from the store and was afraid the two men would identify him.

Authorities also discovered that both Fry and Engh were responsible for the unsolved murder of a Navajo reservation resident named Donald Tsosie, 40, who had traveled to Farmington to sell plasma. The men offered him a ride home, then robbed and beat him and pushed him off a cliff in 1998, Engh admitted to police.

on Our Door (2003), a book written by Danny's parents, Rev. Larry and Carol Vine.

When authorities finally did put the Bruce brothers on trial, one witness, a local mussel diver, got so scared that he checked out of his government-paid hotel room and fled to Kentucky, the Vines recalled.

Nonetheless, the boys were convicted, and all got life in prison without parole.

The brothers' mother, Kathleen Bruce, who had lied to police about her sons' whereabouts on the night that they robbed Danny and committed the murders, received eight years in jail for providing a false alibi.

This particular *Forensic Files* episode fascinated me for a number of reasons. First, of course, was the reality that such horrifying cruelty could take place over a sum of money that would barely pay for a used Ford Focus.

Second, "Shell Game" provided some interesting backstory to the way mussel shells are procured. I'll never look at all those Etsy picture frames inlaid with mother-of-pearl the same way again.

Most compelling of all was something federal prosecutor Steve Parker said toward the end of the episode: "A lot of people were very happy [that the Bruce brothers were convicted]. It lowered the crime rate significantly in Benton County and the area."

Fortunately, most of us have never lived in a town terrorized by felons like Gary, Jerry Lee, and Robert Bruce.

But I've had jobs in a number of offices where the departure of one particular ogre or B-on-wheels washed away stress and conflict among the remaining coworkers.

I'm curious to hear tales from someone who lived in Benton County before and after the Bruces' incarceration—and whether the residents ultimately felt like crocuses that could finally break through the March snow and feel the sun after a U.S. version of the *Seven Samurai* gave them their freedom.

The aforementioned federal prosecutor, Steve Parker, answered some of my questions about the case during a phone interview shortly after I started my blog. Parker, who prosecuted the brothers, went on to work as a lawyer in private practice. But he still vividly remembers the aftermath of Danny and Della's murders. The following are some excerpts from our conversation:

> **Rebecca Reisner: Were you surprised that someone would murder two people over $2,500 worth of mussel shells?**
>
> Steve Parker: I was a police officer earlier in my career—that's how I put myself through law school—and then a federal prosecutor for 30 years. So, no, I wasn't surprised.
>
> **RR: The show mentioned that the Bruces used witness intimidation in their earlier crimes and, in one instance, blew up a building near the site where a witness was being interviewed. Did you know of any other such attempts by the Bruces?**
>
> SP: Robert asked one of his ex-girlfriends to provide an alibi, and Mrs. Bruce began following the woman around to intimidate her. Some neighbors saw this and reported it to the police. There was a Tennessee Bureau of Investigation agent named Alvin Daniels, and he was out there working at the crime scene just after he got a cancer diagnosis and wanted to finish this case before he died. The Bruces would cruise around Daniels's house to try to intimidate him. Members of the Bruce family got in their trucks and followed Rev. Vine to intimidate him. The Bruces thought they were invincible. And that made it easier to prosecute their case because they weren't very smart about covering their tracks. They were very impulsive. We had an eyewitness who saw them at the gas station. [The Bruces bought 10 gallons of gasoline to use as an accelerant.] We also had someone who was there the night they planned the murder and tried to recruit others to participate. They had a huge argument outside with someone who refused, and we found neighbors who heard the fight.
>
> **RR: How did law enforcement contend with witness intimidation?**
>
> SP: Normally, murder is a state crime, not federal, and normally we don't have jurisdiction. But we accused them of robbery affecting interstate business. The shells travel and sometimes even go

to Japan. We took the case federal, so we had a federal grand jury about 90 miles away from Camden, so witnesses didn't feel intimidated. We had a good team of the FBI, Tennessee Bureau of Investigation, and ATF [Alcohol, Tobacco, and Firearms]. The ATF did the arson investigation. The Bruce brothers and their mother were held without bail before the trial. We were able to prosecute J. C. Bruce* early, so that let everyone in the county know they weren't invincible.

RR: Is the mother still in jail? And where was their father during all this?

SP: She was released and passed away. There were no dads in the picture. I referred to the Bruces as Ma Barker and her boys during the closing argument at the trial.

RR: What reaction did you get to the conviction?

SP: Our phone started ringing. The sheriff's office and other local law enforcement were very appreciative. We took out a whole crime wave.

RR: Do you miss the drama from your days as a federal investigator?

SP: Yes, as a fed you get to both investigate and try cases, which is compelling.

RR: Did you feel *Forensic Files* was fair in the way the show portrayed the story?

SP: Yes, very fair. It was a year-long investigation before we charged the Bruce brothers, and it was hard to get that all into 30 minutes. I was very happy with the way *Forensic Files* presented the case.

*****

Today, all three of the brothers convicted of the murders live courtesy of the Federal Bureau of Prisons, with Gary at medium-security USP Lewisburg in Pennsylvania and Jerry Lee and Robert in different parts of the high-security Coleman Federal Correctional Complex in Florida.

Steve Parker spoke to me for a second time, in late 2021, after he retired from his legal practice. He noted that the Bruces lost their most recent legal salvo and had no litigation pending—for the time being.

J. C. is a fourth Bruce brother. Although not implicated in the Vine-Thornton robbery and murders, he had a history of other criminal behavior over the years, most notably raping a teenager, strangling her, and throwing her off a bridge (she survived) in the 1970s. He served only a few years in prison for that crime thanks to a pardon from Governor Roy Blanton. More recently, J. C. was arrested for suspicion of poaching, as reported in a December 17, 2015, article in the Tennessee newspaper the Daily Herald, *which called him a "career criminal."*

Avis clearly came from a strict background. During his *Forensic Files* appearance, Frederick Banks said that Avis asked for forgiveness upon telling him that she and Keyon Pittman were having a child. But she intended to make things right by marrying Keyon.

The two of them got engaged and bought a house in Ridgeland, Mississippi.

But their future together ended on November 30, 2006, when Keyon, 31, returned home from work to find Avis, 27, in a pool of blood on the garage floor.

He called 911 and summoned Avis's mother and father to come immediately, but he wouldn't say what was wrong.

The Bankses told *Dateline Mystery* that they thought Avis had lost the baby. But the news was much more grim. They arrived to the sight of police tape. The coroner told them their daughter had died a horrible death.

It looked as though someone had ambushed Avis, who was five months along in her pregnancy, after she stepped out of her car at around 6 p.m.

She had been shot four times with a .38-caliber pistol and stabbed repeatedly in the upper body. The assailant had slashed Avis's throat. One of the bullets had been fired at close range and had struck her in the back of her head, police ascertained.

"People were shocked," Brandon I. Dorsey—who later became one of Carla Hughes's defense lawyers—told me during a phone interview. "It's always been a quiet community."

Investigators found shoe impressions where they believed the assailant kicked a door before breaking into the house and creeping into the attached garage.

The intruder had ransacked some rooms, leaving drawers open, but didn't steal anything.

Lab testing identified some gunshot residue on Keyon's hands, and he had some bloodstains on his clothing. Police later concluded the forensic evidence came from his handling the body, not firing a gun.

But there were other indicators that didn't look so good for Keyon. The video footage of him talking to his lawyer shortly after he discovered the slaughtered mother of his unborn child revealed a man utterly without grief or anguish. His only noticeable emotion was disgruntlement because police considered him a suspect.

Investigators found out that Keyon usually entered the house through the front door, but on the night of the murder, he went in through the garage. Maybe he knew he'd find a body there.

There was also the question of why he ran to a neighbor's house to call 911 when he had a cell phone with him. He also reportedly called Carla Hughes before summoning help for Avis.

And Keyon—whom local TV reporter Kathryn Kight described as "not a looker" but with "lots of confidence"—was clearly a womanizer, according to *Forensic Files*.

Staff members at Chastain Middle School said that, in addition to the affair with Carla Hughes, he'd been getting close to the mother of one of the basketball players he coached. That woman denied a relationship, and she had a solid alibi anyway.

But so did Keyon. He was at school when the murder happened, and numerous witnesses could vouch for his whereabouts.

Police had a better suspect in cheerleading coach Carla Hughes, who had been enjoying a not-so-discreet relationship with Keyon. Colleagues saw them carrying on out in the open.

Carla was a former beauty pageant winner and mother of a three-year-old boy. At first, she told police that she had no dog in the race, that she and Keyon were just friends. But she lacked a convincing alibi.

Phone records showed that Carla was near Avis and Keyon's house around the time of the murder.

Soon enough, Carla Hughes reversed herself and admitted to the affair with Keyon but denied having anything to do with Avis Banks's murder.

The big break in the case came when Patrick Nash, one of Carla Hughes's cousins, told police that, on November 26, 2006, Carla had borrowed his folding hunting knife and Rossi .38-caliber gun, which was loaded with five bullets.

The ammo was gone when she returned the firearm to him on December 1, 2006. She said she had gone target shooting.

Although Carla would later deny it, Nash said that she was crying when she brought back the gun.

Investigators matched the bullets recovered from the victim's body to Nash's gun.

Police discovered that the footprints from the crime scene matched a pair of size 10 Tredsafe shoes found in Carla Hughes's closet, and they had Avis Banks's blood on them.

Carla Hughes was indicted on charges of capital murder.

Still, those who knew Carla Hughes weren't willing to connect the dots—she was too nice.

So who was this woman, and what made her stake her happiness on a long shot like Keyon Pittman?

Carla Hughes was born June 12, 1981, to a mother who already had more kids than she could support, according to *Dateline Mystery*.

Fortunately, her relatives Lynda and Carl Hughes, who were both schoolteachers, adopted her at six weeks of age. She would be their only child.

Carla excelled at horseback riding as well as her regular schoolwork, according to information from Murderpedia.org, and she grew into a tall, pretty, young woman with even features and high cheekbones. Friends described her as bubbly and fun-loving.

She belonged to student council and Key Club and was a majorette, a cheerleader, and a page in the Mississippi state senate.

And she had charm. Carla Hughes's pageant wins included Washington County Junior Miss and Miss Greenville Teen.

She graduated from the University of Southern Mississippi and went on to earn a master's degree in education at Belhaven College.

During her upward trajectory, she met the man of her dreams and got engaged, but he suddenly panicked the day before their scheduled wedding in 2004.

He left her single and two months pregnant. That was the first sign her fairy tale was not to be.

She gave birth to a son and eventually took a job as a language arts teacher at Chastain Middle School, where she met Keyon Pittman.

As the internet meme says, "If you don't like the end of your story, write yourself a new beginning." In Keyon Pittman, Carla Hughes saw a fresh chance at Camelot.

There's no way of knowing what Keyon Pittman really told her about his intentions, but he would later testify that Carla Hughes knew that she was merely a secret side dish and he had made it clear to her that he intended to marry Avis Banks, according to court papers.

But Carla, 25, insisted upon referring to him as her "future husband," he said.

Investigators believed Carla Hughes wanted to eliminate and basically replace Avis Banks. Carla longed for a home with a husband and probably imagined Keyon would adopt her son and help her replicate the life her baby's father should have given her.

Prosecutors contended that Carla broke into Keyon and Avis's house and ransacked drawers to make it look like a burglary. She lay in wait for Avis in the attached garage and shot her, stabbed her, and slashed her throat. *Forensic Files* didn't mention it, but Avis Banks's pants had been pulled down, perhaps in an effort to make the crime look like a burglary that turned into a rape-murder, according to *Dateline Mystery*.

When questioned by detectives, Carla didn't implicate Keyon.

At the trial, however, Carla's defense team pointed out that Keyon sometimes borrowed her shoes—their feet were the same size.

On the witness stand, Keyon denied having anything to do with the murder. He admitted to the relationship with Carla, and his testimony clearly indicated the two were very close. Keyon said that, on the day of the murder, he had dropped off some groceries at Carla's house to refrigerate while he coached basketball. (Although investigators suspected he had some involvement in the homicide plan, they never had enough evidence to charge him.)

Carla Hughes sobbed in the courtroom when the jury returned with a guilty verdict after deliberating for eight hours. Although eligible for the death penalty, she received life without parole for capital murder on October 14, 2009.

The victim's mother, Debra Banks, later told *Snapped* that she felt a huge burden lifted from her upon hearing the verdict.

Carla Hughes went off to prison.

She lost a 2012 appeal based on the defense's claim that the judge hadn't made it adequately clear to jury members that Carla's refusal to testify in her own defense was not an indicator of guilt.

Carla's mother, Lynda Hughes, maintained that Keyon Pittman wanted to get rid of Avis Banks—and that he framed Carla for the murder. She set up a GoGetFunding page to finance a new investigation, the *Clarion Ledger* reported in 2016.

Those in Carla's camp also lay blame on forensic pathologist Dr. Steven Hayne, a witness for the prosecution. They noted that he was doing 1,500 autopsies a year—bagging more than $1 million annually, according to the Innocence Project—and that the state of Mississippi had voided some convictions from trials where Hayne testified for the prosecution.

And the pro–Carla Hughes *Justice4Carla* blog said that her own lawyer was at fault, too. His specialty was tobacco litigation—not defending clients against murder charges.

Right or wrong, the *Justice4Carla* website seems to have some integrity. Dissenting opinions are allowed in its comments section. For example: "She killed my cousin over a guy that didn't want her the way she wanted him. I hope you raise millions because you will need it for representation that will allow a jury to ignore facts," wrote one commenter.

Today, Carla Hughes is serving her life sentence at the Central Mississippi Correctional Institution. At a trim 140 pounds, the five-foot, seven-inch Carla has apparently resisted the siren song of heavy prison food.

Her son is being raised by his maternal grandparents.

As for Keyon Pittman, there's no telling whether he's creating a fairy tale for any woman in his life today, but it's sure to have a happier ending than what Carla Hughes and Avis Banks got.

CHAPTER 7

Chris Marquis

Death of an E-tailer

A TEEN ENTREPRENEUR PAYS DEARLY FOR FRAUD
Forensic Files *episode "Over and Out"*
Many a duped consumer has thought for a moment or two about sending a bomb to the culprit on the other end of the transaction.

A 35-year-old Indiana truck driver named Chris Dean distinguished himself by actually doing it.

It's a particularly sad case because the dishonest seller, also named Chris, was only a teenager.

Forensic Files told the story of the clash of the Chrises in "Over and Out." The tragedy spans the internet, surface mail, and citizens band radio.

For this chapter, I looked around for an epilogue for the bomber. But first here's a recap of the episode along with information from internet research and an interview with one of the teen's former business associates.

Chris Marquis bought and sold CB radios and parts over the internet.

Although *Forensic Files* depicts him as an obscure hobbyist, the tall, blond Vermont native actually had established himself as a widely known entrepreneur among CB radio enthusiasts.

To inflate his image, Marquis portrayed himself as a married, 27-year-old dad with a retail shop called the CB Shack, according to an investigative piece that appeared in *Wired* magazine.

In reality, Marquis was 17, single, and childless, and he ran the CB Shack online out of his bedroom in his mother's house in Fair Haven—there was no store.

35

Although *Forensic Files* hints that Chris, who had some visual impairment, was a loner, he managed to score a serious girlfriend who was a year ahead of him in school.

The relationship didn't seem to do much for his maturity, however. Marquis acquired a bad personal reputation by making obnoxious comments on the CB. "He'd get on the radio—and his had the strongest transmission, so he could talk over everyone—and he'd insult people," recalls Mark Cutsinger, who did repair work for Marquis. "He didn't have any male role model at home. But he could piss people off because he knew his mom would protect him."

Marquis also gained ill repute as a business owner. He routinely misrepresented the merchandise he sold and traded. UPS had already received a number of complaints about Marquis from customers who said he cheated them.

A bit of a grifter herself, Chris's mother Sheila Rockwell was very close to her son, sometimes working with him as a DJ at events, and the two engaged in a little parent-child shoplifting from time to time, according to the *Burlington Free Press* and *Wired*.

"She taught him how to steal," Cutsinger says. "They only got caught once, but they were shoplifting in Vermont, New Hampshire, and New York. At Sheila and Chris's house, I saw the stuff they stole. They told me they stole it."

Chris Dean had told friends about being cheated by Marquis in a trade involving a Cobra 2000 radio. Marquis sent a broken radio—not the one he promised—to Dean, who repeatedly contacted Marquis to complain but got no answer.

Neither mother nor son imagined the scale of the retribution coming their way.

On March 19, 1998, UPS delivered a package for Chris Marquis with a return address he didn't recognize, from a Samantha Brown in Bucyrus, Ohio.

When Marquis opened it, a pipe bomb exploded, severing his femoral artery. His mother, who had just handed him the box, lost several fingers and part of one knee.

Police heard and felt the explosion and saw smoke (Rockwell's house sat right behind the municipal building) and ran inside the residence.

They saw huge craters in the floor and ceiling and found the mother and son still alive.

Sheila survived, but Chris soon bled to death.

The murder was colossal news for a town of fewer than 3,000 people, and it stunned the CB radio community.

"I was afraid to open a box for a year," Cutsinger says.

Rockwell didn't have to wait long to win justice for her son, who was her youngest child (his father died before he was born).

The FBI and ATF joined up with Fair Haven's three-officer police department to hunt for the bomber.

They quickly zeroed in on Chris Dean.

The house in Pierceton, Indiana, that Dean shared with his wife held a cache of incriminating evidence, including the types of hex nuts, wires, and pipes used in the bomb. A package of nine-volt batteries in Dean's drawer had the same lot number as the mangled one found at the crime scene.

Dean, who apparently didn't watch *Forensic Files* often enough, thought he had permanently erased a computer file with the CB Shack's address and the fake "Samantha Brown" return address used on the package with the bomb.

Police retrieved that file as well as information Dean had downloaded about how to create an explosive device.

The package with the bomb had been mailed from a UPS store in Mansfield, Ohio. Sprint North Supply, the product-distribution company Dean worked for, confirmed that Dean was in Mansfield on the day it was sent.

To top it off, one of Dean's buddies told authorities that Dean said he "was going to send the guy [Marquis] a package in the mail and boy is he going to be surprised," the *Washington Post* reported.

U.S. marshals transported Dean to Burlington, Vermont, where federal district court judge William Sessions charged him with offenses including murder and "sending an explosive device on an airplane, knowing it could endanger the safety of the aircraft," the *New York Times* reported.

To avoid capital punishment, Dean pleaded guilty to first-degree murder. He also met with Sheila Rockwell one on one and apologized for killing her son.

Rockwell said that while she couldn't forgive Dean, she didn't want to see him get the death penalty either.

As far as why Dean, who had no prior criminal record, committed capital murder over a few hundred dollars, it may have been a case of a tightly wound guy stewing until he snapped. According to the *Wired* story by writer Scott Kirsner: "Dean was obsessively neat. Neighbors remember him constantly washing his cars—a Corvette and a Blazer. Joe Stump, his landlord, recalls that Dean kept his lawn buzzed down practically to AstroTurf length. 'And the house was always spotless inside.'"

Dean got life in jail without parole after federal prosecutors alleged that, in addition to the bombing, he had hatched a plan to break out of St. Albans jail and threatened to kill witnesses.

The judge in the case also ordered Dean to pay Rockwell $50,000, although the *Burlington Free Press* noted that it was unclear whether Dean was able to come up with the money.

As he was led out of the courtroom, he mouthed "I love you" to his wife, Diane.

But just because Dean pleaded guilty didn't mean that he accepted his punishment. Early on, he trotted out complaints about having an unhappy childhood.

That didn't get him anywhere.

In 2006, he argued that a U.S. Supreme Court decision that said federal sentencing guidelines weren't mandatory should apply to his case.

A federal magistrate in Vermont ruled against him.

Today, Dean resides in Hazelton, a high-security federal penitentiary in Bruceton Mills, West Virginia. Hazelton is a rough place. In 2018, an inmate died after a fight with a fellow prisoner.

Dean himself is unlikely to exit prison on two feet. As a prosecutor told the judge, "It will be just as easy for Dean to construct a [bomb] at age 70 as it was at 35."

Meanwhile, in the aftermath of the murder, Sheila Rockwell received much sympathy and support from members of the community, who, according to Cutsinger, were willing to overlook any history of her own transgressions because she certainly didn't deserve to lose her son over them.

She was very close to her mother. Crystal had confided in Bonnie that best buddy Ken Register, 18, got a little out of line with her once. But neither could foresee the savagery he unleashed on the night of November 17, 1991.

After Crystal and a girlfriend attended a party that evening, the friend dropped Crystal off in a mall parking lot where she'd left her brand-new Toyota Celica.

When Crystal didn't come home by her midnight curfew, her mother called the Horry County police. She was so overcome with anxiety that the police at first could barely make out her words or tell whether the caller was a man or a woman, according to the 1999 book *An Hour to Kill: The True Story of Love, Murder, and Justice in a Small Southern Town* by Dale Hudson and Billy Hills.

Next, she contacted Ken Register, who said that he hadn't seen Crystal all night and that he would check the local hospitals, according to the Investigation Discovery Network series *Stolen Voices, Buried Secrets*.

Bonnie located her daughter's vacant blue 1991 Toyota, which she'd given her for an early graduation present, in a middle-school parking lot.

Sadly, Bonnie didn't have to wait long to justify her sense of dread.

Hunters found the body of a teenage girl in a ditch the next day. She was wearing a class ring with a shiny purple gemstone and "Crystal Faye Todd" engraved inside the band.

The murder scene horrified even veteran homicide detectives. Crystal had a defensive injury on her left hand, but she was no match for the attacker's weapon, which investigators believe was a 3.5-inch knife with a locking blade.

In addition to bruises and abrasions, Crystal had 31 cut and stab wounds, including an ear-to-ear gash across the throat, according to court papers from *State v. Register* (decided on August 12, 1996). The attacker had also sodomized her.

At first, police had a promising suspect in dark, handsome Andy Tyndall, a grown man who liked to hang around teenage girls. Crystal had known him for a week and already had a little crush on him, according to "Killer Instinct," a 2011 episode of *Stolen Voices, Buried Secrets*.

Although Crystal and her friends could tell Andy Tyndall was past high school age, they probably didn't know he was married and wanted by Alabama authorities on a felony charge.

When law officers came to arrest him in South Carolina, he fled on foot into the woods. Police chased him down with tracker dogs.

But all the drama was for naught. Andy Tyndall was quickly cleared.

Next up, investigators turned to criminal profilers. They predicted that the killer would be an angry, young, white male who was confident the law wouldn't catch him—and he was probably a friend of the victim.

Horry County homicide detective Bill Knowles, who had just visited the FBI Academy, suggested adding the then-new science of DNA testing to the investigation.

Police asked 51 of Crystal's male friends and acquaintances to give DNA samples.

All of them, including Ken Register, said yes. But Ken changed his mind and tried to back out of it. Two agents "basically shamed him into taking the test," Bill Knowles told me during an interview. "Then Ken went to Bonnie and said that she shouldn't trust DNA. That's when he really became a suspect."

Sure enough, a lab determined that DNA from the rape kit matched that of none other than Ken—full name, Johnnie Kenneth Register II—the blond-haired, blue-eyed, onetime varsity football player whom Crystal considered her best pal.

Police arrested him in February 1992.

Bonnie knew that Ken Register had once offended Crystal by propositioning her for sex despite having a girlfriend, but he was the last person she suspected of the murder.

"He's been our friend for years and years," said Bonnie, the *Rock Hill Herald* reported. "He was everybody's friend around here."

Ken and Crystal had dated briefly in their early teens and stayed happily friend-zoned afterward, and he seemed like an asset to the community. He got good grades in school and helped out by scrubbing floors and playing guitar at the little church his family attended. He and his father had recently built a wooden altar for the congregation, according to *An Hour to Kill.*

Little did Crystal's mother know that Ken had a police record for exposing himself to two Coastal Carolina University students not long before Crystal's disappearance.

It was not the first time that Ken had gone out of bounds. At 15, he did something that suggested he was no ordinary budding pervert.

He made an obscene phone call to a grown woman and described in sickening detail how he wanted to slit her body open and kill her—in the same way he eventually murdered Crystal, according to *Stolen Voices, Buried Secrets*. The woman reported it, but Ken had a relative who worked at the South Carolina Department of Social Services—and conveniently forgot to pass along the complaint, according to Knowles.

Once the DNA evidence pointed to Ken in the crime against Crystal, another relative, his mother Shirley, tried to intervene. In an on-camera interview, Shirley Register sweetly explained that her son got home from a date too early to match the time line of the crime.

Ken's girlfriend said they were together at the Dodge City go-cart track in the town of Aynor on the night Crystal died.

Nonetheless, law officers arrested Ken Register on February 18, 1992.

While riding in the police car, he asked twice for his mother, according to court papers.

At first, Ken didn't want to answer questions without his mother present, so officers went to Shirley Register's house to pick her up, but instead she gave them a note to hand off to her son.

According to *Forensic Files*, the note told Ken to clam up until they got a lawyer. But court papers said that she simply wrote that she loved him and knew he was innocent.

It mattered little because police, who are allowed to lie while questioning a suspect, told him that they had found his footprints at the murder scene (they didn't) and that the note from his mother instructed him to tell the truth (it didn't).

The interrogation tricks worked. Ken cracked.

The night of the murder, he and Crystal spotted each other at a traffic light, he said. She then parked her car at the middle school and got into his vehicle, where they had consensual sex—but she threatened to accuse of him of rape, so he panicked and stabbed her, he contended.

Investigators begged to differ. There was no consensual sex. She had severe wounding consistent with rape.

They never found the murder weapon. Ken said he tossed away the knife as far as he could near the scene of the crime, according to an Associated Press account.

As if Ken needed any more bad publicity, in a separate court action before his homicide trial kicked off, he was found guilty of exposing himself to the college students. Ken claimed he was actually clothed during the incident and that he stood up in his car and shimmied himself around because the women "wouldn't give me the time of day" and "made me feel like trash," according to *An Hour to Kill.*

The homicide trial didn't go so well either.

In front of 400 spectators, Ken Register was convicted of Crystal Todd's sexual assault, murder, and kidnapping.

The jury declined to give him the death penalty because of his young age. Circuit Court Judge Edward B. Cottingham sentenced him to 35 years plus life to be served consecutively.

Ken's sweetheart, Angela Rabon, made a few "dutiful" visits to him in prison and then wrote him a breakup letter and headed off to college, according to *An Hour to Kill.*

Over the years, Ken and defense attorneys Morgan Martin and Tommy Brittain Sr. made efforts to get him out of prison on two feet.

In 1996, the supreme court of South Carolina was not impressed by Ken's claims that police violated his rights during questioning and that the DNA testing method was below par. In fact, the prosecution had given the defense an opportunity to do its own independent DNA tests, but Ken told his lawyers not to, according to *An Hour to Kill.*

Ken also tried the requisite smear-the-victim ploy in hopes that some nefarious acquaintance of hers would take the fall. He said that he heard rumors that Crystal used drugs and had seen her drink alcohol and smoke marijuana, contradicting his own statement from 1992 that he had never seen Crystal using marijuana, according to a February 3, 2000, report from the *Horry Independent.*

He claimed he initially lied because he didn't want Crystal's alleged drug use to somehow sully his own reputation—he had only used the recreational drug a few times in his life when someone happened to pass around a joint, Ken said, as reported by the *Horry Independent* story.

Always a gentleman, Ken also said he didn't know whether it was true, but he heard rumors that Crystal "slept around" and that she had helped distribute LSD, the *Horry Independent* reported.

Shirley Register chimed in, saying she heard Crystal would sometimes leave a party with one guy, then return to pick up another guy or two. She also tried to lend credence to the drug-dealing theory by suggesting that Bonnie and Crystal had too meager a legitimate income to afford their lifestyle—and that Crystal rode to school with a student rumored to sell LSD, according to the *Horry Independent*.

Ken claimed that, at the same time that Crystal's morals were deteriorating, he himself was embarking on the straight and narrow, thanks to his serious relationship with Angela Rabon.

Though disturbing to Crystal's friends and family, the character assassination was merely a typical diversion technique, Knowles said.

The truly outlandish twist in the case came after a world-famous author caught the trial coverage on court TV.

Mickey Spillane, writer of the 1940s detective mystery novel *I, the Jury*—and 25 other books in that genre that sold a total of 200 million copies—thought Ken Register got a raw deal.

He and his wife, Jane Spillane, who lived in Murrells Inlet, South Carolina, believed prosecutor Ralph Wilson framed him.

The Spillanes met with Ken in person and "came to the conclusion that the young man was incapable of committing such a heinous act," the *Washington Post* reported on August 22, 2001. Jane Spillane went so far as to run for county prosecutor herself so that she could personally bestow justice upon Ken. (She lost.)

The judicial system, however, hasn't found Ken Register particularly endearing and has refused his post-conviction requests—including the one he made to the U.S. Supreme Court.

"It's the best thing I've heard in a while," Bonnie Todd commented upon the ruling, as reported by the *Charlotte Observer*.

Today, Ken Register resides at the Broad River Correctional Institution, a high-security prison that houses South Carolina's death chamber.

The Department of Corrections doesn't list any escape attempts or disciplinary problems for Ken. And at five feet eight and 223 pounds, he isn't staging any hunger strikes either.

It would serve him well to keep a low profile. In 2019, police charged a female Broad River guard after she allegedly unlocked an inmate's door and allowed 11 other prisoners to enter his cell and beat him up, according to reporting from WISTV Channel 10 on December 16 of that year.

Fortunately for Ken, he still has a large support network of family members living in and around Conway, South Carolina, to speak up for him should he face abuse while on the inside.

Meanwhile, Bill Knowles, who now does private investigative work in civil cases, has pledged to attend all future parole board meetings to fight against Ken's release.

BUT ENOUGH ABOUT KEN REGISTER—WHAT ABOUT THE MOTHER OF THE MURDER VICTIM?

By the time Bonnie appeared on *Forensic Files* in 2002, Crystal had been gone for 11 years, but her melancholy clearly hadn't lifted. The murder "devastated her more so than any other family member I've ever dealt with," Knowles would later tell local ABC affiliate Channel 15 in September 2014.

But Bonnie, who told *Forensic Files* that the only time she wasn't thinking about Crystal was when she was sleeping, did get to have a bit of an adventure.

In the 1990s, she traveled to New York with Bill Knowles and county prosecutor Ralph Wilson to appear on Sally Jessy Raphael's popular talk show. Wilson later recalled that Bonnie packed instant grits in her travel bags in case local eateries didn't serve them, according to a *Sun News* account. (They didn't, so she got some hot water at a Manhattan McDonald's and stirred up her own, according to Knowles.)

The producers sent a limousine to pick up Bonnie and company at the airport, but the real surprise happened when she got to the TV studio. Shirley Register and Jane Spillane were also appearing in person on the show, and Ken was on a video monitor.

After exchanging unfriendly words in front of the cameras, Bonnie discovered the next day that both Shirley and Jane were booked on her flight back to South Carolina. "I had to keep an eye on Bonnie on the plane," Knowles recalls. "Otherwise, Bonnie would have beaten them up and ended up in jail."

Bonnie Faye Todd died at age 79 on September 3, 2014.

Toward the end of her life, she had become close to a niece whom she "affectionately referred to" as her "adopted daughter," according to Bonnie's obituary.

Local music group Grace Revealed—featuring another of Bonnie's nieces, Lorraine Howard—made a video with the song "More than Memories" as a tribute to Bonnie and her lost daughter. It has scored 13,920 hits on YouTube so far.

CHAPTER 9

Daniel and Cynthia McDonnell

Good Cop, Bad Wife

MURDER, INSURANCE FRAUD—WHAT COULD GO WRONG?
Forensic Files *episode "Bed of Deceit"*

As *Forensic Files* villains go, Cynthia McDonnell distinguishes herself as the queen of self-sabotage.

In a bid to collect on her husband's life insurance policy, the freelance writer shot him as he slept in their Michigan house, then blamed the crime on an anonymous robber.

But Cynthia's storytelling competencies didn't exactly exceed expectations.

She staged the phony home invasion so poorly that she ended up having to fabricate a new explanation. She said that her husband killed himself—which meant no $300,000 insurance payout for her.

For this chapter, I checked into where she is today and looked for more information on Daniel McDonnell's life.

So let's get started on the recap of "Bed of Deceit," the *Forensic Files* episode about the case, along with additional facts drawn from internet research.

Cynthia Lee Johnston and Daniel Joseph McDonnell married in 1975 in Santa Fe, New Mexico. Daniel originally came from Port Chester, New York, and worked as a police officer in New York and New Mexico. A dog lover, he volunteered for an Irish wolfhound rescue group.

By 1998, the couple had children, a house in Bingham Township, Michigan, and what looked like a happy union.

Forensic Files didn't mention it, but the dark-haired, blue-eyed Daniel was a local hero back in Albuquerque, New Mexico, where he served as vice president of the Irish American Society and helped plan the St. Patrick's Day parade.

On Christmas morning in 1978, while off duty, he repeatedly crawled into a burning car in an attempt to reach a passenger trapped inside. After his second try, the gas tank exploded, but he slid into the overturned vehicle a third time. It was too late to save the woman, whose leg was pinned down, but McDonnell's bravery was honored by numerous community groups, the *Albuquerque Journal* reported on January 17, 1979.

Little did he know that, two decades later, it would be his turn to become a victim of circumstance.

On the morning of December 31, 1998, Cynthia McDonnell took the couple's daughter, Erin, shopping in Traverse City for several hours.

Their son, Patrick, 18, was at a buddy's house; his father had dropped him off there the night before.

Cynthia said that, when she returned from shopping, she found Daniel, 58, in his bed with a bullet wound to the head.

Judging from her hysterical-spouse routine on the 911 tape, police should have arrested her on the spot for bad acting alone.

But first responders usually start out by giving the survivor's story the benefit of the doubt. They listened to her tale of shock and woe and missing cash from her husband's wallet.

Investigators eventually noticed, however, that Cynthia didn't have an explanation for how the intruder or intruders broke into the house.

Cynthia then had no choice but to change her story, according to *Forensic Files*. The new version: She went into the bedroom to tell Daniel she was going shopping and found him dead with a suicide note.

He had survived cancer but was depressed over the side effects of the treatments, she said. A note he left explained that he wanted Cynthia and the kids to get the insurance money—and instructed her to stage the scene like a murder so his policy would remain valid, she claimed.

So, Cynthia told police, she got rid of his note, then wiped his prints from his service revolver and threw it in a field. Then she went shopping.

But Cynthia, who aspired to publish a murder-mystery novel, botched the plot in a number of ways.

The bullet wound was in the back of the victim's head—people don't generally shoot themselves that way. Blood evidence around his arm and pillow also contradicted her narrative.

And, as *Forensic Files* fans have seen many times, little things murderers inadvertently do or say often scream "guilty" even louder than the forensics (see Brian Vaughn, chapter 4).

In Cynthia's case, on the morning of her husband's death, she went into the bathroom where her daughter, Erin, 20, was showering and turned up the radio.

A Mom Who Pumps Up the Volume on Her Child's Music?

(It seemed fishy to Erin, too, because she would ultimately side against her mother.)

Clearly, Cynthia was attempting to mask the sound of the gunfire. A bullet hole in the pillow next to the body suggested another effort to muffle the noise, investigators believed.

In April 1999, Cynthia was arraigned on murder charges and held without bail.

At the trial in 2000, defense lawyer Pete Shumar argued for the suicide theory and said that Daniel had shot himself in the back of the head to make his death look like murder and hence eligible for the insurance jackpot.

Shumar also trotted out a couple of expert witnesses, including a psychologist who said that going shopping after a loved one's death could be a reaction to trauma.

As for Cynthia's story shift from murder to suicide, the *Traverse City Record-Eagle* reported Shumar's explanation: "I believe that all of us have changed our story at one point in time or another. It's human. She did it for her children."

Leelanau County prosecutor Clarence Gomery had plenty of ammunition for his side of the case.

In addition to changing the manner of the death, Cynthia couldn't keep her story straight about what happened to the alleged suicide note, the *Record-Eagle* reported. She threw it in the garbage or burned it or shredded it and flushed it down the toilet.

There was also the fact that Daniel's arms had no splatter, suggesting someone else fired the gun.

And in the months leading up to the murder, Cynthia's purchase of big-ticket items like new computers and furniture coincided with thefts of cash from a trust fund her husband was managing for a disabled relative, according to *Forensic Files*.

The bank had video footage of her multiple withdrawals, which added up to $50,000. She also forged her husband's name at times.

The prosecution fought the notion that Daniel McDonnell would even consider suicide.

He had beaten cancer, still worked part time, was looking forward to a celebration for Erin's 21st birthday, and was planning to buy a fishing boat.

After a trial that lasted a little more than a week, a jury convicted Cynthia, 45, of first-degree premeditated murder.

As *Forensic Files* fans will remember, her daughter, Erin, urged the court to give the maximum penalty. She got her wish, when Judge Thomas Power sentenced Cynthia to life without the possibility of parole. Off to prison she went.

In a 2002 appeal, Cynthia claimed that her husband had been notified of the trust-fund theft—and his failure to take action right away was evidence that he was suicidal.

A three-judge appellate court panel unanimously ruled against the appeal.

Today, Cynthia McDonnell resides in Level II security at the Huron Valley Complex in Ypsilanti.

At five feet three and 240 pounds, Cynthia doesn't appear to have participated in any hunger strikes. She's resisted the siren song of any local artisans—she has no tattoos, according to the Michigan Department of Corrections.

Incidentally, although *Forensic Files* gave her occupation as freelance writer, it's not clear whether she ever had anything published. Nothing turned up online. (But to be fair, back in the day, magazines and newspapers didn't routinely slap stuff on the internet as they do now.)

Her brother-in-law Kevin McDonnell—her children's kindly uncle—who appeared on *Forensic Files* in 2004 and suggested he himself was ready to join his late brother soon, has a presence on social media and posted on Facebook as recently as 2020.

Cynthia's children maintain a Facebook page devoted to Daniel McDonnell's memory including old photos of their happy childhood with their father. When I reached out to them via Facebook, they declined to comment.

The memorial Facebook page doesn't mention Cynthia or identify her in any of the pictures.

Not everyone has abandoned Cynthia, however. Her former lawyer told me during a phone interview in 2021 that he maintains his belief in Cynthia's innocence. "She was just a really nice person," Pete Shumar said. "She's confined, and that's tragic."

In an odd twist, the lawyer who prosecuted her, Clarence Gomery, pleaded guilty in 2015 to a murder-for-hire plot against a fellow lawyer he was warring with over a case.

CHAPTER 10

Denise Davidson

A Jamaican Queen Falls

THE MURDER OF LOUIS DAVIDSON, MD
Forensic Files *episode "House Call"*

The presence of a beauty queen, even if it's Miss Southern Delaware Bartlett Pear, gives a true-crime story the allure of a fairy tale gone awry.

The *Forensic Files* episode "House Call" is especially hard to resist because it centers on a genuine heavy hitter—a former Miss Jamaica pageant finalist.

Denise Davidson probably thought police would never implicate someone like her when her estranged husband turned up dead.

But her poise and fluffy hair didn't help when it really counted, and she ended up in prison. For this chapter, I poked around to find out whether she's still incarcerated—and if so, whether she's enjoying madcap *Orange Is the New Black*–like adventures or it's just plain dismal living behind razor wire.

But first, here's a recap of "House Call" with additional information from internet research and an interview with a detective involved in the case.

In 1982, Louis Davidson, MD, married onetime swimsuit model Denise Davis, and they moved into a large house in Carrollwood, Florida, a few years later. Both of them originally came from Jamaica.

"He was a very well-respected doctor," says former detective Mike Celona. "He treated my daughter once for a soccer injury."

The doctor was described as kind and generous and "so smart he was almost scary" by Kathy Molino, RN, a former colleague who appeared on *Forensic Files.*

sorry, Denise . . .") on her own answering machine in hopes of throwing off investigators.

No luck with that ploy, because detectives found evidence that Denise had made the call herself from Dooley Groves, the citrus fruit store where she worked as a manager. (A *Snapped* episode about the case says that she made the call from a pay phone.)

They also discovered evidence that Denise had bought a gray sweatshirt and size 9 Voit sneakers—like those left behind at the Days Inn—at a Tampa Walmart, according to *Snapped*.

Police arrested Denise at Tampa International Airport as she was waiting to board a flight to Kingston, Jamaica.

She was held without bail.

Whatever charm she possessed during her tiara-and-sash days had dissipated by this time, says Celona, who remembers her as "brash and streetwise."

Florida investigators tracked down the assassins and put them, as well as Denise, on trial in 1995.

By this time, Denise had given birth in jail to Selena, her daughter with Cisneros. According to a *St. Petersburg Times* account, Denise's face lit up when the baby made an appearance in court, which prosecutors complained was an attempt to win the jury's favor.

At the trial, Denise testified that Cisneros had masterminded the murder plot without her cooperation.

"I have no doubt she was as much of a part of it as he was," Celona says. "He was a way to get it done because he had the contacts."

The jury convicted Denise of solicitation for murder, and she got a life sentence.

At the hitmen's trial, Susan Carole Shore, an accomplice who served as a driver, testified for the prosecution. She had met Gordon and McDonald at a Hialeah, Florida, racetrack and accepted their offer to take them to St. Petersburg for $100. But she said she knew nothing about a murder plot, and received probation and deportation back to England.

McDonald and Gordon's jury found them guilty and voted in favor of the electric chair.

"Your honor," McDonald read from a prepared statement, "God Most High told me to tell you that you should override the jury's 9 to 3 recommendation."

Circuit court judge Susan F. Schaeffer, known as "Ms. Death" for her harsh sentencing, was unimpressed and gave Gordon and McDonald the death penalty for first-degree murder.

As for Cisneros's true role in the murder, no one ever got to hear his side of the story. He had vanished and was still missing when *Forensic Files* first aired "House Call" in 2002. In 2008, *America's Most Wanted* sought help in finding him, without success.

"There are reports he's come as close as Canada to see his daughter," says Celona, who now works as an intelligence analyst for the St. Petersburg Police Department. "I don't believe he'll come back to the U.S. He frequents places like Venezuela and Jamaica, which is so corrupt." (Venezuela has an extradition treaty with the United States but doesn't always enforce it.)

Cisneros remains at large.

Interestingly, "Leo Cisneros" is a relatively common name, and the internet has stories about at least two felons by that name, but neither of them is Denise Davidson's former boyfriend, whose full name is Leonardo Anselmo Cisneros.

The two hitmen clearly had no idea where Cisneros was hiding out. Otherwise, they would have used the information to win themselves plea deals.

They both made efforts to get new trials, however.

Gordon filed an unsuccessful 1997 appeal claiming that having an all-white jury didn't count as a jury of his peers and that the court had neglected to hold Denise Davidson accountable to the same standards that had factored into his punishment.

He didn't get anywhere with a writ of habeas corpus with the U.S. District Court for the Middle District of Florida in 2004, either.

McDonald filed a motion for rehearing, which was denied in 2007.

As of this writing, neither Meryl, 76, nor Robert, 60, has been executed. They're prisoners in the maximum-security section of Union Correctional Institution in Raiford, Florida.

Regarding Denise Davidson, she is inmate number 153691 at the Homestead Correctional Institution in Dade County, Florida.

It's a prison with a minimum-security area that sounds a lot like the fictional Litchfield Correctional Institution of *Orange Is the New Black* (*OITNB*) fame.

Davidson's current custody status is "close," which means limitations on off-premises activities. In other words, for *OITNB* fans, no van-driving gig like the one Lorna Morello and Tiffany Doggett scored.

But Homestead offers plenty of other diversions, including four softball teams and classes in art, creative writing, music, aerobics, yoga, and anger management. Inmates also have the opportunity to study PC support services and automotive service technology.

On the down side, Davidson looks somber in recent photographs.

She probably regrets ending her marriage by soliciting two hitmen instead of one divorce lawyer.

Chapter 11

Dr. Debora Green

An Update

An MD Goes Medea on Her Kids, *Breaking Bad* on Her Husband

Forensic Files *episode "Ultimate Betrayal"*

The world loves to hate mothers who kill their children, and Debora Green makes an especially incendiary target.

She not only plotted her kids' demise but also chose the most horrific possible murder weapon, a fire.

Like Medea (the one from Euripides, not Tyler Perry) 2,400 years before her, she carried out her awful deed to punish a husband who wasn't exactly evil but betrayed her just the same.

And like *Breaking Bad*'s Walter White nearly two decades after her, she used ricin poisoning as part of her bid for revenge.

No wonder Debora's crimes, which took place back in 1995, merited an Ann Rule book in 1997, a *Forensic Files* episode in 1999, and a Lifetime movie in 2021.

So, amid all the drama, are there any mitigating factors? Is sympathy possible for Debora Green, a medical doctor who violated her "do no harm" oath in a way that devastated her own family?

I searched for answers and looked for more background information on Debora as well as updates on her and ex-husband Michael Farrar and any hints about the loyalties of the family's surviving daughter.

So let's get going on the recap for "Ultimate Betrayal" along with extra information from internet research.

Debora Jones came into the world on February 28, 1951, in Havana, Illinois, as the second of three children born to Joan and Bob Jones. The couple had married as teenagers. Debora described her childhood as happy, according to *Bitter Harvest: A Woman's Fury, a Mother's Sacrifice* (1997) by Ann Rule.

It became apparent early on that Debora was exceptionally intelligent. She could read and write before the age of three, the entertainment site meaww.com reported.

But she wasn't a nerd. At Peoria High School, she found time for cheerleading in addition to her schoolwork.

Debora, who also played the violin and piano, got a perfect grade-point average and ended up as co-valedictorian of her class. Next up, the attractive girl with symmetrical features completed an undergraduate degree in chemical engineering at the University of Illinois.

Debora married a fellow engineer named Duane M. J. Green in 1974; however, the union lasted only a few years, and he would later complain to police that Debora jilted him after he helped pay her tuition, according to the *Kansas City Star*.

While studying at the University of Kansas Medical School, she met Michael Farrar, and they married in 1979. The former Eagle Scout was four years younger than his new wife but was also a high achiever on the path to earning a medical degree.

Michael went into cardiology, and Debora specialized in oncology and hematology.

They had their first child, Tim, in 1982. Although the 2021 Lifetime movie *A House on Fire* portrays Tim as having only one sister, he actually had two, the younger girl named Kelly and a middle child whom *Forensic Files* identifies as Jennifer and *Bitter Harvest* calls Lissa—but her real name is Kate Farrar.

Debora and Michael had no shortage of room for their kids: By 1994, the family had settled into a six-bedroom Tudor-style house in Prairie Village, an affluent section of Kansas City, Kansas.

At some point, Debora put her career on pause to stay home with the kids, although she still did some freelance medical peer-review work out of her house.

She became a soccer coach so she could spend more time with her children, who attended the private Pembroke Hill School.

Although, by all accounts, Debora was dedicated to her job as a full-time parent, her marriage grew strained as she grappled with depression. She reportedly leaned on alcohol as a crutch even though her doctor had advised her not to drink while taking antidepressants and antianxiety medications.

Still, she enjoyed playing sports and having fun. In a May 1996 *Redbook* article, her onetime tennis clinic friend Ann Slegman recalled: "In this sea of affluent housewives with their smartly cropped hairdos, tennis skirts, and Steffi Graf wanna-be attitudes, Debora was refreshingly different. Heavyset with short, razor-cut hair, thick glasses that were popular among the disco set in the 1970s, faded T-shirts, and sweat shorts, she joked and laughed her way through the tennis drills."

In an effort to prop up their deteriorating union, Michael and Debora, along with son Tim, went on a hiking and boating trip to Peru sponsored by Pembroke Hill School.

Sadly, the excursion to South America did more harm than good. Michael met a good-looking, blonde registered nurse named Margaret Hacker (called Celeste Walker in the Lifetime movie), and they began seeing each other back in the United States.

Debora "saw all the telltale signs" of an affair including "a new wardrobe, new exercise equipment, and a new, distant attitude toward her and the children," according to the *Redbook* account.

She moved into a separate bedroom and started drinking more.

Soon, it was Michael's turn to struggle with his health. He became violently ill with bacterial endocarditis, which causes severe diarrhea. His weight dropped to 125 pounds.

He eventually needed three hospitalizations, each time after he'd eaten food Debora prepared for him, but at first doctors couldn't figure out what triggered his episodes. It was the 1990s, long before *Breaking Bad* made ricin a household name.

Once his health rallied, Michael vacated the family's mansion on Canterbury Court and rented his own place in the Georgetown apartment complex across town.

Debora turned suicidal and ended up in a psychiatric hospital after Michael called police to intervene during an argument on September

25, 1995. In the emergency room, she spat on Michael, called him an obscene name, and said he'd get the kids over her dead body.

Bitter and angry, Debora had also "used the crudest language to tell the couple's children that Michael was having sex with other women," the *Kansas City Star* reported.

At some point amid the melodrama, Michael discovered in Debora's purse packets of castor beans, which contain ricin.

At first, ricin didn't show up in Michael's lab tests, but the chemical is hard to detect because it breaks down quickly. But eventually, a large number of ricin antibodies turned up in his blood.

Michael confronted Debora on the phone about poisoning him. She denied it, and they had an angry discussion. On October 23, 1995, he spent time visiting his girlfriend Margaret Hacker at her house.

On October 24, 1995, Debora and Michael had another argument on the phone. An hour later, the Prairie Village mansion, where she and the kids were still living, caught on fire.

Golden-haired Kelly, who at age six already showed signs of being a gifted student, died of smoke inhalation in bed. Tim, 13 years old and a popular soccer and hockey player, died of burns.

The family dog, a black Lab named Boomer, died of carbon monoxide poisoning, according to Medium's True Crime Edition website.

Debora, 43, exited through a door to the outside.

All sources agree that 10-year-old Kate escaped by climbing onto the roof through her second-floor bedroom window and jumping to the ground without injury. But accounts vary as to whether Debora caught her as she fell or tried to catch her and failed or just watched her descend.

Kate and her mother stood together as emergency workers arrived on the scene. The flames were so intense the firefighters couldn't go inside.

Reports about Debora's behavior at the fire scene differ. Some describe her as without emotion as she watched the blaze that killed two of her children. Another account said she was yelling at emergency workers, accusing them of not doing enough to save Kelly and Tim.

Authorities suspected arson and, at first, believed either parent could have done it.

Debora explained to police that, on the night of the fire, she woke up to the smoke alarm, opened the bedroom door, saw flames, and ran outside.

On the intercom, she told Tim to stay in his bedroom until firefighters arrived and then she ran next door to ask for help from neighbors, Debora said. They noticed that her hair looked wet. A lab would later find singeing to her hair. Her bathrobe, found in a ball at home, had burn marks. Because the doorjamb to Debora's bedroom was covered with soot, investigators believed the door was open when the fire started.

At the house, police found what looked like an empty accelerant bottle. The stairway that the children needed as an escape route had flammable liquid poured on it. The path of the fire led to Debora's door.

Investigators ultimately concluded that Debora both set the fire and poisoned Michael with the castor beans.

Detectives discovered records indicating Debora had made two purchases of castor beans at Earl May Garden Centers around the time of the couple's woes. She claimed that son Tim needed them for a science project and that Tim—who wasn't around to defend himself—might have poisoned his dad.

By this time, Michael had asked for a divorce; he filed the papers the day after the fire. Debora was not happy that gal pal Margaret Hacker attended the memorial service for the kids.

"Michael was in her bed while our house was burning down," she complained to Slegman.

But in between the fire and the time of her arrest, Debora and daughter Kate continued to live as normal a life as possible after such a tragedy.

Kate got a role in a State Ballet of Missouri production of *The Nutcracker*.

On November 22, 1995, after Debora dropped off Kate for ballet practice at the Midland Theater in Kansas City, police arrested her and charged her with two counts of murder, attempted murder, and aggravated arson. A judge set bail at the unheard-of amount of $3 million.

The developments shocked residents of Prairie Village, who weren't accustomed to having drama and police activity in their corner of the world.

According to an Associated Press (AP) account, neighbors had to contend with the smell of smoke that lingered for weeks after the fire and the sight of cars slowing down to look at the charred $400,000 house at 7517 Canterbury Court.

The *Kansas City Star* reported that most neighbors refused to discuss the tragedy with the media. The few who did said that Debora loved her children—and while clearly the couple's marriage had seen better days, no one imagined it would end in a burning hell.

Locals didn't have to look at the wreckage of the once-palatial home for long. By November 1995, the city was making plans to demolish it. (Apparently, it didn't hurt property values—today, some houses on Canterbury Court are priced at around $1 million, according to real estate websites.)

In preparation for the trial, the prosecution noted evidence that Debora had been reading a book about arson and other literature about people murdered by family members.

Authorities believed that after the couple fought on the phone, Debora poured accelerant on Michael's belongings and used the fluid to cut off the children's escape routes from the house. Her hair and bathrobe sustained burns because she used too much accelerant near her own bedroom door. Then she told Tim to stay in the house with little sister Kelly until the fire trucks arrived.

And one more thing: This was not the first time a blaze had broken out in a Green-Farrar household. On May 21, 1994, when the family lived in Missouri and was considering a relocation to Prairie Village, a fire damaged the Missouri house—reportedly right after Michael had nixed the idea of the move over concerns about the future of the marriage, according to court papers available on Murderpedia.

No legal action resulted from the Missouri fire.

But there was no escaping the consequences of the Kansas inferno. The state kept Debora in custody during court proceedings. "She's very surprised that she would be charged with these kinds of crimes," Ellen

Ryan, one of Debora's three lawyers, told the AP. "She lost everything in this fire including her children, everything, and she's astounded."

Debora's defense lawyers floated the possibility that Tim had set the fire.

Meanwhile, Kate Farrar remained loyal to her mother. She left a vase full of roses at the courthouse for Debora. The two still talked on the phone.

Michael, who had to make $5,400 monthly payments to Debora as a run-up to their divorce, showed up in court with a partially shaved head because he'd needed brain surgery to drain an abscess probably caused by the ricin poisoning. He would also need a heart operation to counteract the damage.

The murder case was such big news that true-crime author Ann Rule, who wrote *The Stranger Beside Me* (1980) and *Small Sacrifices* (1987), attended the preliminary hearing and brought an assistant to help take notes.

Prosecutors had assembled a roster of 300 prospective witnesses and planned to start out by calling 20 of them to the stand. Olathe courthouse employees outfitted a backup room for media outlets; there were only 60 seats in the courtroom.

But the trial never happened.

On April 17, 1996, Debora Green pleaded no contest in a deal to take the death penalty off the table. The AP reported that, "in a fast monotone," Debora read a statement maintaining that she wasn't in her right mind on the night of the fire—her psychiatric and alcohol problems set the stage for the tragedy—and she didn't want to compound the suffering of her family with a trial.

"She's accepting responsibility for [the fire]," said Debora's lawyer Michael Moore. "I don't think she ever intended to kill her children. She's a caring, living, breathing human being."

On May 30, 1996, she received a sentence of life in prison with the possibility of parole after 40 years for attempted murder, premeditated killing, and aggravated arson.

Once Debora had spent a few years behind razor wire, she began recasting her story.

According to *Bitter Harvest*, Debora made claims that Michael and his girlfriend might have hired someone to start the fire. She also told Ann Rule that the home-wrecking Margaret drove Margaret's former husband to suicide.

Debora noted that she cut off her singed hair not to obscure it as evidence but rather to look her best for Kelly and Tim's funeral.

In 2000, Debora briefly tried a new tack. She requested new sentencing based on a claim that her no-contest plea to arson resulted from her own confusion caused by prescription psychiatric drugs.

She would also need to defend herself over the ricin allegations. "No one in an alcoholic fog would have been capable of the intricate planning it took to locate, purchase, and grind up the deadly castor beans," Ann Rule wrote in *Bitter Harvest*.

Once Debora realized, however, that the motion might put capital punishment back in play, she withdrew it.

Four years later, she made a bid to have her plea thrown out because new advances into arson investigations refuted the pour pattern evidence against her, she contended. The fire might have come from a vanity in her bedroom that ignited on its own, Debora said.

Kate Farrar, who was then 19, attended a hearing on that matter—and sat with Debora's supporters, according to the *Kansas City Star*. Michael Farrar showed up as well but sat away from his daughter. In 2005, district judge Peter Ruddick ruled against Debora.

In 2015, a judge scuttled Debora's request for resentencing because she based it on recent state and federal rulings on "Hard 40" prison terms (involving the length of a prison term for committing a murder with "aggravated circumstances" before consideration for parole and whether a judge or jury should make that determination) that didn't apply retroactively. Johnson County district judge Brenda Cameron also noted that Debora understood the terms of her plea deal when she agreed to it.

Today, Debora Green resides at the Topeka Correctional Facility in medium-high security, with the first prospective release date in 2035. According to the Kansas Department of Corrections, she has a job in prison.

So, does Debora Green deserve any sympathy? To me, it sounds like a long-sustained period of temporary insanity resulting from her husband's infidelity, her clinical depression, and the loss of a career that brought her respect, personal fulfillment, and a high salary.

"Even though I could not believe she was innocent," wrote Anne Rule, "I thought her tears [for her children] were genuine."

As for the husband she tried to eliminate, Michael Farrar survived and has worked as a cardiologist at North Kansas City Hospital for 29 years. He recently served as medical staff president and "enjoys traveling, bird hunting, dining out, and learning more about history," according to an interview on the hospital's website.

And what of the extramarital relationship that helped fuel the modern-day Greek tragedy? According to Medium writer Lori Johnston, Michael Farrar and Margaret Hacker broke up. He ended up marrying a lawyer.

Apparently, Kate Farrar, the daughter who never abandoned her mother, maintained a good relationship with her father as well. She eventually went to live with Michael Farrar and his wife.

CHAPTER 12

Diane Tilly

A Texas Tragedy

A Giver Is Taken Away
Forensic Files *episode "Transaction Failed"*

Diane Tilly answered a knock at her door one night and found 15-year-old Pearl Ann Cruz, who told a story about car trouble and asked to use the phone. Tilly, 58, knew Pearl because she had at one time hired her father, Ronnie Neal, to do yard work.

Once inside, Pearl pulled a gun on Diane and let Neal in through the side door of Tilly's house in the Alamo Heights area of San Antonio, Texas.

Although the exact sequence of all of the events is unclear, by the end of the night, the 33-year-old Neal had threatened to kill Diane's cat if she wouldn't give him her PIN number, taken a swig of her scotch, raped her, used her ATM card to steal $400, loaded possessions from the house into her car, driven her to a field, and shot her to death.

Then, Neal dialed up Pearl's mother to announce he had come into some money and suggest the three of them go shopping.

"Transaction Failed"—which told the story of the November 22, 2004, murder of the beloved schoolteacher—is my second-favorite episode of *Forensic Files* because it's rich with difficult truths and compelling characters.

Out of all 400 episodes of the series, "Transaction Failed" portrays the most vivid collision between a high-functioning, admirable human being and the most miserable lowlife imaginable.

Tilly cofounded Robbins Academy, an alternative school for kids who had problems learning or were otherwise troubled, and was also the lead teacher there. *Forensic Files* showed brief footage of an interview with one of the students.

"Most students don't talk to teachers about their personal problems, but almost all the students talked to her about theirs," a boy named Alex Rivard said on camera.

Tilly was called a miracle worker for the way she engaged hard-to-reach kids and helped improve their self-esteem.

The episode made me think of my own 12 years of public education, with so many teachers who went into the profession primarily because they wanted summers off or who paid attention to students who were naturally gifted (in gym and home economics, usually) and either ignored or belittled the rest.

As such, it was beautiful to hear how Diane Tilly cared about making her students' lives better.

Ronnie Neal, on the other hand, was in the habit of ruining lives. In a series of *San Antonio Express-News* articles about the crime, reporter Karisa King revealed disturbing facts that weren't mentioned on *Forensic Files*.

According to King, at the time of Tilly's murder, Pearl Cruz was pregnant with her father's child, and he sometimes earned extra money by prostituting her out to older men. He gave her cocaine and alcohol.

One of the articles also mentioned that Pearl's mother, Elisa Stanley, had children with a number of different men and that Pearl was the only one who was biracial—and not entirely accepted by the others because of it.

Pearl's life underscores a sad truth: As much as we like to think that everyone has a chance to succeed in the United States, there are still kids like her out there who face lottery-like odds.

(In fact, in a letter written to the *San Antonio Express-News*, Diane Tilly's daughter, Allison Tilly Carswell, expressed frustration that the articles missed an opportunity to examine how child protective services could have better served someone like Pearl and thus prevented the tragic events.)

The case also is a reminder that there are people in the world who identify kindness as a weakness to be exploited. Tilly had once given a swing set to Neal and made an effort to connect with Pearl by complimenting her on her nail polish, according to "Transaction Failed."

Pearl would later admit that she and her father had started planning their crime after first meeting Tilly. They noticed that Tilly had a lot more than they did and wished to steal it.

As painful as the case was to contemplate, it was fairly straightforward to convict, according to Alfred J. Damiani, then a homicide detective with the Bexar County Sheriff's Office.

"We could have thrown away three-quarters of the evidence and still gotten a conviction," Damiani told me during an interview.

Police arrested Neal and Pearl in a motel parking lot after they were spotted with Tilly's car and security footage showed them using her ATM card at a Shell station.

They found Neal's fingerprint on the Chivas Regal bottle in Diane's house.

But Neal said he had nothing to do with Tilly's disappearance and told the police quite a story about how he came into possession of her things (more about that in part 2 that follows).

After 10 days in custody, Pearl decided to cooperate with the investigation; she led police to Diane Tilly's body.

Sentenced as a juvenile, she received 30 years. Her father got the death penalty.

While in prison, Neal created an online profile in which he proclaimed his innocence and fondness for poetry. He also crafted an (unsuccessful) escape plan in which he told a prospective accomplice to let him be "the brains" in the plot.

At the same time, Neal claimed to have intellectual disabilities in the hopes of avoiding lethal injection by the state. That ploy didn't work; prosecutors maintained that his IQ was at least 70, above the Texas criminal justice system's range for the death penalty.

In 2010, Neal committed suicide in jail, saving Diane's children from having to endure years of appeals from the killer.

"I am thankful that he has taken his last breath on this earth," her son, Stephen, told the *San Antonio Express-News.*

Today, Diane's son and daughter both have kids of their own and successful careers. Their father, Michael Tilly, MD, died in 2020 at the age of 75.

The final reason that I've watched "Transaction Failed" at least five times is that it raises intriguing questions about the mechanics of the case. For example, why did an experienced criminal like Ronnie Neal—he had prior robbery convictions—submit to police questioning instead of clamming up and calling a lawyer?

Detective Damiani agreed to answer some of my questions.

*****

PART 2: A HOMICIDE DETECTIVE DEMYSTIFIES THE CASE IN A Q&A

Ronnie Neal seemed oddly unaware of the way police actually catch criminals, considering that, as a felon, he had plenty of experience with law enforcement.

For example, he made no attempt to disguise himself when trying to withdraw cash with Tilly's ATM card at businesses he must have known had security cameras.

He had Pearl, 15, use the card, too. She wore a hat but did nothing else to hide her identity.

After the authorities apprehended the father-daughter team at a motel, Neal told the police quite a yarn about how he came into possession of Tilly's 1998 Cadillac Fleetwood, .357 Magnum, bank card, and other property.

Neal was at a car wash, he claimed, when he spotted the sedan with the keys in the ignition and the engine running. The vehicle was already loaded up with easy-to-pawn possessions, so he just couldn't resist hopping inside and driving away, he said.

In the glove compartment, Neal explained, he discovered Tilly's ATM card, with the PIN number written on a piece of paper.

When he heard on TV that the beloved Robbins Academy educator had gone missing and authorities were searching for two people seen with her car, he set the vehicle on fire in a field so no one would mistakenly believe he was connected with her disappearance, he said.

I'm curious as to why Neal peddled such absurdity.

Alfred J. Damiani, whom *Forensic Files* watchers may remember for his appearance on the episode "Shattered Innocence," agreed to answer some of my questions.

Damiani, now a sergeant with the Bexar County Sheriff's Office Vehicle Crimes Unit in San Antonio, offered some insight and also indulged my curiosity about his line of work:

Rebecca Reisner: Were you shocked by this case?

Al Damiani: It was disturbing but not particularly shocking. My wife is an educator, and my habit was to have her proofread my reports before I turned them in. She told me recently that she found it [the Tilly case] so disturbing that she had trouble sleeping.

RR: Why was Ronnie Neal so reckless?

AD: He made some attempts. He told Pearl, "Don't worry, the quality is so bad on the security footage that they'll never be able to identify us."

RR: Why didn't Neal just clam up instead of giving police a story that could easily be picked apart?

AD: He didn't have a lot of choices because we caught him dead to rights on video tape using the ATM card on more than one occasion. We caught him with her possessions, and he tried to pull a gun on us—the gun he stole from Tilly's house. It was in his waistband and fell down his pant leg. Then we grabbed him and took him into custody. He had a second gun, which we found in his hotel room. And the interview was more than meets the eye. I sat down with this guy and talked to him and came to the conclusion that no helpful information was coming. At that time, we hadn't found a body yet so I was still involved in trying to find an alive Diane Tilly and didn't want to waste time with the guy giving a fabrication. There was a real close time frame between the murder and when we had him in custody—around 24 hours—and that's why we were still operating under the hope that it was an abduction and we still might find her alive someplace. So I turned the interview over to some other detectives, and they got something from him down on paper. Sometimes it's good to get a story down, even if it's a fabrication. It helps for judges to see what a liar he is.

RR: Did you believe his contention that he had intellectual disabilities?

AD: I don't think he was a genius but, no, I didn't believe he [had intellectual disabilities]. That contention came up later, because he wanted to stay out of the death chamber. This information didn't make it into the *Forensic Files* episode, but once when Ronnie Neal was in county jail in the Houston area [in connection with an earlier crime], he hatched a plan to have his sister bring him a TV set with a gun inside the back—this was before TV sets were so thin. The plan was that he would take the gun out, shoot a guard, and watch him die.

RR: I found some footage online of Ronnie Neal's mother, Annie Pine, in court that didn't appear on *Forensic Files*. I felt a little bad for her when she begged for his life. She seemed sweet.

AD: I think there was more going on at Annie Pine's house than we know. I don't think she was the nice person she seemed. The first time I met her I got a bad vibe off of her and she was incensed that we would be looking at Ronnie Neal in relation to this crime. Annie Pine absolutely refused to cooperate with the investigation back when we still hoped to find Diane Tilly alive.

RR: What about Pearl Cruz's sentence? *Forensic Files* said she got 30 years, but I read that she's already out.

AD: Pearl Ann was as much a victim as anyone else. That doesn't dismiss her behavior. She took an active part in this crime. But she was only 15 years old and she cooperated with the investigation, which is why the district attorney's office allowed her to have a life and walk out of jail. Otherwise, she would have been considered an adult and served the whole 30 years.

RR: Did you feel *Forensic Files'* portrayal of the case was fair and accurate?

AD: Yes, they did a great job, especially considering the time constraints. There were two days of shooting and a lot of stuff going on.

RR: Why did you stop working as a homicide detective?

AD: I had one case after another of some really disturbing stuff. They say a detective has only so many homicides in him that he can deal with, and that everyone has a different body count. One day, it just hit me, I don't want to do this anymore. It was after the Tilly case and later some baby cases.

RR: Could you put your cases out of your mind when you were at home?

AD: To do homicide, you have to be completely involved—it's not something you can forget. It was my life. Fortunately, my wife didn't divorce me.

CHAPTER 13

Frankie Pullian

Deceived and Killed

E. LEE WHITE PREYS ON AN INNOCENT
Forensic Files *episode "Undertaken"*

Frankie Pullian's murder is one of those stories that simultaneously affirm and deny faith in humanity.

A band of fraudsters put into motion a plan to kill Pullian, a 29-year-old errand runner at a funeral parlor, and pocket $980,000 from life insurance policies.

The culprits thought no one would pay much attention to Pullian's death because he lived in relative obscurity with no family near him in Passaic County, New Jersey.

But society cared. The criminal justice system worked. It took them a few years, but authorities determined how Pullian really ended up lifeless underneath a stolen Ford Maverick—and put three of the conspirators in prison.

The crime happened in 1980 and the *Forensic Files* episode about the case dates back to 2006, so I hunted around to find out whether the perpetrators are still alive and what happened to them.

But first, here's a recap of "Undertaken," along with other information from internet research.

Frankie Pullian joined the army after high school but received an early discharge because of what *Forensic Files* called a neurological impairment. An *Asbury Park Press* story from 1982 suggested he had some type of intellectual disability.

Whatever the case, he functioned highly enough to take a job with the E. Lee White Funeral Home in Paterson, New Jersey.

White hired Pullian to wash funeral limousines and perform assorted other tasks. Pullian earned $7,500 to $10,000 a year.

Pullian (as well as *Forensic Files*) apparently overlooked a bit of trouble the business experienced back in 1975.

The state of New Jersey stripped E. Lee White of certification to conduct funerals because of unethical business practices including the "unconscionable" practice of marking up caskets to "four times their wholesale cost," according to an *Asbury Park Press* account from July 15, 1975.

The *New York Times* reported that the revocation was permanent, but somehow, E. Lee White resurrected his reputation and operations within a few years.

Newspaper accounts published after 1980 describe him as a "respected civic leader," and E. Lee White Funeral Home was open for business.

But White had secretly progressed from crooked to homicidal. He hoped to parlay his investment in the innocent Pullian into a six-figure payoff.

In the eight months preceding the murder on April 8, 1980, White and his wife, Erna, and associates Lawrence Scott and William Brown, started taking out insurance policies on Pullian, forging his signature, and naming themselves as the beneficiaries.

Newspaper accounts give Scott's profession as truck driver or construction worker and Brown's as Prudential Insurance employee. The *Morristown Daily Record* reported that Brown, a Rutgers University graduate, had his pharmacy license revoked in 1978 following a conviction for Medicare fraud.

Apparently, Scott and Brown did some kind of work for White's funeral parlor as well.

Erna White, a public school teacher, obtained one of the insurance policies on Pullian by claiming she was his sister. She signed the policy "Erna Boone," her maiden name.

Pullian didn't have a sister.

One of the policies offered an extra $350,000 if the insured party died in an accident.

Investigators believed that E. Lee White was the mastermind behind the crime and had started planning it several years ahead of time—and possibly hired Pullian with the intention of killing him.

Meanwhile, Pullian "idealized White and considered White a father figure," according to New Jersey Superior Court documents dated March 31, 2014 (*Elbert White v. New Jersey State Parole Board*).

With all the insurance policies in place, White arranged for someone—the police never determined who—to kill Pullian, run over his body with the Maverick, and abandon the vehicle in an alley so it looked like an accidental hit and run.

Everything worked as planned at first. Emergency services took Pullian directly to E. Lee White's funeral parlor, where White started the autopsy himself.

The medical examiner arrived and unwittingly declared a car accident the cause of death and cleared the path for the conspirators to begin collecting the funds.

But the position of the body, lack of skid marks, and unlikelihood of a car traveling fast enough on a short alleyway made police suspicious.

One of the life insurance companies requested an investigation.

Three years after Pullian's death, authorities dug up and reexamined his body. They discovered his skull carried a fatal "moon crater" injury— the mark of a blunt instrument, like a hammer—inconsistent with a death by auto.

Investigators had noted that the vehicle contained high-velocity blood splatter in the interior. But someone had taken care to wipe fingerprints away.

They theorized that a White associate lured Pullian inside the car and killed him there with a heavy implement.

Once detectives spoke to doctors who administered the exams required by the insurance companies, it became clear that the plan involved impostors in the run-up to the murder. The men who had claimed to be Frankie Pullian had to refer to notes to answer the doctors' questions.

As the case pressed on, White tried to appear calm, even after his indictment for first-degree murder and fraud.

The funeral director said that he was not worried about the charges and that business increased after his indictment, according to a *Morristown Daily Record* story from 1984.

Lawrence Scott somehow managed to snag William Kunstler, a lawyer world famous for taking on social outcasts as clients, to defend him.

Nonetheless, a jury convicted Scott, Brown, and E. Lee White on January 18, 1985, after a 47-day trial.

The following month, Judge Amos Saunders, citing "pure, evil greed," sentenced White, age 45, to life with eligibility for parole after 25 years. Lawrence Scott, 38, got life but with parole eligibility after 15 years.

The next day, Saunders also gave William Brown—who admitted to participating in part of the scheme but claimed it was Frankie Pullian's idea—life without the chance of parole for 15 years. The judge cited a "cruel and brutal execution of a helpless individual."

Erna White was tried separately and convicted of fraud and theft by deception. She got off with probation.

So, where are these four coldhearted people today?

1. E. Lee White got into trouble while incarcerated at Trenton State Prison.

In 1990, a judge tacked an extra five years to White's sentence after a jury convicted him of soliciting a fellow inmate to take responsibility for the Pullian murder.

White had offered Robert Earl Moore cash and a sports car in exchange for making a false confession.

That disappointment didn't deter White's optimism, and over the years, he vied aggressively for release on the basis of various claims, including the seemingly universal "ineffective counsel."

In 2016, two superior court judges affirmed a New Jersey State Parole Board's decision to deny parole to White.

The court noted a lack of "rehabilitative progress" and that "instead of confronting the facts as proven at trial, petitioner adhered to a version of events that downplayed his culpable actions."

E. Lee White died in May 2019. He was living in Washington, DC, at the time of his demise at age 79, according to an obituary in the *Star-Ledger*. (It's not known if, when, or why he won parole.)

2. Erna Boone White still lives in Paterson. Apparently the 1985 conviction didn't teach the educator much of a lesson. Her name turned up in the news in 1991, when Passaic County won a case against her for bilking impoverished relatives of deceased individuals out of $39,000 for burial expenses—which had already been paid for with public funds, according to the *Morristown Daily Record*. She received a sentence of 300 days.

3. Lawrence Scott won release in 2001 but ended up back in prison later that same year. The New Jersey Department of Corrections lists his current status as "paroled."

4. William Brown is not listed with the New Jersey Department of Corrections. Newspaper accounts of the crime carry little identifying information about him, and the commonness of his name makes it hard to research him. A story from 1985 lists his age as 50, so if he's alive, he's in his late 80s.

No relatives of Frankie Pullian ever materialized to file suit against the conspirators, but the state of New Jersey made sure that they paid at least something for their cruelty and greed.

CHAPTER 14

Helga Luest's Story

Miami Robbery Mayhem

TRAUMA LEADS TO A NEW AVOCATION
Forensic Files *episode "Tourist Trap"*

The whole world pretty much already knew how bad the smash-and-grab tourist robbery epidemic in Miami, Florida, had become by the time of Helga Luest's 1993 ordeal—the subject of the *Forensic Files* episode "Tourist Trap."

Two years earlier, another attack had made international headlines when thieves shot and robbed two British visitors, John and Rose Hayward; fortunately, they survived.

That was only one of the six southern Florida tourist robberies taking place within a single 24-hour period in 1991.

Between 1992 and 1993, the continuing horror show claimed the lives of nine visitors, including Barbara Jensen Miller, 39, who died when a vehicle driven by escaping thieves ran over her in front of her mother and two children.

Shortly before a would-be thief clamped onto Helga's arm with his teeth as she hit the gas pedal and sped away in a rental car, a German man had died at the hands of an assailant on Miami's Dolphin Expressway.

The victim, Uwe-Wilhelm Rakebrand, recognized a bump-and-rob attempt, and as law enforcement recommended, he continued driving, refusing to stop his Alamo rental vehicle. Instead of giving up, the teen-aged thieves pulled their truck alongside Rakebrand's red Toyota Corolla. Patsy Jones fired a .30-caliber sawed-off rifle into the front seat, killing the 33-year-old agricultural engineer.

Newspapers reported on the irony of the murder occurring just moments after Rakebrand's wife had finished reading off a list of tourism safety tips from the Greater Miami Convention and Visitors Bureau.

There's plenty of irony in Helga Luest's tale as well, so let's get going on the recap of "Tourist Trap" along with extra information drawn from internet research and two interviews with Helga.

A producer for German TV, Helga was assigned to cover the Sunshine State crime woes and even produced a segment about tourist safety for German television.

Coincidentally, before the crime wave hit, Helga and her mother, who both lived in the United States on the East Coast, had made arrangements for a vacation to the Florida Keys. They decided to go ahead with the trip anyway.

Unfortunately, forewarned wasn't entirely forearmed. The women got lost near Miami International Airport and pulled onto a side street to turn around. Two assailants suddenly materialized and blocked their rental car.

"We offered to give them everything to leave us alone," Helga recalled in a 2016 interview with me, "but they said they were going to kill us." Seemingly caught up in brutality for brutality's sake, the drug-crazed pair apparently forgot to steal anything from the women.

Instead, one man yelled threats at Helga's mother, and the other pummeled Helga, who was in the driver's seat. He kicked through her window, reached in, disabled the horn, shifted the gear to park, and began punching Helga.

Helga fought back, and as mentioned, one of the men—later identified as 23-year-old Stanley Cornet—bit down on her arm and managed to hang on for a few moments as she raced from the scene in her car.

The assault left Helga with a dislocated jaw, injuries to her back and neck, and a large bite wound. She retained a lack of feeling on one side of her face.

The five-foot, six-inch Cornet apparently bounced off the pavement without major injuries, because he felt well enough four days later to bite and attempt to rob another motorist. The victim's son, a Miami police officer, intervened and took Cornet into custody.

A forensic odontologist made a cast of Cornet's teeth and determined a match to Helga's bite wound. Unlike many other tourist robbery victims, Helga was willing to travel back to Miami to assist with the investigation and legal actions against her assailant.

(The physical distance between the victims' homelands and south Florida wasn't the only detriment to prosecution during the crime wave. Thieves hoped that the dramatic and brutal nature of the smash-and-grab jobs would leave their prey too shaken up or scared to testify, according to the 2006 book *Crime Scenes: Revealing the Science behind the Evidence* by Paul Roland.)

Cornet, who had prior convictions, ended up receiving life in prison. He never gave up the name of his accomplice in the attack. I presumed it was a rare case of honor among thieves, but Helga told me in a 2021 interview that she suspects self-interest.

"I think they were in a gang together," she says. "That's what law enforcement told me. So I think he was better off taking his own punishment than ratting out a fellow gang member."

The *Forensic Files* episode concludes by noting that the south Florida tourist-robbery wave ended after companies stopped marking rental cars as such and police increased their vigilance around rental parking lots.

But southern Florida's efforts to protect travelers were actually more extensive than what the show detailed. The state and Broward County put up additional lighting and signs to help tourists avoid getting lost. Rewards were offered to members of the public who helped the police apprehend robbers. Most important, law enforcement invested $500,000 in a multijurisdictional task force to prevent crimes against tourists—and made hundreds of arrests within a few months.

In 1994, tourist robberies in Dade County dropped 58 percent from the previous year, according to a *New York Times* story dated June 21, 1995.

Stanley Cornet was sentenced to life in prison in 1996. But in 2001, he finagled a new sentencing hearing, necessitating a trip back to the courtroom for Helga.

"He sat there and smiled at me during proceedings—now, for a second time—as he heard what I went through physically and emotionally. The court saw that he was not remorseful," Helga recalls.

This judge sentenced Cornet to life in jail without parole, giving Helga the justice she deserved. But she still grappled with her injuries from the attack.

"My career changed completely," she says. "Because of my physical injuries, I could no longer carry gear in the field when I was producing news stories so I knew I had to make a change. I came to see my life's work as helping to prevent violence wherever possible and making sure victims have the support they need to heal and live well again."

Today, Helga works as director of marketing and communications for the Manhattan Strategy Group, a consulting firm that specializes in social changes, and manages trauma-informed groups on LinkedIn and Facebook.

"I believe the final stage of the healing process is when you can take the dark cloud of what happened to you and make it something positive," Helga says. "I use my experience to try to better inform programs and use what I know as a survivor to inform and help other people. What was once a senseless incident that happened to me became something I could turn into actions with a positive purpose."

Helga, who now lives in the Washington, DC, area with her children—twins, a son and daughter—also serves on the Governor's Family Violence Council in Maryland.

She's an advocate for protecting the environment as well and created the Give a Shift YouTube channel to encourage individuals to make small changes that can ease climate change. "My daughter and I drive e-vehicles and do composting and wash in cold water and line-dry clothes," she says.

Helga's mother, who was also a victim in the attack in Miami but not physically injured, has retired and enjoys spending time with her grandchildren.

Some of Helga's injuries have healed. "I can lift heavy things now and have run 17 marathons," she says. "I've lived more of a great life on the side of life after the attack."

CHAPTER 15

Helle Crafts

Winter of the Wood Chipper

RICHARD CRAFTS IS STILL ALIVE

Forensic Files *episode "The Disappearance of Helle Crafts"*

"The Disappearance of Helle Crafts" tells of a crime 30 years old, but you can bet that the killer will always be part of popular culture.

Richard Crafts was an airline pilot, a part-time police officer, a former Marine pilot, and a father of three. But ever since 1986, he's pretty much been "the guy in Connecticut who put his wife in the wood chipper."

You'd think the criminal justice system would keep a man with his history away from fresh air and heavily bladed equipment forever, but not so: Crafts has already been released from prison.

I'll get to the specifics about why Crafts, born in 1937 and now in his mid-80s, exited razor wire while still breathing, but first here's a recap of the episode along with additional information drawn from internet research.

Helle Lorck Nielson originally came from Denmark and met her future husband in Miami, Florida, in 1969, when she was training as a flight attendant for Pan Am and he was training as a pilot for Eastern Airlines.

They married in 1975 and eventually moved to a $250,000 house on a two-acre lot in Danbury, Connecticut.

At some point, Richard started cheating on Helle.

In 1984, doctors discovered that Richard had colon cancer and gave him only a 2 percent chance of survival, according to a *Newtown Bee* story, although the *Hartford Courant* described it as stomach cancer.

Either way, he survived.

But Richard, whom associates described as nice although a bit introverted, didn't appreciate that Helle had cared for him during his surgery and chemotherapy.

The ingratitude turned out to be the least of his shortcomings as a husband and father.

And although he reportedly made $120,000 a year—a nice bundle in 1986—he didn't like the idea of paying alimony and child support and dividing up the family possessions. He allegedly tried to thwart a breakup by telling Helle his cancer had returned, but she discovered he was lying.

A divorce became imminent in fall 1986, after Keith Mayo, a private investigator Helle hired, confirmed what she had been suspecting: Her husband was having an affair.

The other woman was an Eastern Airlines flight attendant from Middletown, New Jersey, named Nancy Dodd.

The Craftses' marriage had been in bad shape for a while, with Richard disappearing for long stretches. Helle found receipts from Christmas gifts her husband had bought for another woman.

Richard would later nonchalantly admit to state police that he actually had a second girlfriend, yet another Eastern flight attendant, and that his job as a pilot presented a lot of nice opportunities to cheat.

According to Helle's divorce lawyer, Dianne Andersen, who appeared on the *Forensic Files* episode, Richard physically abused Helle at times.

When Helle, 39, filed for divorce, she told Andersen that if she disappeared, Richard did it.

Andersen remarked that it was "an unusual comment" (but not if you watch enough *Forensic Files*).

Richard Crafts had at one time done some piloting for a secret CIA mission, and Helle feared he could track her down anywhere if she tried to flee, the *Hartford Courant* reported.

But Helle's life ended right in the Craftses' own home. Her friend Gertrude Horvath dropped her off there on November 18, 1986, after a trip to Frankfurt, Germany, for her job.

The family's live-in nanny, Dawn Marie Thomas, 19, was out of the house.

When Helle didn't show up for work the next day, her friends turned to Keith Mayo, who started an investigation on his own.

The nanny told Mayo that Richard had ripped up some bedroom carpet with a mysterious dark stain on it.

A large freezer was missing from the house. And then there was the $279 receipt for the rental of a diesel-powered wood chipper.

A snowplow driver named Joe Hine reported seeing a man with a wood chipper on a bridge over the Housatonic River shortly after Helle went missing.

That sighting jump-started police interest in the case.

An investigative team found a pile of wood chips with a letter addressed to Helle Crafts on the riverbank. They discovered blonde hair, bone fragments, and a woman's painted fingernail. In the water, they found parts of a chainsaw with the serial number scratched off.

Police set up a tent near the scene to collect and study the evidence, and motorists started heading to the site to slow down and take a look, according to the *Newtown Bee*.

"The horrifying accounts of the murder stunned and shocked the community, known more for its quality of life than for gruesome deaths," the *Newtown Bee* recounted. (Tragically, Newtown would go on to make headlines after the mass shooting at Sandy Hook Elementary School in 2012.)

Meanwhile, Richard Crafts insisted he didn't know where his wife was. He had previously said that she went to Copenhagen to stay with her mother, Elsebeth Nielsen, because she was ill. He told other parties that Helle had jetted off to the Canary Islands with a friend.

Richard's defense lawyer would later contend that, because Helle was a world traveler who spoke four languages, she could have happily gallivanted off anywhere.

But investigators weren't buying it. They deciphered the obscured serial number on the chainsaw, and it matched the number Richard Crafts had filled out on a warranty form.

They eventually found a total of 2,660 light-colored hairs on the chainsaw and in the chip pile. Dental records confirmed that a tooth at the scene came from Helle.

The authorities concluded that Richard Crafts bludgeoned the slender five-foot, six-inch Helle to death with a police flashlight in their bedroom, froze her body, then annihilated it with the chainsaw and rented wood chipper.

On January 13, 1987, Richard was arrested for homicide and held on $750,000 bond at the Bridgeport Community Correctional Center.

Upon hearing the news of the murder, Helle's mother was so shocked she required a doctor's care.

Meanwhile, more damning evidence against Richard poured in. A few days before Helle disappeared, Richard had used cash to buy a deep freezer and refused to give his name to the appliance dealer, according to *People* magazine.

Investigators believed he used a U-Haul truck to transport the large Brush Bandit wood chipper to the riverbank. After the murder, he scratched the serial number off the chainsaw, dismantled it, and threw it into the river, they concluded.

Richard's lack of concern over his wife's absence didn't exactly help his case. Helle's friend Jette Olesen Rompe testified that when she expressed alarm because Helle hadn't shown up for work, Richard told her, "You've been watching too many movies," the *Hartford Courant* reported.

Elsebeth Nielsen refuted Richard's claim that Helle went to Copenhagen to nurse her mother back to health in November. Helle wasn't scheduled to visit until April 1987, and Nielsen felt fine until she found out about the murder of her only child.

J. Daniel Sagarin, Richard's lawyer, countered her friends' assertions that Helle would never willingly leave her children. "People do things in divorces," he said, the *Hartford Courant* reported.

Richard Crafts's sister and brother-in-law, Suzanne and Malcolm Bird, supported his innocence.

At the 1987 trial, Richard found one more sympathetic onlooker.

Eleven jurors voted for conviction, but a lone holdout named Warren Maskell, 47, defied the judge and walked out of deliberations. According to *People* magazine coverage, "Maskell had visited a nearby church every day at lunchtime, seeking divine guidance, and his belief in Crafts's innocence was unshaken to the end. 'A woman who was sick of trying to change a guy could just take off and say the hell with it,' he explained. 'I think Helle Crafts might still be alive.'"

At least Helle's friends and family had the comfort of knowing that Richard was tucked away in jail the whole time; he couldn't come up with the bail money.

And incarcerated he would stay—a second jury found him guilty of murder on November 21, 1989.

It marked Connecticut's first homicide conviction without a body and the first time the state had allowed cameras in a murder trial.

A judge gave Crafts 50 years.

In 1993, Crafts appealed, contending the circumstantial evidence was insufficient and the nationwide publicity about the crime prevented a fair trial. No luck on that; the state supreme court upheld his conviction.

That same year, a judge refused Richard's bid to extract money from Helle Crafts's estate.

As for the three children, ranging in age from 5 to 10 at the time of their mother's murder, they stayed with some of Helle's friends and continued to attend school in Newtown, according to the *New York Times*.

Two of Helle's flight attendant colleagues launched a campaign to raise money for the kids, which back in pre-GoFundMe days involved posting signs in stores and on bulletin boards in airports.

Another of Richard Crafts's sisters, Karen Rodgers, of Westport, Connecticut, eventually took custody of the kids.

The state saw to it that the children received Richard's pension fund, according to a *Connecticut News-Times* story.

As far as Richard's whereabouts, he spent some of his sentence at the MacDougall Walker Correctional Institute but later moved to the Osborn CI in Somers, Connecticut.

I originally reported that Richard Crafts would become eligible for parole in 2022. So it came as a surprise when a reader notified me that he was actually scheduled for release in the second half of 2020.

How Did This Happen?

Well, it's safe to assume his sister Karen Rodgers didn't write any letters to the parole board to support him. She sided with the prosecution during the trial and encouraged the judge to give him the maximum sentence. She contended that the Craftses' son Andrew was afraid of his father.

Unfortunately, Helle's lawyer wasn't around to fight Richard's release. Dianne Andersen died in 2012. A *News-Times* piece remembered her fondly as the first woman to practice law in town and a "barracuda" in the courtroom.

And Keith Mayo died in a car accident in 1999.

According to a January 31, 2020, story from the *Newtown Bee*, at the time of Richard Crafts's sentencing, the laws in effect enabled a convict to serve "significantly less time" if he "exhibited good behavior while incarcerated."

"Ninety-eight percent of inmates are going to get out," Karen Martucci, a spokesperson for the Connecticut State Department of Corrections, told me. "Richard Crafts did a large amount of time and his sentence was done."

On a somewhat reassuring note, Connecticut put him into Isaiah House, a halfway house in Bridgeport, Connecticut. "Removing someone from prison and releasing directly into the community isn't a good idea. There's more chance of reoffending," Martucci says. "A halfway house is a safer transmission back into the community. It can include drug testing and other programs."

Next up, the state put Richard in a shelter for homeless veterans, also in Bridgeport, after which he was free to go.

As for the 800-pound popular-culture gorilla in the room—whether filmmakers Ethan and Joel Coen got the idea for the wood-chipper disposal in *Fargo* from the Crafts murder—there's not really evidence to confirm or refute, according to research website Snopes.

But *Forensic Files* maintains a narrative free of morbid pleasure and lends compassion to the story of Helle Crafts, a nice woman who married a heartless guy.

CHAPTER 16

Jack and Linda Myers

Killed for the Farm

A LITTLE BOY SURVIVES A HORROR
Forensic Files *episode "In the Bag"*

Jack and Linda Myers were an enterprising couple who operated a food market and pizza shop in tiny Houston, Ohio.

Serving up hot, fresh slices of extra cheese with mushrooms can be an amiable business, but the Myerses had two side gigs that tend not to create many fans.

They rented out residential properties they owned, and Jack fixed up used cars and resold them, often on credit.

So when the Myerses' great-grandson discovered the couple murdered in their own bed, investigators wondered whether an evicted tenant or a repossessed-vehicle owner might have pulled the trigger.

But, as it turned out, the killer was someone the Myerses trusted and knew far more intimately than any of Jack's buyers or renters.

So what ever happened to the great-grandson who lived with Jack and Linda, just four years old at the time of the murder? And where is their killer today?

Let's get started on the recap of "In the Bag," the *Forensic Files* episode about the case, along with extra information from internet research.

On March 27, 2003, a sweet little guy in bloodstained pajamas and boots showed up an hour late for preschool.

Dameon Huffman (*Forensic Files* used the pseudonym "Johnny Huffman") had run a mile to get to the classroom, which was part of the Oakland Church of the Brethren.

Staff member Marlene Harris would later testify that Dameon said his great-grandparents were "melting." She called the sheriff's office.

Police found Jack and Linda Myers shot to death inside their farm-house on Martin Road in Darke County, Ohio.

It looked as though an intruder had disconnected the phone lines, shot Jack in his sleep, and then turned the gun on Linda after she woke up. She had a defensive wound, and the gunshot to her face made her unrecognizable.

The couple had been happily married for seven years and had full custody of Dameon. His mother, Linda's granddaughter Amber Holscher, was too young to care for him and had put him in foster care at one point.

Dameon said that, on the night of the murder, a "green monster" had looked in on him in his bedroom and apparently thought he was asleep. The only other eyewitness was a neighbor who remembered seeing an unknown minivan in the Myerses' driveway before dawn.

Worried that the perpetrator would try to find and kill Dameon, the authorities placed him in protective custody in a secret location, away from all family members, according to "The Green Dragon," an episode of *On the Case with Paula Zahn*.

The killer hadn't stolen anything valuable, so an outsider's grudge seemed like a probable motive—until police started investigating the family.

Suspicion first fell upon Andrew Huffman, Dameon's dad, after Amber told investigators there was a custody dispute between him and Linda, and he had threatened her.

But he was in Kentucky when the murders took place, and his employer confirmed his alibi.

Next up on the list came Jack's firstborn son.

Travis Myers, 28, and his father had warred over some financial matters, and Travis moved to Arizona to put as much distance between them as possible, according to *On the Case*.

Travis had returned to Ohio shortly before the murders, but he also had a solid alibi.

Surprisingly, investigators found a better suspect in Jack's younger son, Gregg Myers, 25.

The mild-mannered Gregg had no criminal record, got along well with his dad, and was best man at his wedding, but Gregg had reportedly been rebuffed when he asked Jack for a loan to save his home.

Due to a bank foreclosure, Gregg was either scheduled for eviction the following month or had already been evicted (media accounts vary) from his house in the town of Piqua, Ohio.

Gregg, who was the father of two small children, needed a new place to live pronto, and he conveniently stood to inherit Jack and Linda's farmhouse and its 39 acres upon Jack's death.

Evidence against Gregg began to stream in.

A family friend named Jon Helmandollar promptly ratted out Gregg, telling authorities that Gregg had asked him where he could get a gun to shoot his father.

Gregg's girlfriend, Jennifer Brown, told investigators that, when she woke up on the morning of the murders, Gregg was already out of the house. It was earlier than he usually left for his job at a business called NK Parts—when he showed up, that is. According to *Forensic Files*, Gregg had an attendance problem as well as a substance-abuse habit.

But it was the physical evidence that really made the case. A Walmart in the town of Sidney, Ohio, had receipts showing Gregg bought ammunition, masking tape, and batting two days before the homicides. Police had found remnants of tape and batting at the crime scene and believed the shooter used them to make a silencer.

A week before the killings, Gregg, who drove a van like the one spotted in Jack and Linda Myers's driveway the day of the murders, had purchased latex gloves, a pair of Route 66 brand shoes two sizes too small, a green windbreaker, green pants, and black stockings.

After the murders, police discovered those items in a bag discarded in the Stillwater River, downstream from where they recovered a 12-gauge Winchester shotgun with the serial number rubbed out.

One of the gloves had Gregg's fingerprint inside, and the old "make foot impressions with the wrong shoe size" trick didn't fool anyone for long.

Investigators uncovered enough of the gun's serial number (Gregg clearly should have watched more *Forensic Files*) to trace it to a private owner named Eugene Adams who said he sold it to Gregg for around $175 on March 25, 2003.

Police arrested Gregg and set his bail at $500,000.

Darke County prosecutor Richard Howell offered a deal that would take the death penalty off the table in exchange for a guilty plea to aggravated battery and two counts of aggravated murder.

Gregg chose to go to trial.

Defense lawyer L. Patrick Mulligan said Gregg had the moral support of many people—even as they had to look at Linda Myers's family members who came to court dressed in T-shirts with tribute silkscreened pictures of the murdered couple.

The jury convicted the baby-faced defendant on all charges after deliberating for eight hours.

Travis Myers "buried his face in his hands" when he heard the verdict against his little brother, the *Dayton Daily News* reported.

"It tears us apart because we were close with Gregg," said Linda's daughter Kim Hudelson, according to the *Dayton Daily News*. "We got along with Gregg."

At the sentencing hearing, defense lawyer George Katchmer played the unhappy childhood card.

He said Travis and Gregg "grew up in an abusive household without their father's support," the Associated Press (AP) reported in a story dated May 2, 2004.

May Williams, Jack Myers's sister, testified that Jack was the "family bully" and didn't nurture his sons, the AP reported.

It probably wasn't much of a stretch to believe that a man who repossessed cars could be intimidating.

The jury spared Gregg the death penalty.

Instead, Gregg, then 26, received life without the possibility of parole plus five years for aggravated burglary and six years for use of a silencer.

The Ohio Supreme Court later upheld the conviction after Gregg filed an appeal alleging unfair jury selection in 2006.

Today, Gregg resides at Marion Correctional Institution, a severely overcrowded medium-security facility that's home to another *Forensic Files* murderer, Jack Boyle (see chapter 27).

Marion was built to accommodate 1,452 inmates but has a population of 2,550, according to PrisonPro.

On the bright side for Gregg, who has no chance of parole, the facility "is known as having some of the most innovative programs of all institutions" and has a high percentage of inmates who complete certification programs. TEDx even hosted an event, which inmates helped plan and host, at Marion.

As for Linda's granddaughter Amber Holscher, she had gotten married shortly before the murders and had been preparing to regain custody of her son.

Amber, who appeared on both *Forensic Files* and *On the Case*, said little Dameon had persistent nightmares about a green monster or green dragon during childhood.

Dameon got counseling to cope with the traumatic events of his youth and began to feel safer as time went on. "He came out of it very well," Amber told me during an interview on September 28, 2021. "He's always been a hard worker. He's just an all-around good kid."

Still blond and good looking today, Dameon is a motorcycle enthusiast who works for a garage-door manufacturing company in Ohio. He has lived on his own since graduating from high school.

As for Gregg Myers, the uncle who resides behind razor wire, Amber told me in the interview that she's glad he'll be in prison for life "not because I think he would do it again but because of his heinous acts."

She also contradicts those who called murder victim Jack Myers a bully or a black sheep—in fact, she says, Jack helped out customers who were "down and out" by extending store credit and doing all he could to avoid repossessing vehicles.

"We all love and miss our grandparents very much," Amber says. "I wish they could see all their grandchildren—there are a lot more of them now."

CHAPTER 17

Janet Siclari's Surfside Homicide

UPDATE ON THOMAS BERRY—RAPIST AND KILLER
Forensic Files *episode "A Cinderella Story"*

If you're looking for a defendant who deserves zero sympathy and makes you thankful the United States has life sentences without parole, Thomas Jabin Berry is your man.

As *Forensic Files* watchers will remember, Berry's excuse for sexually assaulting a 12-year-old girl was that he thought she was 13.

Fortunately, that victim survived the attack. But Berry killed the next person he raped, an ultrasound technician from New Jersey named Janet Siclari.

For this chapter, I checked on Berry's whereabouts today and looked for additional biographical information on Janet Siclari.

So, let's get started on a recap of *Forensic Files* episode "A Cinderella Story," along with extra information drawn from internet research.

Janet Siclari came into the world on December 30, 1957, and grew up in Lyndhurst, New Jersey, with three brothers.

She earned a certificate in radiology in 1979 and got the highest academic awards in her class. Janet moved to North Arlington and worked at General Hospital in Passaic.

For Janet, visiting North Carolina's Outer Banks in the summer was a family tradition that started in her childhood.

In August 1993, the 35-year-old vacationed there with her brother Robert Siclari and two friends, Celeste Bethmann and Nancy Matt. They stayed at a rental cottage in Southern Shores for a week, then decided to spend an extra day in the area and checked into the Carolinian Hotel in Nags Head.

Janet Siclari, who was athletic but tiny at 92 pounds, disappeared after a night out at a comedy club followed by drinks and dancing at the Port O'Call Restaurant & Gaslight Saloon on August 28. Robert was asleep when she came home but remembered waking up briefly and hearing her say she was going outside to smoke.

In the morning, Robert noticed his sister's bed hadn't been slept in and saw police on the beach outside his window, according to an account from the *Bergen Record*.

A local maintenance crew worker had found her body, clothed in a blue tank top, outside the hotel. Someone had stabbed her repeatedly, slit her throat, and left her to die.

"Blood seeped in the white sand 25 feet in either direction," according to a *Bergen Record* account from February 2, 1999. Apparently, Janet had survived for a short time after the attack and tried to crawl back to the hotel.

The day after the murder, Hurricane Emily caused tens of thousands to flee the area temporarily, but police didn't let it get in the way of their work.

A tantalizing suspect soon emerged in a burly bartender, Edward Read Powell, who had flirted with Janet and later admitted to police that he was sitting around eating pepperoni with a knife near the scene of the murder.

Although *Forensic Files* didn't mention it, three additional prospective perpetrators came to light as well, according to "Murder in Paradise," a 2013 episode of *Nightmare Next Door*.

There was Powell's waitress girlfriend, who exchanged surly words with Janet's brother when he sent his food back at her restaurant—and she'd seen her boyfriend socializing with Janet.

The third suspect, a cabana attendant who hit on Janet and reportedly made her a little uncomfortable, was also questioned by police, who discovered he had a past conviction for stabbing a relative.

Next, thanks to a tip from Janet's mother, investigators checked out Janet's ex-boyfriend, a New Jersey mechanic and biker club member. He had served time in prison as an accessory to the murder of a man from a rival gang.

But one by one, the four suspects fell away.

An autopsy revealed that Janet had been raped, so investigators ruled out the waitress as the killer. And none of the DNA samples collected from the male suspects matched the rapist's genetic profile.

The FBI came in to help local authorities, but a year after the murder, they hadn't found a single eyewitness despite interviewing 100 people in connection with the case, according to the *Bergen Record*. The area had a low stranger-on-stranger crime rate, so there weren't a lot of usual-suspect types to haul in for questioning.

Robert Siclari, who owned an environmental consulting firm in Alexandria, Virginia, put together a $20,000 reward for information that would help solve the crime.

"We lost Janet and we can't bring her back," Robert told the *Virginian-Pilot*. "But we don't want something like this to happen to someone else."

Still, the case turned cold.

Then, in 1997, something wonderful happened in the world of forensic science. CODIS—the combined DNA indexing system—was created so police across the United States could share genetic profiles of convicted felons.

When authorities entered Janet Siclari's rape kit sample in the database, they got a match with Thomas Jabin Berry. The roofer and commercial fisherman, who was 27 at the time of the murder, had undergone DNA testing after committing a parole violation.

Berry's ex-girlfriend told police that he always carried a fishing knife and that a pair of shoes and socks found near Janet Siclari's body belonged to him.

The findings about Berry, who lived in the North Carolina towns of Engelhard and Manteo, weren't exactly a shock. His record included "indecent liberty with a child" involving the aforementioned 12-year-old girl; Berry was 26 when he committed that sex crime.

During his on-camera interview with *Forensic Files*, Berry—who had three children by two different women—called his actions toward the girl "consensual."

Apparently no one had informed him that children can't consent.

The girl would later testify that Berry had lured her into the woods under the guise of helping him find a lost nephew. Then he raped her in a fort, according to court papers from *North Carolina v. Berry* in 2001.

Berry got a 10-year suspended sentence for his crime against the 12-year-old girl.

Under police questioning for the attack on Janet Siclari, Berry said he had been smoking crack cocaine at the time and couldn't remember whether he had raped and killed Janet, according to the court papers.

In his *Forensic Files* interview, Berry said that, if he did have sex with Janet, "it would have been consensual" and he never killed anybody. He also said he sometimes had sex with people he just met on the beach and that was how he met his wife.

Doris Berry, the suspect's mother, strenuously defended him, saying he was "not capable of committing murder" even "to save his own life."

Meanwhile, her son had a history of sex crimes dating back to when he himself was 12 years old, according to the *Bergen Record*. His record also includes larceny and breaking and entering into a vehicle when he was 19.

At the trial, a woman named Shelley Perry testified that Berry had tried to rape her after breaking into her house in 1992. She managed to escape and never pressed charges.

In 1999, a jury convicted Thomas Berry of the rape and first-degree murder of Janet Siclari.

At the sentencing hearing, Janet Siclari's mother, Damy Siclari Daber, spoke of how the death had devastated the family and said that son Robert Siclari felt guilty. "I tell him it's not his fault. . . . It's that maniac's fault," she said, as reported by the *Virginian-Pilot* on January 28, 1999.

Meanwhile, Doris Berry portrayed her son as a victim—a sweet guy who was severely abused by his father and used to hide in the woods to escape him, the *Virginian-Pilot* reported.

The defense also attempted to win the jury members' sympathy by showing them a childhood photo of Thomas Berry holding a fish he had caught.

But in the end, the jury didn't think his case held water. Berry received two consecutive life sentences. He lost a 2001 appeal.

Today, Thomas Berry resides at Albemarle Correctional Institution in New London, North Carolina.

According to North Carolina's Department of Corrections (DOC), he is serving his time with the general prison population, as opposed to in segregated status. That doesn't mean, however, that he has behaved himself.

His list of 34 infractions includes theft of canteen inventory or cash, refusing to take a drug or breath test, fighting, offering or accepting a bribe, and creating an "offensive condition." Most recently, in 2020, he disobeyed orders.

The DOC website makes no mention of any parole possibility. Berry, who was born on January 4, 1966, has a lot of years ahead of him, and all of them will likely be spent behind razor wire.

CHAPTER 18

Joanne Chambers and Paula Nawrocki

Strange Lesson

ONE TEACHER ALLEGEDLY SABOTAGES ANOTHER
Forensic Files *episode "Sealed with a Kiss"*
"Sealed with a Kiss" differs from most other *Forensic Files* episodes in that it involves no violence.

If fact, no one touched anyone or stole anything during the extended course of the criminal activity.

But it's a sordid case just the same, and the episode features on-camera interviews with both the accused and the victim, who ultimately trade places.

The drama kicked off when someone began menacing Joanne Chambers—a teacher admired for her warm, unconventional approach to her job—with threatening letters, offensive photos, and, yes, a voodoo Barbie doll.

The episode was produced back in 1997, when *Forensic Files* still went by the name *Medical Detectives*. So what's happened to Joanne Chambers since then, and has she retained any of the respect she earned as a teacher before things got weird?

To find out, let's get going on the recap of "Sealed with a Kiss," along with extra information from internet research and a 2021 interview with Mike Frassinelli, who reported on the case for the Allentown *Morning Call* newspaper.

In 1993, Joanne Chambers and Paula Nawrocki both taught first grade at the Coolbaugh Learning Center, which sounds like a for-profit tutoring business, but it was actually a public school in Pennsylvania's Poconos region.

Joanne, 41, lived in Carbondale with her husband, who owned a painting business, and her 10-year-old son.

She taught reading and liked to make school fun and nurturing. Joanne did entertaining things like dressing up pillars to look like palm trees. She ended each class with the words, "You are wonderful and beautiful. You make my heart happy," according to *Redbook* magazine.

Students and parents loved her.

Paula Nawrocki, who had started working for the district in 1975, was stricter and more formal in her teaching but was well respected, too. The *Morning Call* would later write that Paula "had a record as clean as a new chalkboard."

That seemed to change when the principal of the school where both women worked started receiving anonymous letters trashing Joanne. Pretty soon, Joanne herself began getting the disturbing missives, and other teachers did, too.

So started a strange and upsetting period lasting 18 months.

All the letters disparaged Joanne. At first, they simply mocked her, criticizing her for wearing jeans at school and organizing a faculty water fight.

They progressed to calling the soft-spoken Joanne a bitch and claiming she smoked marijuana.

Other letters accused Joanne of child molestation and threatened to drag her into the woods and torture her to death. The tormenter pasted Joanne's face on nude pictures in sex scenes, then sent them to parents and posted them out in the open.

Someone planted a whiskey bottle in her desk drawer.

Joanne told police that she cut her hand after the anonymous evildoer placed a razor blade under her car door handle—and later sent her a typed note saying, "You're sliced." She needed eight stitches to close the wound on her right middle finger.

As the campaign of terror waged on, Joanne received sympathy and concern from her colleagues.

Perhaps a bit overzealous in their efforts to find the culprit, officials called a faculty meeting in March 1994 and told teachers that the perpetrator "is someone sitting in this room."

Soon, a solid clue came to light when video footage caught Paula Nawrocki entering Joanne's classroom and removing Joanne's mug, which immediately made her a suspect because the anonymous letter-writer had threatened to poison Joanne's coffee.

When questioned, Paula explained that Joanne had asked her to retrieve the mug. She also allegedly said something to the effect of "You'll never prove it's me." That sounded fishy to Coolbaugh Township police chief Anthony Fluegel.

The police wired up Joanne and had her talk to Paula about the terror campaign in hopes that something incriminating would slip out.

But it didn't work. Paula said nothing suspicious on the tape and, in fact, expressed sympathy: "Joanne, I can't, I can't imagine how this person can do what they're doing," Nawrocki said on the recording. "We are all amazed, Joanne, that you can be surviving through the whole thing."

But when both women took polygraph tests, Paula failed. Joanne passed.

Next up, Paula consented to having her house searched. That helped her a little. Examination proved that her typewriter wasn't the one used to send the frightening letters.

Meanwhile, the school had received the aforementioned Barbie. Someone had dressed and coiffed the doll to look like Joanne, then stuck a razor blade in its neck and drizzled red paint on it.

"I said good-bye to my husband like I wanted him to remember me saying good-bye," Joanne told *Forensic Files*. "I lived every day thinking that it was truly possible that it could be my last."

Next up, Joanne told police that Paula Nawrocki had tailgated her and tried to run her off the road on Interstate 380.

That alleged offense was enough for authorities to arrest Paula for the entire horror campaign—100 counts, including making terroristic threats, stalking, and recklessly endangering life.

Paula's husband, Leonard Nawrocki, who worked as an inspector for the Department of Environmental Protection, would years later tell the *Morning Call* of his shock at seeing news of the arrest in the paper just one day later. According to the *Morning Call*, the Nawrockis suddenly felt like the subjects of a witch hunt fueled by overeager investigators and journalists:

> *"Basically we were isolated people," Leonard Nawrocki, father of the couple's son, Kevin, told the Morning Call. "We felt like there wasn't a friend in the world."*

Leonard also said that other teachers ignored Paula at lunch and administrators snubbed her at a basketball game.

The parents of one student asked the school to remove him from Paula's class. Paula was suspended with pay shortly afterward.

Fluegel later told *Dateline NBC* that at least 10 teachers he spoke to said they suspected Paula Nawrocki as the party behind the terror campaign against Joanne. After Paula's arrest, the menacing behavior toward Joanne stopped. But the FBI couldn't find forensic evidence to help build a case against Paula.

Meanwhile, a private investigator and lawyer whom Paula Nawrocki hired were making progress. Paula paid $7,000 to have some of the threatening letters tested for her DNA. The lab found a small number of epithelial cells under one set of stamps. None of them matched the DNA from Paula or Leonard. But those forensics weren't enough to clear Paula.

Paula's private investigator, Jim Anderson, retrieved some DNA-bearing items from Joanne's trash and found that a threatening letter sent to Joanne had Joanne's own DNA under the stamps. Joanne said that the stamps fell off—she was alone with them in some type of evidence room—and she licked them to reattach them.

Public opinion remained in Joanne's favor.

At the trial in 1996, which *Dateline NBC* covered, Coolbaugh's principal and some of its teachers testified that they suspected Paula Nawrocki of creating the terror campaign against Joanne Chambers. Paula had allegedly started acting jumpy and nervous around the time the incidents began.

The courtroom presentation of the hate letters and threats put the jurors in Joanne's corner. "I felt so bad for this woman, this poor thing, to have had to go through all these terrible things," one juror later told *Dateline NBC*, which broadcast a segment about the case.

But Paula's lawyer Phil Lauer changed everything on Saturday, January 20, 1996.

He put colleagues from Joanne's prior employer, the Lackawanna Trail School District, on the stand. They testified that Joanne had said other teachers threatened to torch her house, and she had a history of complaining about anonymous threats. Some of her ex-coworkers from the previous school said that Joanne liked to cause trouble for other teachers and that her arrival made waves in what had been a harmonious workplace.

In a precursor to what happened at Coolbaugh, at the Lackawanna school, a superintendent had called a meeting of teachers to disclose the alleged campaign against Joanne—and announced that the guilty party "is someone sitting in this room."

The effect of the Lackawanna teachers' testimony was immediate. "It was like the movie *Freaky Friday*," Frassinelli said. "They switched places. All of a sudden, the accuser became the enemy and the accused became the victim."

It had also come out that Joanne had made a habit of reporting fires and burglaries—some of them dubiously credible—to the police.

"Every crime she said she was a victim of had some weirdness attached to it," Anderson said in one of my favorite *Forensic Files* quotes.

After five days of testimony and two hours of deliberation, the jury reached a not guilty verdict. Paula cried with relief, and some of the jurors hugged her outside the courtroom. "Our hearts are with you," one of them said.

Paula commented that Joanne "needs help." (Before the trial, Fluegel had said Paula needed help.)

In 1997, Paula faced another hearing of sorts when the Pocono Mountain School District investigated her for "immorality" based on other aspects of Joanne Chambers's accusations.

She was cleared again and allowed to resume her $55,000-a-year job "after months of school board hearings that were peppered with audience cheers for Nawrocki and jeers for Chambers," the *Morning Call* reported.

As for Joanne Chambers, she retired in June 2015 after havin[received the prestigious National Board Certified status.

But just three months later, on September 25, 2015, an article title["Scandalous Past Gives School Board Pause" appeared in the Hazleto[*Standard-Speaker*.

The story noted that the Hazleton Area School District was ready t[hire Joanne Chambers as a Wilson reading specialist—that is, an educa[tor who teaches dyslexic kids. The Pennsylvania Wilson program officia[highly recommended Joanne.

But then the Barbie doll reared its ugly head. Apparently, som[parents put her name in Google and reported the resulting intelligenc[about the terror complaints, decoupage porn, and so on to the schoo[board, which tabled the decision to hire her.

Still, Joanne retained at least one fan of her professional accomplish[ments.

A former colleague named Jamie Schweppenheiser from the Pocon[Mountain School District wrote a letter to the editor praising Chambe[as a professional who "helped countless children and young adults lear[how to read" and saying "what a shame for the teachers and students [the Hazleton Area School District to miss out on the opportunity to b[mentored by Joanne Chambers."

In other words, Joanne Chambers remains a divisive and contradic[tory figure, someone who allegedly created an absolute nightmare fo[one woman but also gave many children the gift of better reading skill[higher self-esteem, and a sense of accomplishment.

"At the time, I said it's the strangest case I've ever seen," says Frassi[nelli. "And it still is."

CHAPTER 19

John Schneeberger, MD

An Epilogue

WHAT HAPPENED TO A CANADIAN RAPIST AND HIS VICTIM[
Forensic Files *episode "Bad Blood"*

When Dr. John Schneeberger drugged and raped a patient in hi[room, he probably figured that she (a) wouldn't know what happe[(b) wouldn't be believed even if she did.

Schneeberger was a family physician beloved by residents of [a farming town of 1,100 people in Saskatchewan. Many of the[been treated by the 30ish blond doctor at one time or another an[him kind and caring.

The *Forensic Files* episode "Bad Blood" told the story [23-year-old victim, usually identified only as Candy or Candice[media. She was a single mother with a high school diploma, a j[gas station, and a reputation as a partyer.

Who was she to disparage an asset to the community like Dr. S[berger? The charming medical professional helped raise funds [town could install a public swimming pool. He was happily marri[four kids—two of them stepchildren he took in from his wife's p[marriage. What a great guy. In fact, he was so agreeable that he w[took multiple DNA tests after Candy reported the Hallowee[sexual assault to the Royal Canadian Mounted Police in 1992.

Just as Schneeberger's admiring public expected, his DNA[match the semen from the alleged rape. The test results seemed t[firm townspeople's suspicions that Candy was lying, that she had [on Schneeberger and was retaliating because he rejected her, acc[to *Autopsy*, an HBO docuseries that produced a segment about th[

CHAPTER 18

Paula agreed to appear on the *Dateline* segment about the case l
later said she found it tedious. She also gave an interview to *Redb*
magazine but soon regretted it, feeling the resulting article cast so
doubt on her innocence.

She filed a $9 million lawsuit against the school, Joanne Chambe
and the police. In 2000, she received a $600,000 settlement from t
school plus $25,000 from Joanne Chambers. (Joanne's lawyer, John
Freund III, said that she settled only because she wanted to avoid t
cost of defense. She lamented that the polygraph evidence couldn't
used in her defense, but ultimately said that she just wanted to move
with her life.)

Paula sued Police Chief Anthony Fluegel as well, but Fluegel went
trial instead of settling and won the case. Court papers from 2002 not
in Fluegel's defense, that other teachers passed lie detector tests. O
Nawrocki failed, so Fluegel had reason to make her the prime suspect

"I thought from the beginning I was just doing my job," Fluegel la
said, calling Nawrocki's allegations against him baseless.

None of the criminal justice system's authorities whom Nawro
accused of malicious prosecution ended up paying any damages to her
and rightly so, considering that they had evidence against Nawrocki tl
seemed credible. The fault lay with Joanne Chambers for allegedly lyi
not with those who had every reason to believe her.

A note from the producers at the end of the episode said that Pa
spent $100,000 in her defense and mentioned that both women s
taught in the Pocono Mountain School District but at different schoc

But that was back in 1997. What's happened since then?

Paula gave an interview circa 2001 to Frassinelli. "She was very ca
and smart," said Frassinelli, who now writes for a publication about hec
funds. "She did say something funny. She allowed herself one indulger
with the settlement money. She bought a new car—I think it wa
BMW—and she paraded it past the school administrators once."

She has kept a low profile since 2002, after she lost her suit agai
the police. She has no presence on social media and no longer speaks
journalists.

Some residents suspected Candy was hoping to profit from a nui-
sance suit, according to *Forensic Files*.

The physician maintained that he gave Candy the injection of Versed
to calm her nerves and that the drug sometimes caused hallucinations of
sexual activity as a side effect. The police halted the investigation in 1994.

What Mrs. Schneeberger and the rest of her husband's fan club
didn't know was that the doctor had foiled the DNA tests by implanting
in his arm a tube containing another man's blood.

Meanwhile, Candy persisted. Although the Versed had incapacitated
her and made her memory hazy that evening on Dr. Schneeberger's exam
table, she felt sure he had raped her. It took seven years, but her efforts
finally landed Schneeberger behind razor wire.

A private detective she hired got hold of Schneeberger's ChapStick.
Candy paid for a DNA test at a private lab and got a match. But Schneeberger pulled his fake-blood routine once more during the hospital's lab
test and evaded justice again.

Then, in 1997, there was a colossal break in the case: Lisa Schneeberger switched sides. She found out her husband had been drugging and
sexually assaulting her 13-year-old daughter.

The court ordered more DNA tests, which this time included a
sample of Schneeberger's hair and blood drawn from his finger. They
matched the semen from Candy's attack.

Schneeberger went on trial in November 1999 in Saskatchewan
for raping both Candy and his stepdaughter. He admitted to the blood
switcheroo; it came from one of his patients. But, he said, it was a matter
of self-defense. Candy had broken into his house, he contended, and
stolen a used condom so she could frame him.

The jury didn't buy it and convicted him of enough crimes to put
him away forever. But he got a sentence of only six years. The *Forensic
Files* episode, first aired in 2001, ends with Candy's jubilation when she
learned the doctor had been denied parole.

So what happened to Dr. John Schneeberger after *Forensic Files'*
closing guitar chords?

Well, it's a mixture of justice and injustice. After four years in the minimum-security annex of Ferndale Institution (now known as Mission Minimum Institution) in British Columbia, Schneeberger won parole.

The ex-convict—who was also sometimes known by his given first name, Steven—promptly moved to Regina, the same town where Candy lived. He'd been stripped of his medical license, so he got work on a demolition crew and also did carpentry. Fortunately, Candy didn't have to worry about bumping into Schneeberger at the supermarket for long.

Records showed that Schneeberger—who originally came from Zambia and later lived in South Africa—had neglected to disclose on his Canadian citizenship application in 1993 that he was being investigated for rape, according to the *Calgary Herald*.

Canada moved to deport him to South Africa—but not before his victims had to witness the residual goodwill Schneeberger had built up in the Great White North. His friends began a letter-writing campaign urging the immigration minister to reverse the deportation order so Schneeberger would have a chance to say goodbye to his biological daughters.

Schneeberger's camp won.

His wife, who was identified as Lisa Dillman after her divorce, was ordered to allow the girls, ages five and six, to see him. She had paid $2,000 for contempt of court for previously refusing to take them to see their father in jail, but she ultimately obeyed the visitation order, according to a *Globe and Mail* story. As writer Margaret Wente quoted the former Mrs. Schneeberger: "At least I can say to my girls when they're older: 'I tried.' They will know that Mummy at least tried to keep us away from him. . . . I still blame myself. Maybe if I had believed [Candy], none of this would have happened to my daughter."

The article also reported that Schneeberger's pals threw him a going-away party. He had a garage sale to get rid of his things prior to deportation.

But if this is sounding more like a kid going away to college than a sex criminal being chased out of North America, don't worry—he faced adversity when he finally landed back in Africa in July 2004.

The man once affectionately known as "Dr. John" in Canada became "Dr. Rape" in South Africa. He tried to join the Health Professions Council of South Africa so that he could work in some field of medicine again, but he soon withdrew his application.

His brother, William "Bill" Schneeberger, a cardiothoracic surgeon, tried to help him get back on his feet professionally. He maintained the charges against his brother were false. "I don't believe my brother is a saint," Bill Schneeberger said in a statement to the *Calgary Herald*, "but I know he is not a fool and rape in a consulting room when you have asked two nurses to join you is ridiculous."

Bill Schneeberger's efforts on his brother's behalf appear to have gone nowhere. Bill himself returned to the United States and works with the humanitarian nongovernmental organization Emergency in Ohio, according to his LinkedIn profile.

John Schneeberger went to live with his mother, Ina, in Durban, South Africa, and reportedly took up work in the catering industry; he had picked up some skills on kitchen duty in prison. He pretty much dropped off the radar screen after that.

But according to a tipster who reached out to me, Steven John Schneeberger is director and owner of two food companies in South Africa and has remarried.

As for the woman whose actions exposed Schneeberger as a sex criminal for all the world to see, she's now known as Candice Fonagy. She continues to live in Saskatchewan and has a long-term boyfriend and a grown daughter she's proud of. Her home includes a Rottweiler, four Pomeranians, a miniature show horse, and two miniature goats.

She cares for human beings as well—as a critical care assistant for senior citizens and people with disabilities for the Saskatchewan Health Authority, where she's worked since 1995. Professionals with her job title are known as "the eyes and ears of the frail and vulnerable," a good fit for someone who has survived a saga like Candy's.

Her appearance on *Forensic Files* has led to many messages of support from viewers around the world who have reached out to her after seeing the show. Numerous victims of sexual assault have contacted her.

"I want to mention how proud I am that my *Forensic Files* friends over the years have gained inspiration and courage to fight and deal with their own perpetrators because I was able to share my story with each of them," Candy told me in a written message.

While she tries not to dwell on the attack, she has at times struggled with depression and posttraumatic stress disorder over the years.

"I have no expectations in this crazy world we live in," Candy wrote. "But I often wonder how much better/different life would have been for myself, my daughter, and my parents had I not been raped by Schnee-berger."

Karyn Slover's Killers

An Update

JEANNETTE AND MICHAEL SLOVER MURDER THEIR GRANDSON'S MOTHER
Forensic Files *episode "Concrete Alibi"*

Although she liked her job as an advertising sales rep at an Illinois newspaper, Karyn Slover was looking forward to making more of a splash in the world after she clinched her first gig as a model.

But her colleagues at the *Herald and Review* never got to throw her a going-away party or publish a story about the local girl who made it to the big time. Instead, her coworkers attended a memorial service and wrote headlines about Karyn's murder—after she turned up dead, her body dreadfully abused, at Lake Shelbyville.

It took more than five years to solve the case, but the justice system convicted ex-husband Michael Slover Jr. and his parents, who probably thought they were too upright-seeming to even be suspected of a homicide.

So where is the Slover gang today? And what happened to Karyn's baby son, who lay at the center of the case?

Let's get going on the recap of "Concrete Alibi," the *Forensic Files* episode about Karyn Slover's short life and horrible death, along with extra information drawn from online research.

On September 27, 1996, a police officer spotted an abandoned car on the side of Interstate 72 outside of Champaign, Illinois.

Inside the black Pontiac Bonneville, police found a purse, a half-eaten candy bar, and scattered coins.

The vehicle was registered to David Swann, who worked as a circulation district sales manager at the *Herald and Review*.

David said he'd lent the car to his girlfriend, Karyn Slover, who was going to pick up her three-year-old son whom *Forensic Files* calls Christopher.

Two days after Karyn's disappearance, boaters spotted a gray plastic bag on the shore of Lake Shelbyville.

It contained a female head with blonde hair and at least six bullet wounds fired to the back with a .22-caliber gun.

Other bags, found in the water, held the rest of her body. The bags as well as the car had chunks of concrete in them. The killer probably used them to weigh down the bags, but body gasses caused them to rise to the surface (another case of criminals who don't watch enough *Forensic Files*).

Investigators believed someone had used a power tool to cut up the body. Dental records confirmed the victim was 23-year-old Karyn Hearn Slover.

She had disappeared after leaving the office for the day.

Publisher Bill Johnston called a meeting to tell employees about the tragedy. "He did spare everyone the gory details," former coworker George Althoff recalled in a *Herald and Review* story from August 2020. "But the emotion was quite raw and evident around the whole place."

"Karyn didn't have enemies," her friend Jill Scribner said in an interview with the series *Cold Blood*. She "was a very lovable person."

Her ex-husband, Michael Slover Jr., had been violent during the relationship, but he had an alibi for the night of the murder. He'd been working as a security guard at Cub Foods. A coworker remembered seeing him in his office with a shoplifter the store had just caught.

After work, Michael Jr. taught a karate lesson, went home to shower, and left for his second job as a bouncer at Ronnie's Tavern.

Police next turned their attention toward David Swann, who had been dating Karyn for just a few weeks. He had some legal problems in his past, including impersonating a law officer—yikes.

David also had a felony conviction for aggravated battery. (Years later, at the trial, he would claim he didn't remember what crime he committed.)

At first, David couldn't account for his whereabouts for 45 crucial minutes on the day of the murder. He'd been late to a rehearsal dinner—he was slated to serve as best man—at Tater's Family Grill. Police interrogated him for four hours before he mentioned that he'd stopped to get money at an ATM during the 45 minutes.

Fortunately for David, the bank had video footage of him that served as his alibi.

Meanwhile, investigators had appealed to the public for help identifying the place where the murder and desecration happened. Surely, there must have been signs of a bloodbath hidden somewhere.

A law enforcement task force including FBI agents said they suspected Karyn met her grisly end in a location with tall grass and a gravel or rock base. They asked owners of remote properties matching that description to look around for signs of foul play.

"Because the offense was so odious, it also left an entire community clamoring for vengeance," according to Dusty Rhodes, a reporter for the free weekly newspaper the *Illinois Times*.

A former FBI profiler cautioned that individuals "can commit these horrendous crimes yet they can act like the person sitting next to you in church."

Funds were set up to pay for a memorial to Karyn and an education for Christopher. The newspaper offered a $10,000 reward for information leading to the conviction of the killer or killers.

But to some extent, the hunt for suspects was primarily a formality and process of elimination.

Early on, police found out that Karyn and her ex-husband's family didn't get along. Mother-in-law Jeannette Slover reportedly hated Karyn.

"There was never any doubt about who was responsible," a local law officer close to the murder investigation told me. "The parents were suspected as major players out of the chute."

Karyn had won custody of Christopher in the divorce, but the court ruled that Jeannette and husband Michael Slover Sr. would have the right to babysit him while Karyn was at work.

Jeannette enjoyed an excessively close relationship with Christopher and acted as though she were the mother.

An ex-boyfriend of Karyn's would later explain that Karyn sometimes had to physically pry Christopher away from Jeannette and that she had told her grandson that "one day you'll be all mine," the *Herald and Review* reported.

Karyn's father-in-law, Michael Slover Sr., who worked as a pipe insulator at the Clinton Powerhouse, claimed that he'd gone to Kmart and bought a Play-Doh Factory for Christopher around the time of the murder, according to *Cold Blood*. But the store said that it had never carried that particular toy.

Jeannette, whose occupation has been described as either full-time homemaker or employee at a drive-through liquor business, also lacked an alibi.

Investigators couldn't find a blood-splattered murder scene, so they concentrated on Miracle Motors, a poorly maintained Mount Zion used-car lot owned by Jeannette and Michael Sr.

The lot had concrete and cinders that resembled remnants used to weigh down the bags with parts of Karyn's body.

Authorities called in the U.S. Army to help sift through the soil on the 5,000-square-foot expanse—although the Slovers had given the property a makeover shortly after the murder (a *Forensic Files* red flag).

Six months into the forensic archaeological dig, the task force hit a small but valuable piece of pay dirt: a metal button that matched the ones on Karyn's jeans. They later found rivets from the jeans and a fabric-covered button that appeared to have come from her blouse.

Authorities uncovered evidence that Michael Jr. had participated in the planning and cleanup—he and his folks talked on the phone 12 times on the weekend of the murder. One theory said that Mary Slover, Michael Jr.'s sister, babysat Christopher while her parents "performed the gruesome work necessary to dispose of Karyn's body," prosecutors would later allege.

Friends said Karyn was thinking about moving away from Illinois to pursue her modeling career after she landed a job in Georgia (more about that in a minute). The Slovers reportedly feared she would move there and take Christopher with her.

Police arrested Michael Jr. and his parents and charged them with first-degree murder.

Prosecutors made a case that Jeannette shot Karyn in the back of the head when she showed up to get her son.

The loving grandparents dismembered her body at the car lot, bagged the pieces, weighed them down with concrete from the property, and then threw the bags in Lake Shelbyville, the prosecution maintained. The presence of the Pontiac on the Slovers' property would have raised suspicions, so they abandoned it along the highway.

Neighbors remembered seeing Michael Jr. trimming weeds along the Miracle Motors parking lot around the time of the murder, important because investigators believed tall grass grew at the scene of the crime. Witnesses also remembered that the Slovers had been burning items at the lot during the same period.

And as though we needed more reason to root against the Slovers, Jeannette and David Sr. euthanized their dogs after a laboratory matched DNA from Cassie—one of the couple's black Labradors—to a hair that was found stuck to tape on a bag from the lake, according to *Cold Blood*.

In 2002, the loathsome trio were convicted of first-degree murder. Jeannette got a 60-year sentence. The men got 65 years each.

The Slovers lost a June 2003 appeal.

Nonetheless, Mary Slover continues to fight for brother Michael Jr. and their parents—who probably still can't believe an outwardly respectable couple like them got caught.

According to an article in the *Illinois Times* from 2005: "'Homebodies' is the word Mary and Michael Jr. use to describe their parents. A night out meant dinner at a fast-food restaurant and maybe a movie. Usually, they were happy to simply hang around their Mount Zion home, grill some pork chops, and watch PBS or the History Channel."

In 2008, a court filing mentioned an untested human hair found at the scene as well as a fingerprint near a spot of the victim's blood on Findley Bridge—and ordered a hearing to consider potential new evidence in the case. The Slovers' camp also called attention to unidentified short blue wool fibers found in Karyn's car and with her body parts.

In an impressive development, the Slovers garnered the support of the Illinois Innocence Project, a legal studies seminar sponsored by the University of Illinois at Springfield. In 2014, they won a ruling allowing

DNA testing on fingerprint evidence from the case. But that went nowhere, and assistant state's attorney Jay Scott, who prosecuted the Slovers, pledged to work to keep the conviction in place. And rightly so. Random fingerprints and fibers can show up anywhere.

So where are the Slover three today?

Well, they're still behind razor wire, but with some chance of release in the next decade.

Jeannette Slover, 72, resides at Logan Correctional Center, with a parole date in 2029 and projected discharge date of 2032.

Michael K. Slover Sr., 74, occupies a bunk in medium security at Pontiac Correctional Center. He has a date with the parole board in 2032 and a projected discharge in 2035.

In the meantime, there's no chance he'll bump into his son in the prison cafeteria. Mike Jr., 50, is incarcerated at the Illinois River Correctional Center, with a parole date of 2031 and projected discharge in 2034.

As for Christopher, Mary Slover adopted him in 1999—but that was before authorities had charged Mary's parents and brother with murder.

Christopher spent some time in a foster home. After a legal battle, a Macon County judge ruled Mary unfit as a parent because the judge believed she took part in concealing her sister-in-law's murder.

At some point, cousins of the Slovers also threw their hat into the ring in the custody competition.

Ultimately, Karyn's parents, Larry and Donna Hearn, won custody of Christopher. (He must have been a sweet little guy—everyone wanted him.)

"We're goofy," Larry Hearn told the *Herald and Review* after defeating Mary in the battle for Christopher. "We're just both giddy as a couple of kids."

So, what happened to Christopher?

Today, he's in his late 20s and uses a different name. According to a social media account, he works in the home-improvement industry as a flooring remodeler.

And on the subject of occupations, I was curious about the legitimacy of the agency that supposedly snagged Karyn a modeling engagement—there are so many scams associated with that industry.

Paris World, the Savannah-based firm, "would seek applicants through newspaper ads and then sign potential models and place their photos on the internet," according to testimony from Paris World owner Alan Tapley at the 2002 murder trial.

Tapley said that he couldn't remember any of the particulars about the modeling job his agency secured for Karyn except for the fact that it was temporary, not longer than a month. Karyn paid $92 in processing fees in order to get the modeling gig, Tapley said, adding that he returned the money to her family after the murder.

Paris World no longer exists and Yelp didn't saunter onto the stage until eight years after the murder, so the modeling agency's repute remains unknown.

(By the way, the Federal Trade Commission offers guidelines to help prospective catwalkers avoid scams.)

Whatever the case, Karyn Hearn Slover seemed like a lovely person who never got the future she deserved.

CHAPTER 21

Kathleen Foley (aka Katy Doyle) Kills for a Player

Q&A WITH PROSECUTOR MICHAEL MCINTYRE
Forensic Files *episode "When the Dust Settled"*
After three hours of fruitlessly combing the internet for an epilogue for so-called "Katy Doyle," I tried watching "When the Dust Settled" one more time.

Sure enough, the end credits of the *Forensic Files* episode said that some names had been changed.

It turns out that the woman who murdered her husband so she could divert all of her bandwidth to a workplace Romeo was actually named Kathleen Ann Foley, according to numerous media accounts.

Her husband, whom she shot four times in his sleep on July 30, 1998, was Joe Foley.

Kathleen, a 36-year-old psychiatric aide at Allentown State Hospital in Pennsylvania, probably didn't know that her boyfriend, George Fleming, was romancing another woman on the side, but she certainly knew that he was married.

Nonetheless, Kathleen happily cashed in a $1,177 savings bond to give George, who worked in housekeeping at the hospital, a down payment on a 1995 Chrysler Concorde. She also bought him clothing, exercise equipment, and jewelry.

He and Kathleen "had sex whenever and wherever possible" including at their houses, in cars, and even at the hospital where they both worked, George would later testify.

While the widow was looking forward to using her husband's $212,000 life insurance payout to underwrite new escapades with her Casanova, the police were slowly building a case against her. They didn't believe her story that an anonymous intruder killed her husband.

Results of an autopsy on Joe Foley, a union official and recreational therapist at the hospital, conflicted with the time line of the story that Kathleen offered. And the clothing at the crime scene was arranged the wrong way.

Still, Kathleen Foley maintained that an unknown thief took her husband's life, and her defense lawyer tried to point the finger at everyone from a local trade organization to a foreign terrorist group.

A Lehigh County jury rejected those contentions, and she received a life sentence on October 2, 2000.

But the Pennsylvania Department of Corrections doesn't list a "Kathleen Foley" as an inmate, and newspapers haven't mentioned her name in years.

What happened to her?

Fortunately, former district attorney Michael P. McIntyre, who prosecuted Kathleen in 2000, agreed to fill in a few blanks about the case. Following are excerpts from our phone conversation:

Rebecca Reisner: Did anything about the case surprise you?

Michael McIntyre: I handled it from the arrest through the trial—I was the one pressing for the arrest. The amazing thing is how she [Kathleen] remained free for 15 months after she shot her husband. It was soon after the time of the O. J. Simpson trial, and the defense came up with the mantra "rush to judgment," and investigators didn't want to do that anymore.

RR: What did you think George Fleming's role was in the crime?

MM: The boyfriend was the whole impetus for this killing. Our theory was that he was selling Kathleen on something like "go ahead and kill him." But he had an iron-clad alibi. We couldn't find anything on him. He testified for the prosecution. In my heart of hearts, I thought he might have had something to do with it, but we couldn't prove it.

RR: I read that Joe Foley was one of nine children. Did you meet any of the siblings?

MM: Yes, I met at least two of them, and they pushed for the prosecution. They assisted me and told me to talk to this person, talk to that person.

RR: Was Joe Foley a prominent citizen around the area?

MM: Joe Foley was well known in the Irish community. He started a program that brought poor Irish kids to the U.S. for the summer.

RR: What do you recall about the defense's attempt to shift the blame away from Kathleen Foley?

MM: I think there was some kind of defense that had to do with Joe's work with the union. Or over the Irish program—they were saying maybe the IRA [Irish Republican Army] did it. I never put any credence in it. It's the defense's job to come up with theories.

RR: Kathleen Foley only made one appeal attempt. Did that surprise you?

MM: It's very rare. There's no downside [to an appeal], nothing to lose.

RR: She served time in the SCI [State Correctional Institution] Muncy prison—what's it like?

MM: I've never been there, but I think it's brutal, one of our toughest prisons for women.

RR: Pennsylvania doesn't list Kathleen Foley as an inmate. Was she released?

MM: No. She died in 2017.

RR: Was a fellow inmate to blame?

MM: I heard it was natural causes, nothing traumatic. [She died from gastric adenocarcinoma, according to the Abolitionist Law Center, a human rights group that tracks inmate deaths.]*

RR: How did you like working with *Forensic Files*?

MM: It was a good experience. They found some gunshot residue on the nightgown that she wore, and we used that as evidence.

RR: Are you still working for Lehigh County?

MM: I retired from the DA's office in 2001, but they brought me back for one more *Forensic Files*, the Patricia Rorrer case. It was my half hour of fame—Foley was my 15 minutes.

*****

The time in the spotlight was even more fleeting for Kathleen's paramour George Fleming. It ended with the trial and the 2003 *Forensic Files* episode.

Incidentally, Kathleen Foley is not the only *Forensic Files* killer to sacrifice everything for a lover who ended up helping the prosecution. Sarah Johnson (see chapter 31) made the same mistake.

They both should have listened to my former hair stylist's advice, "Don't lose your head over a little piece of tail."

Thanks to reader D Zee for writing in with the tip.

CHAPTER 22

Lisa Manderach's Murder

An Unlikely Trap Awaits a Woman and Her Baby
Forensic Files *episode "Shopping Spree"*
Of all the circumstances that led to murders portrayed on *Forensic Files*, those that ensnared Lisa Manderach seem the most improbable.

She walked into a kids' clothing store where a young man working the cash register just happened to be a fantasy-game super fan seething with thoughts of criminal perversion.

Lisa Agostinelli Manderach died because the aforementioned Dungeons & Dragons (D&D) enthusiast, one Caleb Fairley, age 21, reportedly considered her the embodiment of female beauty he'd been wanting to seize.

Fairley also killed Devon, the baby daughter Lisa shared with husband James "Jimmy" Manderach.

The murders initially made Jimmy a suspect because, as we know from countless true-crime stories, "the spouse did it."

Fortunately, investigators found glaring evidence of Fairley's guilt within days of the homicides and built a case so solid that the attacker ended up sentenced to two consecutive life terms for two counts of second-degree murder.

Still, "Shopping Spree," the *Forensic Files* episode about the murders, left me curious about some kind of epilogue for Fairley.

He came from an affluent family, which can, unfairly, favorably tip the scales of justice. On the other hand, the judicial system rarely takes kindly to anyone who kills a mother or child, or both.

Before getting into the most recent information on Fairley, here's a recap of the episode along with some additional facts culled from internet sources.

Lisa Manderach, two weeks shy of her 30th birthday, worked full time as a forklift operator in a food warehouse and also had an entrepreneurial streak.

The Manderachs ran a janitorial service on the side. She also did volunteer work for Meals on Wheels.

The couple had known each other since Lisa was 10 years old. Jimmy was friends with her brothers. Lisa and Jimmy married in 1992.

Devon, 19 months, was their only child.

All three of them were dark haired and striking. Lisa had long, flowing hair, pale skin, and a pretty face.

On September 15, 1995, she and Devon headed to Your Kidz & Mine, a new clothing store in the Collegeville Shopping Center, 10 minutes from her house in Limerick, Pennsylvania.

Jimmy stayed home to watch football.

Lisa left her diaper bag at home because she planned to stay out for only an hour, which makes "Shopping Spree" an odd choice for the title of the *Forensic Files* episode. (To me, it's not a "spree" unless it starts in the morning and doesn't end until it's too dark to find your car.)

After Jimmy reported Lisa missing when she failed to return home from shopping by dinnertime, police found her 1988 Firebird in the shopping plaza's parking lot and located a witness who remembered seeing Lisa in Your Kidz & Mine.

Then, in what has to be everyone's favorite part of the episode, when police brought Caleb in for questioning, they noticed he was wearing beige makeup on his face. At the officers' request, he washed it off, uncovering scratch marks that looked as though they came from someone's fingernails.

He claimed he got them while mosh-pit dancing, although it came out later that he had told friends he got scratched up while rescuing a guy who was being beaten up outside the clothing store.

He allegedly pressured one of those friends, Christopher Lefler, to perjure himself by corroborating the dance alibi in court; Lefler refused.

Police got a search warrant for Fairley's home and discovered a great deal of pornography.

"We found out that he was a real pervert, all kinds of sexual devices and various perverted stuff," District Attorney Bruce L. Castor Jr. told *Forensic Files* rather triumphantly.

In general, I wouldn't be so hasty to assume a link between perverted, well, whatever it was he had in his possession, and criminality.

But fortunately the murders, which horrified the community, created plenty of forensic evidence that made for a stronger case against Fairley.

Fairley, a blond, heavy, powerful-looking fire hydrant of a man who lived with his parents, was described by a friend as a devotee of D&D, a role-playing game that allows people to act out story lines involving medieval warrior heroes, dragons, wicked monarchs, you name it. (For more on D&D, see part 2 that follows.)

As soon as Lisa stepped into Your Kidz & Mine, Fairley, who had a passion for vampire lore, recognized her as having the idealized look of the women portrayed in vampire-related literature, investigators believed.

It's not clear whether Fairley's interest in vampires was part of D&D or a separate pastime.

The authorities theorized that, when Fairley realized he was alone in the store with Lisa and Devon (a customer exiting the store noticed the mother and daughter were the only shoppers left there), he locked the door and attacked Lisa toward the back of the store near some high racks out of view from the windows.

During the struggle, she fought back vigorously, leaving the nail marks on his face. Some of her ribs were broken. The mullet-wearing Fairley strangled her to death in the store and likewise killed the baby, police believed. Devon left saliva stains in the same area. Tests revealed that Caleb might have sexually assaulted Lisa, according to *Forensic Files*—his semen was found on the floor in the store.

Fairley took the bodies out the back door and loaded them into his vehicle, investigators believed. He disposed of the little girl's body in Valley Forge National Park, where hikers soon discovered it. It looked as though someone had tossed her body out of a car from above, according to *Forensic Files*.

At some point that evening, Fairley washed and vacuumed the rug and did so again the next morning, witnesses said.

Police found Lisa's body after Fairley agreed to disclose its location in exchange for a promise that they wouldn't pursue the death penalty. That decision drew public anger—as could be seen in letters to the editor published in the *Philadelphia Daily News* on September 29, 1995. According to one written by citizen Brian Green, "The only deal that should have been cut for this subhuman Caleb Fairley punk should have been: Do we inject him first or let the victim's survivors spend a half hour with him in a closed room with [a] baseball bat!"

After retrieving Lisa's body—Fairley had gone to an industrial area near his health club and left the murdered woman on the ground with her hair arranged to cover her face—investigators discovered Caleb's DNA under her fingernails.

They found some strands of long, dark hair with the roots attached (suggesting a struggle) in the vacuum cleaner bag at the store.

All this culminated in Caleb Fairley's April 1996 conviction for two counts of murder, aggravated assault, theft, and abuse of a corpse. He got life without parole.

Fairley has not found prison existence agreeable. In 2012, he tried to have his conviction vacated and get a new trial following a Supreme Court decision that deemed life sentences without parole for juvenile offenders unconstitutional.

Fairley's argument: The court should have rendered him a minor for sentencing purposes. Even though he committed the double murder at age 21, "a person's biological process is typically incomplete until the person reaches his or her mid-twenties."

That ploy hasn't worked out, and today, Fairley lives in SCI Fayette, a moderately overcrowded maximum-security prison in La Belle, Pennsylvania. It houses 2,114 inmates but has bed capacity for just 1,826.

As for an update on Lisa's widower, Jimmy Manderach, it appears he still lives in the same part of Pennsylvania. Jimmy did not appear on the *Forensic Files* episode and hasn't talked to other media.

In 1998, Caleb Fairley's parents settled a lawsuit filed by Lisa's mother and Jimmy for $1.6 million. According to legal documents, the Fairleys contended: "While the circumstances were indeed horrific, the deaths . . . were relatively and mercifully swift, mitigating their conscious pain and suffering."

That same year, police arrested Caleb's father, James Fairley, who owned a pharmacy in Phoenixville, Pennsylvania, for allegedly providing a customer with the painkiller Darvon illegally. Court papers allege he asked the customer for sex in return for the drug.

But one wholesome thing did happen in the aftermath of the murders. In 1997, a Montgomery County mother of two named Ginger Childs came up with the idea of building a playground in honor of Lisa and Devon—and helped raise $500,000 in cash and materials. Hundreds of local volunteers helped build Manderach Memorial Playground at Limerick Community Park.

The township invested an additional $50,000 for new equipment for the playground in 2012.

In 2017, an opinion piece by *Philadelphia Inquirer* columnist Maria Panaritis called the playground a "wonderland" and "oasis of unbridled joy" and noted it even draws tourists. (Oddly, Panaritis also said that Lisa made a "grave mistake" by going into the clothing store. Lisa didn't make any mistake—the homicidal maniac who worked there did.)

Just last year, a Limerick-area resident sent me a beautiful video of her grandson trotting across the playground's castle and descending on a spiral slide. In the background, the clip shows a tilted merry-go-round with masts, and it looks way more amusing and safe than the fast-rotating disks we had in my school days.

The playground has nabbed 4.5 stars on Yelp and has a lively Facebook page dedicated to it. Most important, it has offered some solace to a community shaken to its core by the murders of Lisa and Devon Manderach.

PART 2: DUNGEONS & DRAGONS, OH MY—SCAPEGOATING A ROLE-PLAYING GAME

Because the homicide of Lisa Manderach in 1995 allegedly arose from obsessive fantasies fostered—at least in part—by killer Caleb Fairley's fondness for Dungeons & Dragons, I looked into whether other D&D superfans have left murder victims in their wakes.

To get right to the point, the answer is yes, a few, although they go back pretty far. In 1984, Steve and Dan Erwin, 12 and 16, respectively, died in a Colorado murder-suicide and were rumored to have left a note saying it was their only way to escape Dungeons & Dragons. "There is no doubt that D&D cost them their lives," police Detective Greg Corrie said at the time, as recounted by an AP story from September 18, 1985.

Three years later, Daniel Kasten murdered his parents in their Long Island home reportedly because a Dungeons & Dragons character named Mind Flayer coerced him into it, according to a recounting in the *New York Post* on December 12, 2000.

But even before those murders happened, Dungeons & Dragons had turned into the subject of public scrutiny because of suicides by a number of boys known to play the game.

After two separate such cases, one in 1979 and the other in 1982, the mother of the second young man (Irving Lee Pulling) started the group Bothered about Dungeons & Dragons, or BADD.

By 1985—a full decade before Fairley generated headlines—BADD had made Dungeons & Dragons the object of some public hysteria, or at least concern.

The BADD folks reasoned that a game involving such supernatural elements as magic spells and curses must degenerate into real-life everyday devil worship, human self-sacrifices, and such.

Evidence existed that Pulling and the other youth who took his own life, a 16-year-old boy genius named James Dallas Egbert III, had underlying psychological problems, but that didn't slow down BADD's momentum.

BADD grew prominent enough to spur a *60 Minutes* segment about the Dungeons & Dragons phenomenon in 1985. Host Ed Bradley described D&D:

An enormously complicated game in which each player chooses an imaginary character he'll assume. There are dwarves, knights, and thieves, gods, and devils, magic and spells. It's a journey into fantasy through complicated mazes where you use your wits to kill your enemies before they kill you, all in a quest for wealth and power. The dungeon master orchestrates and referees the game, creating scenarios both complicated and terrifying.

Gary Gygax, who created Dungeons & Dragons, and Dieter H. Sturm, public relations director for TSR Inc.—the company that sells D&D—told 60 Minutes that correlation doesn't mean causation: With three million to four million users of the game in the United States, it was a coincidence that a fraction of the 5,000 teens who committed suicide in the then-most-recent 12-month period played D&D, Strum pointed out.

An adolescent boy wearing eyeglasses with Reagan-era giant aviator frames (talk about scary) explained that the good game-characters try to stop the bad hombres from raping and plundering—and the role-playing stops once the six-sided dice go back in the box.

"This is make believe," Dungeons & Dragons creator Gary Gygax told *60 Minutes*. "Who is bankrupted by losing a game of Monopoly?"

An online commenter who identified himself as Michael Miller wrote the following retroactive rebuttal to BADD's campaign:

My mom gave me the red Basic D&D for Christmas while this stupidity was going on. She played with me and the rest of the family several times, and we all had a great time defeating monsters, getting out of traps, and amassing sizeable fortunes. She knew how to be an involved, responsible parent.

The BADD publicity died down after a few years. After the *60 Minutes* story aired, Betty Erwin, mother of Daniel and Steven Erwin, said she believed the tragedy that took her sons' lives had more to do with Daniel's dread over repercussions after he pleaded guilty to auto theft, according to the AP story from September 18, 1985. Researchers from the Centers for Disease Control said they found no causal link between D&D and violence.

In fact, one could make a case for a connection between the game and healthy creativity.

A number of accomplished authors, including George R. R. Martin, the father of *Game of Thrones*, have given credit to Dungeons & Dragons for sparking their imaginations as writers.

A 2014 *New York Times* article quoted Pulitzer-prize winner Junot Díaz as saying that, via Dungeons & Dragons, "we welfare kids could travel, have adventures, succeed, be powerful, triumph, fail, and be in ways that would have been impossible in the larger real world."

Still, it's not hard to imagine anti-D&D activism reappearing today. (As a Wiccan told me many years ago, every so often, when there's nothing better to worry about, some concerned citizen sounds an alarm about devil worship.)

It can be enough to make even a sane person worry about his own affinity for fantasy and superhero-related culture. Fairley's crime prompted self-reflection from one writer somewhere along the nerd continuum. A passage from a 2015 post by blogger Benjamin Welton on *Literary Trebuchet* reads:

> *Whereas Fairley spent his days alone in his parent's home with his porn, his vampires, and Dungeons & Dragons, I killed many hours alone in my father's apartment with my comic books, my horror novels, and my favorite television shows. Fairley loved heavy metal; I still do. As much as it pains me to say it, Caleb Fairley, who was convicted of murdering and sexually assaulting Lisa Manderach and her 19-month-old daughter Devon in 1995, is the darkest version of people like me and my friends.*

But surely he knows that paranoia and substance abuse—not football—fueled Aaron Hernandez's homicidal rage, and greed—not tennis—compelled the Menendez brothers to make themselves orphans.

One can point to an id lurking in practitioners of just about every avocation and vocation. Fortunately, very few lead to horrifying crimes.

And perpetrators are far outnumbered by the authorities who protect us from them. Who knows, some of those hardworking law enforcement types just might shake off stress with a little witch and wizard role-playing in their off hours.

CHAPTER 23

Madison Rutherford

Con Man Walking

HE SWINDLED A SENIOR CITIZEN, THEN SOLD PIZZA

Forensic Files *episode "Past Lives"*

If Yelp existed back in the 1990s, maybe Brigitte Beck would have enjoyed the retirement she deserved.

Unfortunately, she had no way of knowing that Connecticut financial adviser Madison Rutherford was a con man born with the name John Sankey.

He probably didn't tell his clients about the six months he spent in prison for larceny in 1993, shortly before he persuaded Beck to let him take charge of her six-figure nest egg.

Rutherford ruined Beck's finances as well as his own, then tried to fake his own death for $7 million in insurance payouts.

Like other *Forensic Files* fraudsters (Barbara Stager, Cynthia McDonnell) who thought they were smarter than the insurance companies and police, Rutherford was done in by the forensics.

"Past Lives," the *Forensic Files* episode about Rutherford, first aired in 2004 while he was serving his second term in prison, so I looked around to find out what happened to him after he exited federal lockup in 2006.

I also searched for an epilogue on Brigitte Beck, the mild-mannered German immigrant whose *Forensic Files* appearance always makes me teary. So let's get started on the recap of "Past Lives," along with additional information from internet research.

John Patrick Sankey was born circa 1964, the son of a New York City police officer, according to the *Hartford Courant*. He started to use the last name Rutherford at some point during his adulthood and filed for bankruptcy under that name in 1990.

After his stretch in prison in 1993, John Sankey legally changed his name to Madison Rutherford and worked as a financial adviser in Connecticut.

He had a talent for making good investments for his clients, according to *Forensic Files*. His friend and neighbor Brigitte Beck, in her late 60s and with no family in the United States, named him as her executor and gave him power of attorney over all that she owned.

Brigitte had moved to the United States at age 24 and worked as a nanny, then as a massage therapist at Graf Studio, a Stamford, Connecticut, business owned by an older German couple who had taken a liking to her. When they died, they left her everything, and she took over the business.

She got to know Rutherford through his wife, an attractive older woman named L. Rhynie Jefferson who was a client at Beck's massage studio. The three became trusting friends.

Brigitte was also a neighbor of the couple, who reportedly delighted in spending their newfound riches on cars, travel, and their huge colonial farmhouse on five acres in Bethel, Connecticut.

Multiple media sources list Rhynie Jefferson's occupation as fortune-teller, but if she had any premonitions about the stock market, she stopped sharing them with her husband. His luck at picking winning stocks ran out in the late 1990s, and he eventually lost more of his own and his clients' money than he could ever hope to recoup on Wall Street.

The 34-year-old Rutherford had also spent all of Beck's savings and taken out a mortgage on her house.

Instead of telling his clients the truth and starting over, he decided to chase after $7 million in payouts from CNA Insurance and Kemper Corporation.

In 1998, police discovered his rental SUV ravaged by fire in a ditch near Monterrey, Mexico, where he traveled to either buy or sell (sources vary) an exotic dog.

At first, it looked as though the car had ignited after skidding off the road.

Inside the vehicle, first responders found a body reduced to charred bones. An inscribed wristwatch and a medical alert necklace enabled investigators to tentatively identify the victim as Madison Rutherford.

Rhynie Jefferson gave police one of Madison's teeth that she said was removed during a dental procedure. Its DNA matched that of the teeth from the burned-out Suburban.

Mexican authorities signed off on the case as an accidental death even though their forensic specialists had doubts.

One of Rutherford's U.S. insurers decided to do some of its own sleuthing before forking over $4 million to the widow.

Kemper Corporation hired private detective Frank Rudewicz to search for an alive Madison Rutherford and engaged forensics expert William M. Bass to study the bones. Bass found that the teeth weren't consistent with those of a Caucasian person and the skull fragments came from someone older than 34.

Before authorities blew the lid off the fraud, Rhynie confided in Brigitte Beck that Rutherford was still alive. Soon after, he even showed up at Beck's house with an outrageous story—that the FBI had staged his death because organized crime figures wanted to kill him.

The kindhearted Beck allowed him to hide at her house for a couple of weeks. She had recently had a windfall of nearly $100,000 and handed it over to Rutherford to manage.

Then he disappeared again.

When the FBI showed up at her house, Brigitte at first denied seeing Rutherford. He and Jefferson had manipulated her into opening a checking account in the name B. Beck & Associates, which the con man used to launder money.

The authorities soon found Rutherford by tracing a car he owned to a "Thomas Bey Hamilton" who worked as a comptroller for Double Decker Studios in Boston.

Management liked his work and was considering elevating him to CEO.

FBI agents ambushed Hamilton in his apartment in Boston on November 7, 2000, and arrested him.

His fingerprints matched Rutherford's. Thomas Bey Hamilton—who had books about how to change one's identity in his Boston pad—was Madison Rutherford.

"He was very good with credit reports, which helped him with creating new identities," Rudewicz told me in an interview.

The court kept him in jail pending legal action.

When authorities showed Rhynie Jefferson evidence that Rutherford was cheating on her with other women, she spilled the whole story: On July 11, 1998, he staged the accident with a body stolen from a tomb in Mexico and then pedaled away on a bike. He sneaked her a tooth from the pilfered corpse after returning from Mexico.

A year later, Rutherford had planted a bag of clothes stained with his own blood in Mexico as a backup explanation for his "death."

"He did his homework," says Frank Rudewicz. "He knew that in Mexico he wouldn't get scrutiny as he would in the States."

Once Rutherford was formally charged, Brigitte Beck revealed that, between spending her cash and mortgaging her house, he swindled her out of $782,000. She had virtually nothing left.

Meanwhile, Rutherford tried to blame everything on his wife.

Rhynie Jefferson, he claimed, had seduced him when he was a 16-year-old lifeguard and later "manipulated and pressured him to maintain a lavish lifestyle that included providing for all manner of pets and livestock, including scores of free-range chickens," according to a Hartford Courant story from July 21, 2001. (A neighbor said that Rutherford considered the birds to be his children.)

In a Bridgeport, Connecticut, courtroom, Rutherford's father, John Sankey Sr., pinned his son's problems on Rhynie as well, according to a Connecticut Post story. The elder Sankey also mentioned that his other son had recently died of leukemia.

In the end, Rutherford pleaded guilty to fraud. Without going into detail, he apologized for his crimes and said his eight months in jail so far were "hell" and that he promised to make the rest of his life "worthwhile," according to the Hartford Courant.

U.S. district judge Stefan R. Underhill gave him five years in a federal prison for fraud and "leaving a lot of pain and loss in his wake."

The authorities couldn't charge him with embezzling Brigitte's money because she'd given him power of attorney.

Rhynie Jefferson got 18 months in prison and three years of supervised release for her part in the scheme.

So what contribution to society has Madison Rutherford made since exiting the penitentiary?

Well, he's not incinerating skeletons anymore, but he's left a trail of disgruntled diners thanks to his foray into the restaurant business.

Rutherford, who now goes by the first name "Bey," owned a restaurant called Pop's NY Pizza that opened in Columbia, South Carolina, in 2006. By 2011, the place had a Yelp rating of one star and scathing reviews: "If you care about your health," wrote Sam V., "please do not go." According to Julie R., "There was a hole in the door of the restroom, the toilet looked like it had never been cleaned and the toilet paper was on the floor with flies buzzing around it."

Rutherford also allegedly neglected to pay his bills from local ad agencies, according to a post by writer Paul Blake in a blog dedicated to the now-defunct *Columbia City Paper*.

The con man was also known to brag to employees about having served prison time, according to Frank Rudewicz.

Pop's closed in shame, but Rutherford's other business—the nearby Bey's Sports Bar—lived on. His Yelp rating rose to 1.5 stars, but customers scorched him and the place: "Picture yourself in the worst bar of your life X 10," wrote Michelle M. A former customer named Keith S. confirmed that the man with a fondness for the names of founding fathers took his standards of hygiene from their era. "Bathrooms are disgusting," he wrote on Yelp. "There's never been soap in the guy's when I'm there."

DirecTV sued Rutherford for allegedly pirating its services in order to broadcast games at Bey's Sports Bar, according to the Columbia City Paper blog. Even worse, Rutherford allegedly stole tips from employees, according to a reader comment imported from the newspaper's archives.

"It was a lawless place," says Lex, a former Bey's bartender who spoke with me. "No ID needed, dollar drinks. It was cheaper to drink there than anywhere else. When we were working, we could drink on the job, and it was the ultimate party bar."

According to Lex, who asked that her last name not be used, the establishment closed in 2013 amid tax woes. (Not that it didn't leave some joy in its wake—Lex ended up meeting and marrying a fellow Bey's bartender. Today, they live in the Midwest and have a baby daughter.)

The shuttering of the business didn't stop the Yelp reviews—people who watched the episode wrote in. "What a piece of garbage this guy is," wrote Andy C., "stealing $500,000 from a trusting old woman."

Rutherford pretty much disappeared after he closed his sports bar. His spare, outdated LinkedIn profile lists him by his last-known name, Bey Rutherford, and gives his occupation as owner of Pop's NY Pizza.

Regarding what happened to his wife, Rhynie Jefferson, she was living in Oakville, Connecticut, and was single and 75 years old as of 2019. According to a reader who wrote in with a tip, she died in May 2020.

Finally, on to the emotional centerpiece of the story, Brigitte Beck. Once swindled out of everything and having had Chase Manhattan Bank foreclose on her house, she received some financial help from friends and continued to live in Connecticut, according to the *Hartford Courant*.

Beck died on January 18, 2008, at the age of 78. Two brothers and a sister, all living in Germany, survived her, according to her obituary. She's buried in the East Norwalk Historical Cemetery.

At least she can rest in peace and be remembered. No one ever identified the deceased man whose grave Madison Rutherford desecrated.

CHAPTER 24

Mark Winger

No Great Catch

DIABOLIQUE, AMERICAN STYLE
Forensic Files *episode "A Welcome Intrusion"*
If I ever brought a guy like Mark Winger home to meet my parents, they would have died.

Of ecstasy.

"A nuclear engineer for the state of Illinois," I can hear my mother saying in awe. A graduate degree and solid job would be a nice parcel of news to relay to the extended family in Miami Beach.

Winger also seemed to have a pleasant personality—mild mannered and friendly.

Unbeknownst to his future wife Donnah Brown and her approving mother and stepfather, he was no prize.

Donnah, a medical technician, married Mark in 1989. By 1995, he was having a secret affair with her best friend, DeAnn Schultz, even though he and Donnah had recently adopted a baby girl. Donnah, who was medically unable to have children, was thrilled to be a mother.

Meanwhile, Mark's apparent plan was to get rid of Donnah, marry DeAnn, and keep the baby, named Bailey, for the two of them to raise.

That would mean no need to strain his $72,000-a-year-job with alimony or child support.

To accomplish his goals, he thought up the most devious murder scheme ever portrayed by *Forensic Files*.

"A Welcome Intrusion" is probably my favorite episode of all because it illustrates how (a) the surface only tells half of the story, (b) even the most stable-appearing family is just a house of cards, and (c) people who get away with murder once—literally or figuratively—just can't stop pushing their luck.

So let's get going on a recap of the story along with extra information from internet research. Here's what happened.

Mark Alan Winger, who up until 1995 had been an in-law-pleasing pillar of society, grabbed a chance to put a diabolical plot in motion after his wife's chance encounter with a young man suffering from psychiatric problems.

Roger Harrington, 27, an airport shuttle driver, had driven recklessly and muttered some disturbing thoughts during a ride Donnah took from Lambert International Airport in St. Louis, Missouri, to the couple's home in Springfield, Illinois. At Mark's urging, she wrote a letter of complaint to the shuttle service owner.

The company suspended Harrington.

Mark, 32, then lured Harrington to the Winger home on August 29, 1995, under the pretense of wanting to smooth things over.

When Harrington showed up, Winger shot him in the head.

Donnah, 32, ran into the room to find out what the commotion was. Winger beat her about the head with a claw hammer.

Then he called 911 and, doing his best impression of a hysterical, grief-stricken husband, blamed the carnage on Harrington.

"I just found this man in my house. He beat my wife. . . . He's lying on the floor with a bullet in his head," Winger said in a breathless state of rehearsed melodrama.

"Yes, I shot him—he was killing my wife!"

Both victims died of their injuries without speaking.

Winger wanted the world to believe that Harrington was a deranged malcontent who invaded his home to seek revenge—by bludgeoning Donnah to death for making him lose his job—and that Winger shot Harrington to halt the attack.

Winger's plan worked.

The authorities and the media believed him. Shortly after the crime, a *South Florida Sun Sentinel* article reported: "'How [Harrington] got into the house, we don't know,' Springfield Lt. Bob Shipman said. Mark Winger was exercising in the basement when he heard his wife's body thud to the floor. [Mark] grabbed a .45-caliber pistol and shot Harrington fatally in the head. Police said Harrington had a history of mental illness, and that Mark Winger shot in self-defense and will not face any charges."

(Donnah's mother and stepfather, Sarah Jane and Ira Drescher, lived in Florida, hence the Sunshine State media coverage.)

It's not clear whether Winger knew this in advance, but Springfield Police detective Charlie Cox was already familiar with Harrington. Years earlier, Cox had to break up at least one physical fight involving Harrington and Harrington's then wife. (Cox owned the trailer park where the couple lived.)

It established a pattern of violence for Harrington, giving police all the more reason to accept Winger's story without question.

Winger received $25,000 from a fund for crime victims and a $150,000 payout thanks to Donnah's life insurance, according to the *Chicago Tribune*. The grieving husband wrote a letter to a local paper to thank residents for their support during his "ordeal."

He resumed his life, hiring a nanny, Rebecca Simic, to care for Bailey. He married Rebecca (instead of DeAnn Schultz) and converted from Judaism to Christianity for his new bride. The couple added three more children to their family.

The Dreschers stayed loyal to Mark Winger, and they remained part of one another's lives.

Meanwhile, Mark apparently decided that $175,000 wasn't payment enough for committing a double homicide.

He sued the shuttle company.

Bootheel Area Rapid Transportation, however, wasn't going to just hand over the millions Winger demanded, and began an investigation of its own.

Springfield police reopened the case in 1999.

Evidence of the deception trickled in. DeAnn Schultz told investigators about her relationship with Mark and that he had talked to her about wanting Donnah dead, although at the time she didn't take him seriously.

Lead detective Doug Williamson, a member of the Springfield Police Department who had always harbored doubts about Winger's narrative, now had a second chance to examine evidence. The original placement of the bodies, visible in rediscovered Polaroids, contradicted parts of Winger's story to police.

After reviewing Winger's 911 call—which picked up the sound of Harrington moaning in pain from the first bullet wound—and talking to a neighbor who had heard gunshots, investigators concluded that Winger hadn't immediately fired his gun twice at Harrington as he'd claimed.

"My baby's crying, my baby's crying. I've gotta go," he told the operator on the 911 recording after he realized Harrington was still alive. Then he used the gun a second time to finish him off.

Investigators also turned their attention toward a note found in Harrington's Oldsmobile. It listed the Wingers' address and "4:30," suggesting that, rather that showing up unexpected, Harrington was attending a prearranged meeting. Harrington's roommates said they remembered his receiving at least one phone call from Winger.

In 2001, Winger was indicted, arrested, and held on $10 million bond. He asked a childhood friend, a successful Florida real estate developer named Jeffrey Gelman, to put up the money. Gelman said no.

In 2002, a jury convicted Winger of two counts of premeditated murder.

Now Mark Winger was once again a great catch—this time for the criminal justice system. He received life in prison without parole.

*****

That's where the *Forensic Files* episode ended, but Mark Winger had more in store. From his new home at Pontiac Correctional Center in Illinois, he dreamed up an even more complicated scheme.

It started around 2002, when Winger established a rapport with another inmate.

Terry Hubbell didn't have a degree from the Virginia Military Institute or a family prominent enough to land a wedding announcement in the *New York Times*, as Winger did. But the biographies of the two men overlapped in that each had beaten someone to death: in Hubbell's case, a teenager named Angel Greenwood, in 1983.

Winger asked Hubbell to execute a murder-for-hire project intended to exonerate Winger and wipe out all those who had offended him. According to an Illinois state court document filed in 2011:

In May and June 2005, [Winger] approached Hubbell in the recreation yard and mentioned his desire "to get rid of a witness in his case." Defendant [Winger] named the witness as DeAnn Anderson or Shultz. Hubbell initially blew it off "because everybody that is in prison pretty well says they would like to get rid of a witness in their case." Hubbell stated the issue came up "repeatedly" and he eventually contacted a private investigator who worked on his case. Hubbell hoped to receive consideration for himself. In June 2005, Hubbell received a written plan from defendant [Mark Winger].

Winger's 19-page handwritten note called for a hitman to kidnap Jeff Gelman and extract a huge sum of money in return for promising not to hurt Gelman's family.

That jackpot would pay for the kidnapping of DeAnn Schultz. She would be forced to write and record statements saying that she lied during the trial and Winger was innocent.

Another provision in Winger's plan, as paraphrased by Donnah's stepfather, Ira Drescher, was revealed during an interview with *48 Hours*: "Oh, by the way, if there's any money left over, kill Ira Drescher also because he's the son-of-a-gun father-in-law that I dislike."

Winger also wanted Gelman and Gelman's family killed once they came up with the cash. The hitman would murder Schultz, too, but make it look like suicide.

The hired killer would need to follow elaborate instructions every step of the way. Winger's plan specified, for example, that the hitman ensure that the only fingerprints on Schultz's suicide note and its envelope would come from Schultz herself and only her DNA could be found on the stamps and flap of the envelope.

Given Winger's past crimes and his background as an engineer, the elaborateness of the blueprint doesn't seem too surprising. But his belief that he could phone in a plan with that many moving parts does. It sounds like a job for a team of CIA agents and Navy Seals, not some freelancer hired sight unseen.

Also, in his fixation on the details, Winger seemed to forget the larger picture. Once the hitman received the ransom from Gelman, what would keep him from taking the money and running? Why would he risk committing all those capital murders?

And wouldn't investigators connect the dots between Winger and Schultz, Gelman, and Drescher? No one else had a motive for seeing all of them dead.

The 2013 book *The Perfect Patsy* by Edward Cunningham contains transcripts of Winger's conversations with Hubbell. As murder-for-hire dialogues go, these are actually a little tiresome to plow through. They're riddled with repetition and passages noting unintelligible spans of tape. But there's enough incriminating conversation to ease the minds of any folks still worried that Winger is just a good guy victimized by the system.

In the resulting 2007 trial, Winger claimed that his plans were just a fantasy, fueled by anger over his belief that Springfield police detectives had lied about his murder case and that his conviction was in part politically motivated.

Winger explained that he was merely managing his anger when he did such things as verbalize his desire to cut out DeAnn Schultz's tongue and use it as toilet paper.

He also blamed his own bloodthirsty reveries on the dehumanizing conditions at maximum-security prisons. "They are warehouses of men, but they're also insane asylums," Winger said.

Winger characterized Hubbell as a "sly fox" whom he feared. Hubbell was scamming him, he alleged.

Apparently, Winger's parents couldn't or wouldn't help him get a lawyer for his second trial. Livingston County public defender Randell Morgan represented him.

In a twist, a special agent who had helped arrange for Hubbell to wear a concealed recording device while talking to Winger in the prison yard ended up testifying for the defense. Casey Payne said that Hubbell came forward in the first place only because he wanted his mother's phone bill paid and a transfer to another prison.

Winger insisted he was a sociable soul, not a sociopath. "I love people," he said in his presentencing statement to Livingston County Circuit Court judge Harold Frobish. "The only thing I love more than people is more people."

Nonetheless, after deliberating for three hours, the jury convicted Winger.

Morgan asked for a minimum sentence, arguing that no money changed hands between Winger and Hubbell and that none of the kidnap-murder plans came to fruition.

Frobish handed Winger—then 44 years old and already serving two life sentences without parole—two sentences of 35 years. The judge called him a "threat to the public."

Donnah Winger's mother, Sara Jane Drescher, told *48 Hours* that the additional sentence eased her worries that her former son-in-law would go free if a technicality caused the murder convictions to be overturned.

Ira Drescher recalled looking at Winger in chains after the trial and telling him, "Your miserable life is over."

*****

Actually, you wouldn't know he was miserable from his prison mugshots over the years.

He grew a long, gray beard and looked like a friendly organic food co-op manager or a department store Santa. Later, he trimmed his facial hair and the fringe around his receded hairline. But in all the photos, he manages what looks like a warm little smile. Perhaps the onetime nuclear engineer from Springfield, Illinois, has lost just about everything except hope.

Although audiotapes captured Winger complaining about becoming ill from a "meat sandwich" served in prison, he's been able to find ample culinary delights.

The five-foot, 10-inch formerly small-framed prisoner now weighs in at 215 pounds, according to the Illinois Department of Corrections, which also notes he has an eagle tattoo on his left leg.

Winger has tried to make the most of his time in captivity by mounting a legal fight over where he can exercise. His litigation in its various incarnations dragged on for years.

At Tamms Correctional Center, he complained that forcing him to stay in his concrete-walled cell all day constituted cruel and unusual punishment that led to "physical illness, depression, and panic attacks."

He said that running in place and doing jumping jacks in his cell caused his knees to hit the wall or bunk, sit-ups made his bed too sweaty, and the floor was too dirty for push-ups.

Court papers noted that intent is essential for liability under the Eighth Amendment and there was no indication of malice toward Winger and no evidence the exercise restrictions caused his alleged psychological problems.

In 2013, a Chicago U.S. Court of Appeals affirmed a lower court ruling that defeated Winger's suit over exercise. That seems to be the last of Winger's efforts to shake things up from supermax. As of this writing, Winger is serving his time at the Western Illinois Correctional Center in Mount Sterling, Illinois.

But what about those victimized by Winger? Where are they today?

- Sara Jane and Ira Drescher took comfort in philanthropy. They raised $42,000 to build Donnah's Playroom in Joe DiMaggio Children's Hospital in Hollywood, Florida, in 1998.

  At that time, they still believed Roger Harrington was the hammer-wielding killer. Once the truth about their son-in-law came out, the Dreschers turned their attention toward domestic violence.

  They established Donnah's Fund at the Women in Distress shelter in Broward County, Florida, to help victims pay for security deposits, furnishings, and babysitting once they exit the facility and start anew.

- Rebecca Simic, the nanny Mark married, kept a low profile for a long time after he went to prison in 2002. She lost the family's house and declared bankruptcy.

  She moved to Louisville, Kentucky, along with Bailey—whom Simic adopted—and the other two daughters and son she shared with Winger.

  In a 2012 article in the *Southeast Outlook*, a publication of the Southeast Christian Church, Simic said her marriage to Winger had been a happy one. According to the piece by writer Patti Smith: "They were active in their church, and Winger did construction projects as a volunteer around the building. Simic said she believes Winger's conversion was real. She never suspected him until he was sent to prison for life and she asked for a divorce. His letters, she said, were threatening and hostile."

  In a 2016 interview with the *Southeast Outlook*, Simic said that she had begun to open up more about her history as a means of giving moral support to other single moms.

  "No one seems to think about the family when someone is incarcerated," Simic said. "I call them living victims. It's a humiliating, embarrassing role to play, although you have done nothing wrong. That spouse is alive but dead to the family." As so with the earlier story, the more recent article asserts that Winger threatened Simic's life when she took steps to end their marriage.

  Despite everything, she said that the whole experience has strengthened her religious faith and that she's grateful to have brought up Bailey.

  In a surprising turn of events in 2021, Rebecca and the four kids appeared on camera on a *20/20* episode called "The Perfect Lie." They had all changed their last names from "Winger" to "Simic"—and considered it a fresh start.

  The Dreschers and the now-adult Bailey, who actually resembles Donnah Winger, recently renewed their relationship. Sara Jane and Ira still consider her their granddaughter.

- Doug Williamson, one of the lead detectives on the case starting with the deaths of Donnah Winger and Roger Harrington, went on to appear in "Invitation to a Murder," a 2008 episode of *48 Hours*.

In more recent years, it seems, life has not gone so well for Williamson. He failed firearms training and left the police force in 2011.

As of 2014, he was locked in a conflict with the city of Springfield over a disability claim, as reported in the *Illinois Times*.

Williamson, whose father and brother also were police officers, said the job brought on posttraumatic stress disorder and made him unable to function in his position.

Investigating murders, including one involving the suffocation death of an infant, gave him disturbing dreams and night sweats and caused other trauma, he said.

The city countered that Williamson's problems stemmed from his drinking and willful wallowing in memories of homicide cases. He went on vacation with the surviving family of Donnah Winger, according to the May 22, 2004, issue of the *Illinois Times*.

• Charlie Cox, the other lead detective on the case, it seems, has had an easier time. He retired as Springfield chief of police in 2009.

He later appeared in "The Devil You Know," an episode about Donnah's murder featured on the *Final Witness* series.

• Ralph Harrington, the father of Roger Harrington, lived until the age of 73 in 2010—long enough for him and his wife, Helen, to see Mark Winger convicted of not only Roger's murder but also the jail-yard plot to kill DeAnn Schultz and the Gelman family in 2007.

Regardless of their connection to the case, all of the survivors must have felt relieved when Judge Richard Mills rejected Winger's latest appeal in November 2021.

Michael Peterson

An Update

A *FORENSIC FILES* MURDER THAT WENT ON A BINGE
Forensic Files *episode "A Novel Idea"*

Forensic Files produced "A Novel Idea" back in 2006, but any murder story that includes well-educated mansion owners plus a cheerful male escort on the witness stand is sure to be revisited many times.

Throughout the years, *Dateline* has continually covered the case of how writer Michael Peterson's wife, Kathleen, ended up dead at the base of a staircase in their 19-room house. The NBC series most recently broadcast an update of "Down the Back Staircase" in 2017.

But public interest in the case didn't really explode until the following year, when Netflix expanded and updated a documentary by French director Jean-Xavier de Lestrade to create a 13-part binge-fest called *The Staircase*.

For this chapter, I looked into what's happened to Michael Peterson since the Netflix series ended in 2018 and whether a theory that a rogue owl played a role in Kathleen's death ever got any traction. But first, here's a recap of "A Novel Idea," along with extra information drawn from internet research

Michael Ivor Peterson graduated from Duke University, where he was editor of the school newspaper. He joined the Marines and earned silver and bronze stars for service in Vietnam.

As a young man, he divided his time between North Carolina and Germany. He and his first wife, schoolteacher Patricia Sue Peterson, had sons Todd and Clayton—then acquired two daughters, Margaret and Martha, when the couple's friend Liz McKee Ratliff died. Ratliff had assigned Michael as guardian of her kids and left him her entire estate.

Michael later became a novelist, weaving his real-life experiences in the military into the plots of his books.

He and Patricia split up, and he began a relationship with his neighbor Kathleen Hunt Atwater in Durham, North Carolina, in 1992.

Kathleen Hunt grew up in Lancaster, Pennsylvania, and was so bright that she took advanced Latin classes at a nearby college while still in McCaskey High School, according to the *Lancaster New Era* newspaper. She graduated first in her class.

She was the first woman accepted into Duke University's School of Engineering. At the time of her death, she was a vice president at Nortel Networks at the company's Research Triangle Park offices. She had a net worth of around $2 million, according to *Forensic Files*.

By the time Michael and Kathleen became a couple, his two daughters and Kathleen's daughter from her first marriage, Caitlin Atwater, were already good friends.

Michael and Kathleen married in 1997. By then, one of Michael's books, *A Time for War*, had made its way onto the *New York Times* bestseller list and generated enough cash to pay for the Colonial Revival–style house containing the now-famous staircase.

The couple combined their families into one household in the five-bedroom, six-bath abode in the Forest Hills neighborhood of Durham.

By all reports, Michael and Kathleen enjoyed a close, happy marriage and were sought-after guests on the local social scene. The *New York Times* would later describe Michael as having a "theatrical personality." Kathleen was a live wire, too. The couple threw dinner parties for dozens of friends at their spread, which included a swimming pool with decorative fountains.

But Michael hit a rough patch when he decided to run for mayor of Durham. It came out that a leg injury he said happened during battle actually came from a car accident. He lost the election.

Still, there was no serious drama until December 9, 2001, when Michael Peterson made a desperate-sounding 911 call to report his wife had fallen down the stairs but was still breathing.

Kathleen was dead by the time first responders got there.

Michael said he and Kathleen were relaxing by their pool, and she went inside to work on the computer. He stayed outside to smoke for 45 minutes or so and found her at the bottom of the stairs when he came back in.

She had been drinking and was wearing floppy shoes, so she probably tripped, Michael told police.

But there was one circumstance that Michael Peterson couldn't explain away.

The accident scene was a bloodbath—inconsistent with a tumble down the stairs. Homicide detectives were called to the Peterson residence.

They noted that Michael was wearing shorts and a T-shirt. Investigators later brought in a forensic meteorologist who determined it was 51 to 55 degrees outside that night, a little too cold for beach clothes, which made investigators question whether he was really at the pool when Kathleen fell.

That part of the prosecution's case doesn't seem impressive. Everyone knows at least one wacky guy who wears shorts in cold weather. (And those investigators must have had money to burn—they could have just looked online to find out the temperature that evening.)

But other evidence pointed convincingly to Michael's guilt. Paramedics said that Kathleen's blood had congealed, suggesting she died hours before he called 911.

Todd Peterson, 25, was at the house when the police came but refused to talk to them, according to *Forensic Files*.

And it looked as though someone had tried to clean up blood from the wall near the stairs.

The police found blood splatter between the legs of Michael's shorts and his bloody footprint on Kathleen's clothes, which suggested he was standing over her and beating her.

Although testing would later confirm that Kathleen had some alcohol in her system, it was nowhere near the stagger-and-face-plant level.

And one more little thing: Investigators found thousands of gay male porn images and hookup conversations on Michael's computer.

In one of his messages, Michael wrote that he was happily married to a "dynamite" wife but that he was "very" bisexual. Other online correspondence allegedly proved he was trying to hook up with men on the side, including a chipper prostitute called Brad.

Prosecutors would later contend that Kathleen stumbled upon the trove of photos and messages while using Michael's computer—she had left her own machine at work that day. She confronted Michael about cheating on her, there was an argument, and he beat her to death with a fireplace implement, they alleged. He made a futile attempt to get rid of blood evidence and then called 911, the prosecution contended.

According to *Power, Privilege, and Justice*, which produced a 2004 episode about the case, titled "Murder He Wrote," Peterson went upstairs to work on the computer while police were still working on the murder scene. Perhaps he was trying to delete some files.

In addition to the salacious activity, investigators discovered evidence of financial woe in the family. Michael hadn't generated any income in two years, and Kathleen was the mainstay.

The couple had three daughters in college and credit card debt of $142,000. The value of Kathleen's Nortel stock had dropped from more than $2 million at its peak to $50,000.

But Kathleen had life insurance worth $1.2 million to $1.8 million, with Michael as the beneficiary.

Soon enough, yet another bombshell came up. Investigators found out how Liz Ratliff, Margaret and Martha's mother, died.

On November 25, 1985, when Michael was living in Germany and married to his first wife, Ratliff turned up dead at the bottom of a staircase—just as Kathleen Peterson did 16 years later.

Previously, Michael had told people Liz Ratliff died from a brain hemorrhage, never mentioning a fall on the stairs, according to an interview with Kathleen Peterson's sister, Candace Zamperini, on *Power, Privilege, and Justice*.

The authorities exhumed Liz Ratliff's body in 2003 and discovered multiple scalp lacerations, similar to those found on Kathleen Peterson.

Ultimately, no charges involving Ratliff were brought, but North Carolina used the information about her death to strengthen the

Kathleen Peterson case, which lacked a murder weapon. Police believed it was a fireplace blow poke that someone took outside to hide, leaving bloodstains on the door.

Nonetheless, all five of Michael's children believed in his innocence at first.

Caitlin Atwater, Kathleen's daughter from her first marriage, later switched sides.

Friends of Liz Ratliff, who lived on the same German military base as Michael and his first wife, testified about the bloodiness of the scene of her demise. A medical examiner testified that Ratliff's cause of death was homicide via blunt force trauma.

And as if the trial needed more sordidness, Brad the hooker was called to the stand, where he congenially answered the prosecutor's questions about his services. They ranged from simple companionship to "just about anything under the sun" sexually, according to the pert and perky Brad.

The defense, led by David Rudolf—the same lawyer who represented NFL player Rae Carruth in his murder trial—had some impressive courtroom drama to offer, too. A live in-court splatter demonstration was presented to refute some of the blood evidence against Michael.

Team Michael also displayed a fireplace blow poke they said they found in the house. It had cobwebs on it but no blood, which appeared to snuff out the prosecution's theory that the implement acted as the murder weapon.

Michael claimed that Kathleen had been suffering from blackouts due to stress. Nortel had forced her to lay off some well-liked employees, according to an Associated Press (AP) account. Kathleen worried that she would lose her own $145,000-a-year job amid the downsizing, the AP reported.

Nonetheless, in the end, there was just too much evidence against Michael Peterson. His 2003 trial ended in a first-degree murder conviction and a sentence of life without parole.

Off he went to North Carolina's correctional facility in Nash.

Corrections officers at the prison didn't always find him as charming as his old dinner party friends did, and he earned some time in solitary for mouthing off, according to the Raleigh *News & Observer*.

A 2009 motion for a new trial based on the owl attack theory (details on that in a minute) was unsuccessful.

Then, after serving eight years in prison, Michael got a huge break.

He won the right to a new trial after authorities discovered that "expert" prosecution witness Saami Shaibani had misrepresented his own professional credentials.

And the happy hustler was off the table too—the seizure of Peterson's computer messages was ruled unlawful, so Brad couldn't testify again. Plus the death of Liz Ratliff in Germany was deemed inadmissible.

North Carolina released Michael Peterson on bond in 2011.

In 2017, the then-73-year-old avoided a second trial by taking an Alford plea to voluntary manslaughter in return for six years of house arrest. (An Alford plea is an arrangement whereby a defendant doesn't admit to the crime but acknowledges that there's enough evidence against him to likely convince a court that he did commit it.)

But there was no 9,429-square-foot palatial home with a redwood-paneled author's study for Michael to return to. The family had sold the Cedar Street showplace, reportedly the largest house in Durham. Michael moved into a two-bedroom condo, according to *Cosmopolitan*.

So what about the owl? The *Cosmopolitan* story includes information from ornithology experts who believe a barred owl could have tangled its claws in Kathleen's hair and made the gashes in her head that prosecutors alleged came from a metal implement. Kathleen might have fallen down the stairs while struggling to extricate herself from the bird of prey's talons, they opined.

Nonetheless, Michael Peterson's lawyers never brought up the owl theory in the courtroom—it was too bizarre and potentially fodder for, well, hoots of laughter.

Instead, Michael laid the blame for his murder conviction on humans. The police were out to get him because he criticized them in columns he wrote for the *Herald-Sun* before Kathleen's death, he told *Dateline*.

So what's happened to Michael Peterson since the 2018 Netflix series turned his story into an international entertainment sensation?

Michael told the *News & Observer* that well-to-do friends from his and Kathleen's napkin-ring-and-place-card days had deserted him. He did find himself a post-lockup girlfriend, however, in one of the editors of *The Staircase* docuseries. The couple lived together for a time after his release, he said.

Also in 2019, Michael Peterson made a two-part appearance on *Dr. Phil*. Although skeptical, the TV psychologist gave Michael a chance to defend himself.

Michael told Dr. Phil McGraw that medical reports confirmed Liz Ratliff died of a stroke.

He also explained that after Kathleen's death, he engaged legal help immediately—a move that raised suspicion at the time—only because his son insisted upon it, calling in Michael's lawyer brother, Bill Peterson.

A video accompanying the in-depth *News & Observer* piece gave Michael an opportunity to talk about his everyday post-prison life. He mentioned receiving a chilly reception from the primarily white upper-middle-class shoppers at Whole Foods. But at Target, a less afflu-ent, more diverse crowd welcomes him because they know firsthand how unfair the law can be, he said.

Meanwhile, Michael kept busy plying his trade as a writer. In 2020, he self-published two autobiographical books, *Beyond the Staircase* and *Behind the Staircase*. The latter book "shares the devastating events of Kathleen's death" and documents the "many grueling years that he spent with murderers, rapists, gangbangers, and pedophiles," according to a jacket synopsis. Any money Michael receives for the literary effort will have to go toward a $25 million award Caitlin Atwater won against him, he said.

And because this story isn't over until it's over, HBO Max came knocking.

The upscale streaming platform is presenting its own version of the drama called *The Staircase* and starring Colin Firth, Toni Collette, Sophie Turner (yes, Sansa Stark herself), and Patrick Schwarzenegger (that's right, President John F. Kennedy's grandnephew).

Regardless of the way media and entertainment outlets tell their father's tale, you can bet that Margaret, Martha, Todd, and Clayton will always believe the justice system failed their father. Although I tend to agree with those who think that Michael Peterson is responsible for Kathleen Peterson's and Liz Ratliff's deaths, it's still sweet to see the loyalty of his children and their willingness to accept him as he is.

CHAPTER 26

Michael Prozumenshikov

A Success Story Dies

**AN IMMIGRANT BECOMES A MILLIONAIRE BUT BETRAYS HIS OWN
PEOPLE**
Forensic Files *episode "Going for Broke"*
For a while, Michael Prozumenshikov seemed to be doing everything
right.

In hopes of a more prosperous life, he came to the United States
from Soviet-era Russia, where he'd grown up in an apartment crammed
with 30 other people.

He got a job as a janitor for $63 a week after arriving in Minneapolis,
studied finance, and earned a stockbroker's license.

Amid the 1980s Wall Street bubble, Prozumenshikov grew into
a tiger of a salesman. He nabbed a $240,000 signing bonus when
Prudential-Bache Securities recruited him as an investment adviser.

Within seven years of coming to America, he was driving a Mercedes, living in a newly constructed 20-room house, and making $1
million a year.

But his American dream turned into a cautionary tale.

Prozumenshikov's story, however, differs a bit from the usual because
he ended up as the homicide victim rather than the perpetrator.

I did some research into Prozumenshikov's background and how he
botched the financial fiefdom he created.

So let's get going on the recap of "Going for Broke," along with
extra information culled from online research, the 1994 book titled *The
Pru-Bache Murder: The Fast Life and Grisly Death of a Millionaire Stockbroker* by Jeffrey Taylor, and an interview with defense lawyer Joe Friedberg.

At 10:30 p.m. on January 28, 1991, Michael Prozumenshikov called his wife, Ellen, to let her know he was on his way home.

He never arrived.

Police found his Mercedes, with his checkbook, credit cards, and some cash inside, in a parking lot in Wayzata, Minnesota.

Soon after, a headless torso and two legs from a Caucasian male turned up under some abandoned Christmas trees. The severed tip of a left pinky finger found at the scene and scars on other body parts helped police identify the victim as Michael Prozumenshikov, age 37.

So who would want to harm this respectable family man?

Well, lots of people, it turned out.

Although he labored long hours and aimed high, Prozumenshikov also liked to take short cuts. It was a pattern that started when he still lived in the Soviet Union.

After excelling in hammer-throwing as a boy in Leningrad, Prozumenshikov used his athletic connections to get into dental school there, according to Taylor's book.

He was a poor-performing student but still managed to network his way into a job as a dentist in a clinic in Russia, according to Taylor.

But the United States had more strenuous requirements, and Prozumenshikov failed his dental exams in his new home.

Fortunately, he landed in a more lucrative field thanks to a friend who encouraged him to try a career in finance. He learned quickly and pursued clients—many of them fellow Russian Jewish immigrants—aggressively.

But Prozumenshikov was in too much of a hurry. Greed overtook him, and he made impossible claims to prospective clients, engaged in unauthorized trading, and falsified information.

Like most good con men, he had a knack for putting on an optimistic front even as things headed south. He persuaded clients to stay with him despite their losses, according to Taylor.

Although the police had no specific murder suspects at first, they found that a lot of people didn't feel all that bad to hear about Prozumenshikov's demise, according to Rocky Fontana, a Hennepin County Sheriff's detective who appeared on *Forensic Files*.

First off, Prozumenshikov had begun to separate himself, literally and figuratively, from the Russian Jewish émigré community who had helped make him successful.

He, Ellen, and their sons, ages 11 and 13, had moved to Wayzata, a lakeside town with a yacht club and median house price of $600,000.

And he liked to flaunt his Rolex watches and Montblanc pens. On his desk, he kept framed photos of cars and houses he aspired to purchase, according to Taylor's book.

While his family was enjoying the high life, Prozumenshikov was busy erasing the personal fortunes of the people who trusted him to help them attain better lives for their own kids.

A former client who appeared on *Forensic Files* said that Prozumenshikov went rogue with $20,000 of her money.

He had also used clients' money to make disastrous investments in Texas Air, which promptly lost 75 percent of its value (and no longer exists), according to *Forensic Files*.

Even as his clients' accounts were shrinking, Prozumenshikov would make as many as 100 trades on a single account in a year so he could pocket the commissions.

He wiped out the $70,000 life savings of a World War II veteran named Clem Seifert, who would later enthusiastically volunteer to testify in the killer's defense.

Prozumenshikov had also persuaded clients to invest in developing a Reno, Nevada, resort that was an utter scam. The project never happened.

Clearly, Prozumenshikov's death was somehow related to his work. His wife told police that, on the night he disappeared, he had called her to ask for his supervisor's number (this was back in the days when people kept address books at home, rather than cell phones in their pockets).

Next, he called his boss from a pay phone to ask for $200,000 in cash for a client. The supervisor refused.

Then, Michael Prozumenshikov disappeared.

Police were able to connect a brown 1986 Mazda 626 seen parked near Prozumenshikov's black Mercedes on the night of the murder to a handsome 39-year-old dam inspector named Zachary Persitz.

The Prozumenshikov and Persitz families were close friends. Their sons had sleepovers together. Both families sent their kids to private school.

Persitz, also a member of the local Russian Jewish community, entrusted Prozumenshikov to invest $150,000 for him. A lot was riding on that investment.

Although the Minnesota Department of Natural Resources surely paid Persitz a decent salary, his wife, Julia, a concert violinist, had been needling him about why he couldn't be as successful as his buddy Michael Prozumenshikov, Fontana told *Forensic Files*.

But Persitz wouldn't be buying his wife a McMansion or an E-Class Cabriolet anytime soon. A combination of Prozumenshikov's misman-agement and the 1987 stock crash diminished Persitz's wealth by any-where from $37,000 to $120,000 (sources vary on the amount of the loss).

Joe Friedberg, who later represented Persitz in court, actually dis-putes the claim that Persitz's wife drove him to take foolish risks. "Julia was a lovely lady and unaware that her husband was investing so aggres-sively," he told me. "I think Zachary was the one trying to keep up with the Prozumenshikovs. It took everything Julia and Zachary made to support their family. They really didn't have the money to send their kids to private school."

Persitz had more of a motive to kill Prozumenshikov than his other disappointed clients. "They could afford to lose money," Friedberg says. "Persitz couldn't."

Around the time of the homicide, a car wash employee wrote down the license plate number of Persitz's Mazda after noticing the driver trying to wash blood from inside its trunk. Persitz told the workers he hit a deer.

Police discovered that some paint found on Persitz's bumper looked similar to that from an orange gate near the crime scene. And bumper fragments found there matched those missing from Persitz's Mazda, whose interior revealed blood splatter.

Authorities also learned that an ax Persitz kept in his locker at work had gone missing, according to an Associated Press account from 1991.

And the Persitz family had a Bernese mountain dog whose hair matched a strand found at the murder scene (not that the family pet was in on the homicide—shed fur carries and transfers like crazy). Then-county prosecutor Kevin Johnson remarked that it was the "first time a search warrant has been executed on a dog in Hennepin County."

On February 4, 1991, authorities arrested Persitz and set his bail at $750,000.

There was circumstantial evidence against him in addition to the forensics.

The day before the homicide, Persitz had gone out shooting at Bill's Gun Range in Robbinsdale, Minnesota, with family friend Rudolph Lekhter, who reportedly sold him a gun. When Lekhter asked him whether he wanted to use a bull's-eye target or the silhouette of a person, Persitz opted for a silhouette, according to Friedberg.

Prosecutors think that Persitz later set up a meeting with Prozumenshikov, then threatened the six-foot-tall, 200-pound-plus stockbroker with a gun and demanded $200,000 to cover his losses plus interest. Friedberg believes that Prozumenshikov had persuaded him to invest his money by promising that he would refund the principal if he failed to make a profit from it.

When Prozumenshikov couldn't produce the cash, Persitz shot him (possibly with one of Lekhter's guns, although he wasn't implicated), threw him in the trunk, and then headed to a compost site 60 miles away the next day. He crashed through a gate there and dismembered the body.

Once charged, instead of going the usual *Forensic Files* killer route by claiming the victim attacked him first, Persitz declared himself not guilty by way of insanity.

"He'd never done anything against the law in his life," Friedberg says. "He was a nice, quiet, gentle man in the throes of depression and desperation."

Judge Robert Schiefelbein delayed the trial so the defense team could obtain Persitz's 1970s records from a psychiatric hospital in Russia.

Mental health professionals for both the defense and prosecution ultimately agreed Persitz suffered from OCD and severe depression. In fact, the judge agreed to another delay so Persitz could undergo electro-convulsive therapy.

Persitz said that, as a child, he had witnessed violence between his parents and had tried to kill himself at age 11.

His claim of suicidal tendencies was credible. While awaiting trial in 1992, Persitz and fellow inmate Russell Lund made a pact to suffocate themselves with plastic bags. Lund succeeded, but deputies reached Persitz in time to save him.

The defense argued that the crime itself was crazy enough to prove insanity. Persitz admitted to shooting Prozumenshikov once on the frozen Lake Minnetonka and again in the Mazda, then hacking up the corpse the next day.

"Clearly, chopping a body up in the early morning hours when it's 20 below is nonsensical," said Paul Engh, a lawyer who was part of the defense team.

Still, prosecutor Kevin Johnson made the state's case that Persitz had been plotting the murder for months and was sane enough to know that killing Prozumenshikov was wrong.

The jury convicted him of the murder on June 23, 1993. In a separate hearing, the panel rejected the insanity plea. He received a life sentence with the possibility of parole after 27.5 years.

Widow Ellen Prozumenshikov blamed the murder on Persitz's "envy" and "greed," the *Tribune Star* reported. "Michael was living his American dream," she said. "His dream was suddenly ended by someone who couldn't bear to see it realized, who couldn't accept Michael's life in comparison to his own."

With the trial over, Ellen, a dental hygienist, said she hoped to begin the "healing process for our family." A 2013 obituary for her mother noted that Ellen had a new man in her life.

As for Persitz, his parole eligibility would have come around in 2021, but he couldn't wait.

He hanged himself in Stillwater in 2010.

Persitz had admitted that he threw Michael Prozumenshikov's head and hands—the instruments of his deceits—into the St. Croix River, but they were never found.

In another tragedy related to a key figure in the case, Kevin Johnson, who later rose to administrative law judge, saw his career cut short after a 1997 traffic accident that left him with a severe brain injury. In 2008, he died of a heart attack at age 57.

CHAPTER 27

Noreen Boyle

A Death Encrypted

JOHN "JACK" BOYLE CREATES A BISTATE HORROR SHOW
Forensic Files *episode "Foundation of Lies"*

Noreen Boyle's murder sounds more like a page from an Edgar Allan Poe short story than an episode of *Forensic Files*.

After killing Noreen, her husband decided on a macabre way to conceal her body. Dr. John "Jack" Boyle created a grave beneath the concrete basement floor of their new house in Erie, Pennsylvania.

The story surrounding the homicide, however, is pretty typical as true-crime tales go: A spouse finds a new love and murders the old one to avoid a battle over the kids and money.

But Jack Boyle, a University of Pennsylvania graduate who was a tremendous success as a physician, failed miserably as a hit man and landed himself in a crypt of his own—a cell at the Marion Correctional Institution in Ohio.

The murder took place on New Year's Eve in the hours before midnight struck 1990, but people from the Boyles' old hometown of Mansfield, Ohio, have never stopped talking about the case. The Investigation Discovery Network produced the documentary *A Murder in Mansfield* about it in 2018.

Jack Boyle is still alive. So where is he now, and what about the children he and Noreen shared? Here's a recap of the episode titled "Foundation of Lies"—along with extra information drawn from internet research and interviews with the Boyles' now-adult son, Collier Landry, as well as local newspaper reporter John Futty.

Noreen Schmid Boyle, an elegant mother of two, managed to cope with her husband's various affairs throughout the years of their marriage.

Maybe she cared more about maintaining a stable home for Collier, 11, and his baby sister, 3, than she did about her own hurt feelings.

Or perhaps she soothed her pride with shopping trips and her Range Rover and BMW. Her husband's medical practice, which specialized in Medicaid and Medicare cases, was a money machine. One in every 13 residents of Richland County, Ohio, was a patient there, according to *Forensic Files*.

Surely, Noreen enjoyed Jack Boyle's status in the community.

Not that she didn't make an impression on her own. "Some people just plod along—my mother would glide into a room," Collier, who legally changed his last name to Landry, told me in an interview. "When she would walk in a room, you would know it. But not just because she dressed well. It was her energy and personality."

According to the *Akron Beacon Journal*, Noreen was something of a Holly Golightly. She came from a working-class background, the daughter of a secretary and a machinist.

But she liked people to think otherwise.

She told friends that she grew up in a mansion and had an MBA from the Wharton School.

"My mother would fib a little about her background because she was embarrassed," Collier says. "At the end of the day, she wasn't trying to perpetrate a fraud."

According to Collier, she really had received a better-than-average education. Her parents sent her to a private girls' academy, and she graduated from the University of Pennsylvania School of Dentistry as a dental hygienist (and worked to support Jack Boyle when he went to medical school).

At some point before New Year's Eve 1989 rolled around, Noreen made the educated decision that being the wife of Dr. Jack Boyle wasn't worth the pain. In addition to having to contend with her husband's violent temper, she found out that Collier had witnessed him kissing another woman.

Citing mental cruelty and neglect, Noreen, 44, filed for divorce. But Jack, then 46, persuaded her to make a fresh start with him in Erie, Pennsylvania. "He was charming, as most narcissists are," Collier says.

Jack bought a house in Erie and arranged for the sellers to vacate it right away.

All along, however, Jack planned to make Noreen disappear, then marry his girlfriend, Sherri Campbell, and live with her and the kids in Erie, where he intended to establish a new medical practice.

On December 31, 1989, Jack struck Noreen and suffocated her to death after an argument at their residence in Mansfield, Ohio.

Over the course of the next few days, the doctor began driving the three hours from Mansfield to Erie, saying he was preparing the new house for their big move. He didn't mention that he was renovating the basement into a cemetery.

He used a rented jackhammer to make a hole in the concrete floor. Then he secreted Noreen's body inside, filled in the opening, repainted the floor, and covered it with indoor-outdoor carpeting.

In what must have been a strenuous job, Jack gathered up the pieces of broken concrete and dumped them on property owned by Mark Davis, a business associate who was also Sherri Campbell's uncle.

Now Jack was free to move in with Sherri Campbell, who was 26 years old and very pregnant with his child. He told Collier that Noreen had gone on a little jaunt out of town. Jack would later contend that he saw his wife leave the house and that she was picked up by someone in a car.

Why did Jack Boyle think that his wife's disappearance would quickly fall off the radar screen?

Maybe he figured the new friends and associates he planned to acquire in Erie would know nothing of Noreen and have no reason to inquire about her.

Jane Imbody, a local Mansfield news anchor who appeared on the *Forensic Files* episode, said that the doctor considered his deceptions good enough for not only the public and his family but also for himself. "He was such a good liar he believed those own lies," Imbody said.

But 11-year-old Collier wasn't having any of it. He felt sure his mother would have never taken off without him and his sister.

"When it was a missing persons case, I was the one who told police she's dead," Collier told me during a recent phone interview.

Collier told investigators everything: Jack's affair with Sherri Campbell, the scream and thump he heard while his parents were arguing on New Year's Eve, the trips to Erie, and how his father complained of being sore when he returned. His three-year-old sister reportedly told police she saw her father strike Noreen.

The authorities found the patch of newly paved basement flooring in the Erie house and discovered Noreen's decomposing body beneath it. She had a plastic bag over her head.

The real estate agent who handled the $300,000 house deal told investigators about the woman who accompanied Jack to his office. She signed her name "N. Sherri Boyle," in an apparent effort to impersonate Noreen. (When later asked about it in court, Sherri Campbell pleaded the Fifth Amendment.)

The prosecution ordered forensic tests to make sure the discarded concrete fragments dumped in Mark Davis's yard came from the concrete in the Erie basement.

They matched, but the real smoking gun was the rental receipt for the jackhammer.

Jack said he used it to break up ice on his property. I grew up near Erie, with the lake effect and six-month-long winters, but never saw a homeowner use a jackhammer to get rid of ice. People either left the ice alone, put rock salt on it, or ruined their shovel blades hacking away at it.

By the end of the month, authorities had arrested Jack and were holding him on a $5 million bond. The trial kicked off just a few months after the murder in 1990, and the doctor testified in his own defense for nine hours.

It came out during questioning that Jack had arranged for Sherri Campbell to cook a pork roast and bring it over on New Year's Day—evidence he knew there was no chance Noreen would show up at home, according to Richland County prosecutor James Mayer Jr.

Stories published in the *Mansfield News Journal* on June 26, 1990, gave extensive coverage of Jack Boyle's various evasions under oath.

In addition to the lies he told to cover up the murder plot—for example, he denied purchasing concrete mix at a local Busy Beaver store—there were self-aggrandizing claims regarding his military service.

He said that he was a former Navy man (true), that he flew an F-14 during the Vietnam War and logged more flight time than any other pilot (false), that a sniper shot him during the Iranian hostage crisis (false), and that he was a flight surgeon (false).

The trial's real sensation was Collier, age 12 by then, who impressed the courtroom with his articulate testimony about his parents.

"The streets would be pretty much deserted because everyone was watching that testimony," recalls local journalist John Futty, who covered the case for the *Mansfield News Journal*.

On the stand, Collier revealed that he and Noreen feared Jack's nastiness and temper.

Despite his outward calm while testifying, Collier worried the whole time about what would happen in the event of an acquittal. "He would probably kill me," Collier says. "That's the reality when you're dealing with someone who's a sociopath."

Fortunately, the jury sided with the prosecution. Jack received a sentence of life without the possibility of parole for 20 years for aggravated murder and a consecutive 18 months for abuse of a corpse.

As if losing his mother once didn't hurt enough, Collier had to go through it again in 1994, when Jack Boyle claimed the body found underneath his basement didn't belong to Noreen and that she might still be alive.

Some of the autopsy details, including her eye color, were wrong, and the doctor's brother claimed he'd received a phone call from Noreen after the night she officially disappeared.

Around the same time that Jack was pushing for a new trial, his aforementioned brother, Charles "C. J." Boyle, began a smear campaign against Noreen.

A lengthy account appeared in the *Akron Beacon Journal* on July 25, 1994.

Charles Boyle claimed that Noreen's adoption of her daughter from Taiwan was illegitimate.

He also alleged the adoption was "the 'first operation test' of a baby-selling organization for which Noreen Boyle became an agent" and that she and an associate had nabbed "several hundred thousand dollars in clear profits" from the illegal enterprise.

What's more, Noreen was an international gold jewelry smuggler, according to Charles. And she had planned to burn down the new house in Erie out of jealousy—and she had multiple affairs of her own with men, including a contractor and a police officer, Charles claimed.

He also suggested that Noreen staged her own death and then disappeared of her own volition.

Noreen's friends never believed any of the disparaging words about her, according to John Futty.

And while Noreen wasn't around to defend herself from the character assassination, the authorities were able to refute the story that she had fled on her own accord.

They exhumed Noreen's body, and a mitochondrial DNA test reconfirmed its identity.

The misinformation on the coroner's report was simple human error.

On June 2, 1994, Jack Boyle lost his appeal of the case, when a panel of circuit court judges ruled that evidence of his guilt was "overwhelming."

In 2000, the *Mansfield News Journal* reported that Boyle was making noise about his attorneys not representing him competently. He said they failed to advise him against testifying in his own defense. That effort went nowhere, and he remained behind razor wire. In 2010, he failed in his first bid to win parole.

He has reportedly changed his story about Noreen's death. He says that she tried to attack him with a knife, so he pushed her and then he blacked out. When he woke up, he claimed, Noreen was dead.

Okay, whatever you say, Jack.

More about him in a minute. What about the kids?

The little girl was adopted by the family of a local school principal. No other information came up about her in internet searches, and she probably prefers to remain uncontacted by the media.

Collier found himself alone after the murder.

As a *Daily Mail* story quoted filmmaker Barbara Kopple, who directed a 2018 documentary about this case, "He . . . had a lot of rejection from both sides of his family. His father's family probably felt that he betrayed them, and they didn't want to adopt him or have him live with them, and the mother's family probably had some trouble embracing a murderer's son."

Fortunately, a nice local couple named Susan and George Zeigler eventually adopted Collier. He credits them with helping him recover from the traumatic events of his childhood.

Today, he works as a cinematographer out of Los Angeles and hosts the *Moving Past Murder* podcast.

He conceived of the idea for the documentary *A Murder in Mansfield*, which was produced by Cabin Creek Films.

It shows Collier's homecoming to Mansfield and his reunion with his mother's best friend as well as with lead detective Dave Messmore, who also appeared on the *Forensic Files* episode. (Messmore and his wife actually wanted to adopt Collier, but legal problems prevented it, Collier told me.)

The creative effort, which had "explosive ticket sales" for its showing in Mansfield, included a jailhouse visit Collier paid to Jack. Somehow, Collier has managed not to hate him.

"Is it going to bring back my mother? No. It's wasted energy. My mother wouldn't want that," Collier explained. "He's my father. He just happens to be a horrible father."

At the same time, he makes it clear he doesn't believe Jack's version of Noreen's death and that he has no intention of helping him get out of prison.

The documentary, later shown on the Investigation Discovery Network, didn't win Jack any fans among members of the parole board either. They denied his 2020 request for freedom because of the "extreme brutality" of the crime and the "undue risk to public safety" he poses.

The Ohio Department of Rehabilitation and Correction website lists Boyle's next parole eligibility date as October 1, 2025.

"I don't know to this day that he's taken responsibility and shown real remorse," says John Futty. "Now he's saying she died in a fight she started. That doesn't necessarily play well with a parole board."

CHAPTER 28

Patricia Rorrer

Double Murderer or Victim of Injustice?

CONTROVERSY OVER JOANN KATRINAK'S DEATH CONTINUES
Forensic Files *episode "A Woman Scorned"*

Patricia Rorrer has been portrayed as a bully, petty thief, neglectful horse owner, and heartless killer—or a sweet, caring friend railroaded by state and federal authorities desperate to solve a harrowing double-murder case.

After Joann Katrinak, the wife of Patricia's former flame, turned up dead along with her infant son, investigators suspected Patricia.

Her accusers theorized that she resented Joann's domestic bliss with the tall, athletic Andrew Katrinak. They allege that the North Carolina resident stealthily drove 500 miles to Pennsylvania and killed out of a sense of deadly indignation. Strands of the accused's dyed-blond hair at two crime scenes proved it.

Or did they? Aside from the hair, there was almost zero forensic evidence pointing to Patricia as the killer. The state made a case fueled by circumstantial evidence and public outrage over the deaths of a modern-day Madonna and child.

More than 20 years after her conviction, Patricia Rorrer still has advocates working to exonerate her.

For this chapter, I looked into Patricia's innocence advocates' reasoning and searched for information about Patricia's whereabouts today. And because some of her advocates have suggested Andrew Katrinak had a motive for murder, I checked into whether he had a life insurance payout to gain upon Joann's demise.

I also communicated with Patricia via e-mail to get her input on some matters.

So let's get going on the recap of the *Forensic Files* episode "A Woman Scorned," along with extra information drawn from internet research:

Joann Marie O'Connor was born on October 11, 1968, the youngest of Sarah and David O'Connor's four children.

The Irish Italian girl had full, fluffy dark hair, olive skin, and a pretty face. She made an effort to look perfectly groomed "even when she took out the trash," according to her mother, who appeared on *Forensic Files*.

Joann was "fun, likable, beautiful, always happy," said her sister-in-law Cindy Wiard.

After a very early failed marriage, the 24-year-old Joann scored a new husband in Andrew Katrinak, 38, whom she met at a club. He had worked as a semi-pro boxer in Las Vegas in his youth and later settled into his own construction business.

The couple moved into Andrew's sturdy brick house at 740 Front Street in Catasauqua, Pennsylvania. They had a son, Alex Martin, in August 1994.

On December 12, 1994, Joann answered a phone call from a woman she'd never met—Patricia Rorrer, her husband's onetime girlfriend.

Patricia asked to speak with Andrew, who was home during the call; Joann refused.

Three days later, Joann had plans to pick up her mother-in-law, Veronica Katrinak, to go Christmas shopping.

Joann never showed up.

At 10:30 p.m., Andrew reported his wife missing. And, yikes, he discovered that someone had cut one of the house's phone lines and pried the hinge on the basement door.

Family members found Joann's tan Toyota sitting vacant in the parking lot of McCarty's, a nearby bar. Inside the locked 1992 vehicle, police discovered some strands of blond hair stained with dried blood. DNA testing revealed the blood came from either Joann or her son.

Forensic Files didn't mention it, but the hairs were actually brown at the top and the rest dyed blond, according to the episode titled "A Fatal Attraction" from the TV series *Autopsy Six: Secrets of the Dead*.

At first, local police suspected Andrew.

Detective Barry Grube found it odd that Andrew fixed the severed phone line before police examined it—in essence tampering with evidence. And Andrew's explanation of how the intruder got in through the basement door seemed contrived, according to Grube, who gave an interview to *Wrong Man*, a 2020 true-crime docuseries from the Starz network, which produced two episodes called "The Hang Up" about the Rorrer case. (The series was produced by Joe Berlinger, who made the *Paradise Lost* documentaries, which garnered actor Johnny Depp's attention and ultimately helped free the West Memphis Three.)

But investigators conceded they had no solid evidence against Andrew. Plus, he had only a "minimal" life insurance policy on Joann and he passed polygraphs, according to *The FBI Files: Family Secrets*. His father confirmed his alibi that at the time of Joann's disappearance, they were doing construction work together, putting an addition on the house of friends Tom and Kathy Holschwander.

Andrew described his existence with Joann and Alex as a "little Camelot."

"I can't lose them," he told the media. "That's my life."

The state police dropped him as a suspect.

Joann's first husband, New Jersey construction worker Michael Jack, who had reportedly abused her during their marriage, also had a solid alibi.

The police considered the possibility that Joann ran away, a theory disputed by her family. "She's just extremely happy with Andy," her brother, Michael O'Connor, told the media. "She's extremely, extremely happy with the baby. In a million years, she wouldn't do anything to harm that."

No activity on her bank account or credit cards took place after the day she went missing, so investigators dismissed the theory that she took her child and bolted.

Meanwhile, the case of the missing mother and baby turned into colossal news throughout the United States and internationally. State police and the Philadelphia division of the FBI appealed to the public for leads. Authorities set up a phone line for tips and released a poster of Joann and Alex, noting that the baby had "almond-shaped blue eyes," weighed 18 pounds, and was circumcised.

Federal and Pennsylvania agents searched the neighborhood for clues, removing the tarp and examining the swimming pool belonging to one of the Katrinaks' neighbors and also using dogs to follow any scents, the Associated Press (AP) reported on December 30, 1994.

A neighbor told the AP that she had begun copying down license plate numbers of unfamiliar cars. One area woman vowed to keep her Christmas tree standing until Joann and Alex turned up.

Still, no good leads materialized. "It's definitely getting rougher every day," Andrew told the *Morning Call*. "I don't even know it's Christmas." Frustrated by the wait, Andrew traveled to Louisiana after a psychic predicted he would find Joann and Alex there, according to an April 12, 1995, *Morning Call* story. (The psychic was wrong.)

Four months after Joann's disappearance, farmer Paul Kovalchik reported seeing what at first looked like a pile of clothes on his land in Heidelberg Township, about 15 miles from the Katrinaks' house.

On closer inspection, he saw it was the body of a woman. An infant was lying face down on her stomach. Both were deceased.

Police identified the pair as Joann and Alex Katrinak. Alex's favorite rattle, shaped like a phone, lay near the crime scene.

Someone had shot Joann in the face with a .22-caliber pistol, then beaten her about the head—hitting her 19 times in all—with a blunt object. Police couldn't determine whether the baby died of exposure or suffocation. On Alex's diaper bag, police found strands of the same type of hair from the car.

"I tried to prepare myself for this," Joann's sister, Peggy Courter, told the *Morning Call*, "but I just didn't expect so much violence."

In April 1995, the family buried Joann and Alex in a single bronze casket after a funeral mass at a Bethlehem church.

Andrew mentioned to police that his former live-in girlfriend Patricia Rorrer once managed a horse stable two miles from the bodies' location and would have been familiar with the riding trails close to the murder scene. (Media sources vary as to whether she actually worked at the stable or just rented a stall there for her own horse.)

Patricia "seemed like the girl next door but all of a sudden, something snapped," Katrinak remarked about their onetime relationship when *Wrong Man* investigators interviewed him.

Patricia Lynne Rorrer made for a good suspect. Then 31 years old, she had lived a rocky existence.

She was born on January 24, 1964, in eastern Pennsylvania and moved back and forth between there and Davidson County, North Carolina, according to a June 25, 1997, article in the *Morning Call*.

At 17, Patricia dropped out of high school and married landscaper Gary Gabard.

Later, they both worked 12-hour graveyard shifts at a textile factory. Her mother, Patricia Chambers, provided day care for their baby son, Charles.

Patricia Rorrer "was a cold woman. She was always looking for a fight," Gary Gabard told the *Morning Call*, which noted that he was "a head shorter" than Patricia.

Once, when a gun-wielding farmer and his buddy caught Patricia and Gary riding motorcycles on his field, Patricia walked up and "got in their faces" and argued, Gary recalled to the *Morning Call*.

"She is a tough one," Sheriff Gerald Hege would later tell the *Morning Call* in a June 29, 1997, interview. "I don't think she was ever scared until we put the cuffs on her."

Patricia's professional life included short-lived gigs as a Century 21 real estate agent and an Oldsmobile salesperson. In North Carolina, she reportedly enjoyed some success as a horse trader, riding instructor, and rodeo competitor.

But her reputation wasn't exactly sleek and shiny. She got 12 months of probation for shoplifting at a Walmart in Lexington, North Carolina.

She was also accused of breaking into barns, stealing horses, and underfeeding the ones she owned, according to a June 25, 1997, *Morning Call* story. But none of those charges ever stuck.

Tragedy also touched Patricia's life. Charles Robert, the three-month-old son she had with Gary Gabard, died of sudden infant death syndrome; Patricia found him blue in his crib.

Patricia and her husband broke up after the baby's death.

After relocating to Pennsylvania, Patricia met the six-foot, two-inch Andrew in a restaurant. They moved into her house in Salisbury County, staying together for about two years. They broke up in 1993.

Patricia defaulted on her mortgage and then returned to North Carolina, where she eventually moved in with a boyfriend named Brian Ward. Together they had a baby girl, Nicole.

When police traveled to North Carolina to interview Patricia about the murders of Joann and Alex, she said that, on the day of the homicides, she had visited a feed store, a tanning salon, and a country music club.

Andrew told investigators that the unpleasant phone call between Joann and Patricia happened just three days before his wife's disappearance.

Patricia's phone bill showed no record of a call to Catasauqua that day, but police noticed she didn't make any calls at all from her house in North Carolina that day either—suggesting she could have been out of state and used a pay phone to dial up the Katrinaks.

As for the words exchanged on the call between the two big-haired women, Joann told Andrew that Patricia had used profanity; Patricia said it was the other way around. Both sides agree Joann hung up on Patricia.

Police slowly built a case against Patricia. Her alibi about going to the Cowboy's Nitelife club got fuzzy when investigators discovered she hadn't signed the guest book on that day. And dance instructor William Jarrett couldn't remember whether or not she attended his dance class at the club the night of Joann's disappearance. On a secret recording, Patricia asked Jarrett to vouch for her attendance or she might go to the electric chair.

"Why would somebody tell you, 'they're going to fry me,' if they didn't do it?" Jarrett later told *Wrong Man*.

As for the murder weapon, police didn't find a .22-caliber gun on Patricia's property, but an ex-boyfriend claimed that she owned one—and it would always jam after one shot.

They also found a photo of Patricia taken 11 days before the homicide. It showed her usually all-brown hair haphazardly highlighted blond. Forensic tests suggested the hair found in the Corolla and at the murder scene came from Patricia.

According to court papers from Patricia's 2017 appeal, "DNA on the cigarette butt found near the two bodies belonged to Appellant." (Prosecutor Michael McIntyre, however, told me in an interview that the cigarette butt was never actually tested.)

At 6 a.m. on June 24, 1997, police arrested Patricia at her modest house in Linwood, North Carolina, and took her back to Pennsylvania.

Lieutenant Christopher Coble and Sergeant Suzanne Pearson would later testify that Patricia cried and apologized to 18-month-old Nicole, telling the baby, "I'm sorry for doing this to you" and lamenting to the officers that she would never see little Nicole again after her arrest. Pearson didn't actually take part in the arrest but was present during it following the sheriff department's policy of having a female officer present at "an interdiction that involved the arrest of a female," according to court papers filed May 26, 2016 (*Commonwealth of Pennsylvania v. Patricia Lynne Rorrer*).

"If I had known I was going to get caught, I would have never brought you into this world," Suzanne Pearson would later testify that she heard Patricia say to Nicole when Patricia was arrested at her home. Pearson said she was taking notes during the arrest, according to the May 26, 2016, court papers.

The authorities charged Patricia with two counts of murder. After her arraignment, she had to walk past a crowd of dozens of locals screeching, "Hang her!" and "baby killer!" Patricia clung to a Polaroid picture showing her and her own little girl.

Prosecutors offered Patricia a plea deal that would take the death penalty off the table, but she declined. "How could I explain to my daughter years later that I took a plea for something I didn't do?" she said.

At the trial, prosecutor Michael McIntyre alleged that Patricia remained obsessed with Andrew Katrinak long after their breakup—despite testimony that she'd had "many boyfriends and live-in lovers" to occupy her bandwidth.

Ex-boyfriend Walter Blalock said that Patricia wanted him to be more like Andrew. (Another former boyfriend said she talked about Andrew frequently and liked to gaze at old photos of him, according to what Michael McIntyre said on *Autopsy Six*.)

The prosecution alleged that Patricia called the Katrinaks' house from a pay phone in Pennsylvania. Angry that Joann hung up on her, she stalked her for three days, then broke into her basement and cut the phone line, put a gun to Joann's head as she was placing Alex in the car, and forced her to drive to the rural area, the prosecution contended.

After one bullet didn't kill Joann, the gun locked up, so Patricia had to beat her to death, according to the prosecution. The five-foot, nine-inch Patricia was physically strong, no match for five-foot, four-inch Joann.

Testimony from Walter Blalock contradicted Patricia's claim that she never had a gun. He said she did own a firearm, with its serial numbers filed off.

And in a piece of salacious testimony, Patricia Rorrer's half sister, Sandra Ireland, said that, in May 1995, about six months after the murder, their mother, Patricia Chambers, stopped by the house and asked her to hold on to or hide a gun, or both. Ireland's husband buried it in the yard because he didn't feel comfortable with a firearm inside, she said.

During Patricia Rorrer's hours-long turn in the witness chair, Michael McIntyre grilled her relentlessly. According to a *Morning Call* account from March 5, 1998: "McIntyre leaned forward conspiratorially like someone trying to persuade another to tell a secret, lowered his voice and said: 'Here's what I want to know: After you killed Joann Katrinak, did you kill that baby or just leave it to die?'"

"Sir I would not kill somebody and I definitely wouldn't kill somebody I never met," Rorrer said.

The prosecution alleged that, after the murder, Patricia drove Joann's car to McCarty's parking lot and backed it into a parking space. Those who knew Joann pointed out that she didn't like to drive in reverse and would have never parked that way.

But defense lawyer Robert Pfeiffer said that plenty of evidence supported Patricia's innocence. For one thing, her mother never asked Sandra Ireland to "hide" the gun, and she retrieved it on the way home the next day. She worked as a bus driver and couldn't take it with her to school.

Plus, baby Nicole's father as well as a friend of his testified that they saw Patricia Rorrer at the line-dancing club the night of the homicide.

Pfeiffer and Burke claimed that police sergeant Suzanne Pearson fabricated quotes from Patricia—including Pearson's claim on the witness stand (as reported by the *Morning Call* on February, 18, 1998) that Patricia said, "I'm going to the electric chair" upon her arrest—because a conviction would boost Pearson's career.

And Patricia wasn't all edges. She was bubbly and likable, not disgruntled, according to friend Kathy Barber, who visited Patricia in jail.

Other loyal friends and associates attested to Patricia's kindness toward horses and devotion to her daughter, whom she took along as she worked in stables.

A newspaper account described Patricia as a soft-spoken, demure woman who had a sweet southern accent and wore feminine clothes in court.

It all gave jurors a lot to think about—but only for six hours. They returned with a guilty verdict and a sentence of two life terms.

Advocates for her innocence complain of hype surrounding the case. "Men who murder are conventional, women are sensational," posits the Worldwide Women's Criminal Justice Network. "The media love the femme fatale."

The organization purports that "if there were awards for distorted reporting, the *Morning Call* . . . would win high honors."

The Worldwide Women's Criminal Justice Network's website also points to a bombshell: In 2015, the Justice Department acknowledged that most of the team members from an FBI microscopic hair comparison unit gave prosecutors flawed data from 1980 to 2000 that could have unjustly contributed to a number of convictions—including Patricia Rorrer's.

Some lawyers call microscopic hair analysis junk science that today wouldn't qualify as evidence in a trial like Rorrer's.

Further, an early FBI report said the hairs found in the car had no roots, hence no DNA for conclusive testing.

But that's just some of the ammo on Team Patricia's battleship. She's attracted the help of writer Tammy Mal (full name Tammy Malinowski O'Reilly), author of *Convenient Suspect* (2017), a book about the case. And James Pfeiffer and Jim Burke have remained on her side.

They theorize that Andrew Katrinak framed Patricia and that the hostile phone call between Patricia and Joann actually took place not on December 12 as Andrew said but rather on December 7. Phone records confirmed Patricia placed the earlier call from North Carolina, not Pennsylvania.

Patricia's defenders also say Andrew Katrinak staged the scene at his house by prying the door and cutting the phone line. The phone wire was located at the opposite end of the basement, which was dark. How would an intruder find it?

And the fact that Patricia called Andrew even after he married someone else didn't mean she was still carrying a torch for him, according to one of her friends. "She just stayed in touch with everybody," Kathy Barber said in her interview on *NBC's Murder in Lehigh Valley: Keith Morrison Investigates* in 2017. "And she would just call out of the blue."

According to a quote from Patricia on the patriciarorrer.com website, "On December 7, 1994 I called Andy to let him know that me and my team had won the National Championship at a team penning competition in Oklahoma. It was a pretty big deal, and I was excited enough to call everyone I knew. Joann answered that night, told me that Andy was married and they had baby and not to call her house again. I honestly didn't think too much about it. And it certainly didn't make me mad enough to jump in my car, drive 500 miles one way and kill two people I'd never met—one an infant child."

The Free Patricia Rorrer page responds to comments from supporters ("How is this even possible that this woman is still in jail?!?!") and detractors ("This is another bs attempt to free a psycho").

Barry Grube, one of the few, if not only, police officers sympathetic to Patricia's cause, noted that Andrew didn't seem particularly frantic while authorities searched desperately for his wife and son. In TV clips, Andrew didn't come off as anguished.

Mal told Keith Morrison that Patricia's dance teacher originally confirmed her alibi that she was in class on the day of the murder, then changed his mind later. At the state's request, the instructor wore a wire during a phone conversation with Patricia. Although the prosecution used it as evidence that she was trying to create a false alibi, it actually sounded more like Patricia was simply trying to nail down the facts he had already asserted to her.

And even prosecutor Michael McIntyre, who wrote the book *Hair Trigger* about the case, acknowledged to Keith Morrison that it was a little odd that the police found blood on the hairs in Joann's car but nowhere else in the vehicle. If Patricia drove it back from the murder scene after she shot Joann and then beat her to death, luminol—which allows investigators to see the remains of bodily fluid—would have lit up the interior.

There's also the matter of a woman who suddenly remembered she saw Joann with another man at a Food Mart store five days after the disappearance. (Disclaimer: I'm not a big fan of eyewitnesses who come forward years after the fact, but it's possible.)

Another witness, Walter Traupman, who never testified, had told state troopers that, on the day of Joann's disappearance, he saw a couple who looked like Joann and Andrew arguing about the paternity of a baby. Traupman claimed that, when he reported the dispute, trooper Robert V. Egan III got mad and practically kicked him out of his office. The police report misspells his name ("Troutman") and doesn't include his address, suggesting authorities didn't want anyone to track him down, according to Patricia's side. (McIntyre said that Egan ignored Traupman because they thought he was a nut; he also said that the man he saw arguing with the woman in a car was Hispanic but wearing a fake mustache and a toupee. Traupman died in 2016.)

Wrong Man investigators Ira Todd and Joe Kennedy have some theories of their own. They noted houses near the murder scene would have heard a gunshot in December, when no farm equipment was making noise, and question why the murderer didn't just kill Joann inside her house instead of risking being seen in public in her car. (A good point.)

And in another bombshell, Joann's good friend Karen Devine said Joann planned to leave Andrew after the holidays, according to *Wrong Man*. "She had a suitcase packed," Devine said. "She had money put aside. He wanted to move to Colorado and she was against it."

The Free Patricia Rorrer page points to a sliver of a fingernail found at the murder site that didn't come from either Patricia or Joann.

Despite the new evidence and hypotheses, the courts have rejected all of Patricia's bids for a new trial.

The Innocence Project has declined to take her case.

In the meantime, ex-flame Andrew Katrinak moved to Colorado and has kept a low profile since the trial ended. He gave an audio interview to the *Wrong Man* investigators when they made a surprise visit to his house, but he declined to appear on camera.

His mild-mannered mother-in-law, Sarah O'Connor, died in 2019 at the age of 83.

Today, Patricia Lynne Rorrer resides in the State Correctional Institute at Muncy, a medium-security and maximum-security facility that has the highest rate of cancer of all prisons in Pennsylvania, according to a story from northcentralpa.com.

The article also notes that most inmates earn around 19 cents an hour at their jobs and must pay $5 each time they need medical attention or medicine.

I was able to e-mail Patricia via the PrisonConnect platform around Christmastime.

Patricia pointed out that when author Tammy Mal "started her research and speaking to me, she was not an advocate at all"—but she reversed and ended up advocating for Patricia's innocence.

Wrong Man also spent money to investigate the case and ended up unconvinced of her guilt, Patricia notes.

Most of all, Patricia said, she would like a rematch with prosecutor Michael McIntyre.

Now retired, he declined my invitation to spar directly with Patricia via a podcast.

"I most definitely will not personally afford Patricia a platform," Michael said in an e-mail to me. "She had her chance to answer my questions and tell her story in court over 20 years ago. She failed miserably to convince me, or anyone else who mattered, of her innocence."

Meanwhile, Patricia is continuing with legal salvos. "We are currently in federal court, trying to get the lab reports through discovery," Patricia wrote to me from prison in an August 23, 2021, e-mail.

So who does Patricia blame for Joann's and Alex's deaths? "I don't know and wouldn't want to print an opinion," Patricia wrote, "as that would be doing the same thing that was done to me. I will say, Joann and Alex did not get justice, and because of the blunders in the case, probably never will."

She also says that her story—unlike the prosecution's—about where she was and what she was doing at the time of the murders has never changed.

"People don't want to believe their system could fail so horribly," says Patricia. "But it does."

CHAPTER 29

Paul Taylor's Murder of Kathy Woodhouse

HE RAPED AND KILLED BEFORE TURNING 21

Forensic Files *episode "Clean Getaway"*

Anyone who watches the news or reads the paper knows the frustration of finding out that the justice system could have prevented a rape and homicide if only it doled out a longer sentence the first time the perpetrator committed a sexual assault (see chapter 17, Thomas Jabin Berry).

Kathy Woodhouse's 1992 rape and murder fall into that category. "Clean Getaway," the episode about the case, mentions that the killer spent some time in a juvenile detention facility before he committed the deadly attack on the mother of three. But the show doesn't mention what he did to earn his bunk there or why he got out early.

I did some research and learned of the horrible crime he committed at the age of 14. I also looked into his whereabouts today.

So let's get going on a recap of "Clean Getaway," along with extra information from online sources as well as my interviews with *Murder in the Heartland* author Harry Spiller and former Herrin police chief Mark Brown.

On Saturday, January 18, 1992, a caller told police that a woman had been raped and murdered in the back of a dry-cleaning store in Herrin, Illinois.

It sounded like a legitimate concerned-citizen call except for two things: The man didn't give his name, and murders didn't usually happen in the small town of about 12,000 people in Williamson County.

At first, some police believed the call might be a prank.

But when they arrived at Fox's Laundry and Dry Cleaners, they found a deceased woman beaten about the head, the murder weapon probably a mop wringer that remained on the scene.

The victim was Kathy Ann Woodhouse, a petite 40-year-old Herrin native with lush, blonde hair and delicate features. The mother of three worked at Fox's and had been married to Joe Woodhouse for 18 years.

After hearing that something out of the ordinary had happened at Fox's, Kathy Woodhouse's mother headed to the scene.

"I saw all these cops around and they wouldn't let me go inside," Sybil East later recalled, adding that Kathy's employer had been planning to transfer her to a store in Marion in just a couple of days.

Police questioned a customer who had left a check for $14.30 on the counter and retrieved her own dry cleaning.

She gave a police artist a description of the tall white man who poked his head out of the back room and asked if she needed help as she was exiting the store. The customer guessed the man's age at 30 to 35.

Unfortunately, lab work on semen recovered from the victim revealed it came from a nonsecretor—someone whose bodily fluids carry no indication of blood type.

A fingerprint found on the pay phone used to make the 911 call didn't match that of any known offender.

In the meantime, state police captain William Barrett warned the rattled community to stay alert but not give in to "excess hysteria." But they had reason to worry.

"The killer was pretty brazen," says Mark Brown, who was an investigator at the time. "The dry cleaner was right on the main street." And Fox's acted only as a pickup and drop-off operation—there was no heavy equipment to mask the noise of an attack.

Early on, police got a tip about a slightly perverted young customer.

Kathy had told a friend that an anonymous man called the store and asked what color toenail polish she was wearing.

Investigators tracked down the gentleman via phone records and visited his house. Under police questioning, the suspect, a 25-year-old construction worker, disclosed that he knew Kathy from visiting the store and eventually admitted he made the call. He said it was something he liked to do every so often. "He was petrified," says Brown. "He was sort of a prominent person in another town. That was probably the last time he did that."

The curious fellow denied any connection to the murder, and fortunately for him, he had an alibi that checked out.

Next up, an anonymous source suggested that the police look at a local man named Paul E. Taylor.

Paul had led a turbulent life. In fact, many *Forensic Files* YouTube viewers who saw his photo expressed surprise that he was only 20 ("in dog years," wrote one).

His parents divorced when he was two, and his mother was reportedly an alcoholic. She remarried, to a man named Douglas Jackson, and he allegedly would physically assault her and verbally abuse young Paul.

"It's my understanding that as he grew up and in school, he was picked on because he was extremely poor," said Harry Spiller.

Paul also ran away and spent some time in a foster home.

By his mid-teens, he had landed at the Louisiana Training Institute, a detention facility for juveniles. But his offenses were much more serious than vandalizing cars or shooting garden gnomes with a BB gun.

In 1984, at the age of 14, Paul entered the women's bathroom at a Baton Rouge hotel that was hosting a school administrators conference. He grabbed an attendee named Sandra Lott while she was drying her hands, according to court papers (*People v. Taylor*, June 22, 1995), which gave a detailed account of the nightmarish crime.

After dragging her to a stall, the teenager brandished a butcher knife, told her to take off her clothes, and sexually assaulted her; he made a failed attempted at penetration. When another woman entered the bathroom, he threatened to kill Sandra Lott if she made a sound.

Next, Paul let Sandra dress, forced her to go to a nearby field with high grass, and made her disrobe a second time. The victim, who weighed 84 pounds, said she suddenly realized that if he raped her, he would probably kill her. Sandra fled and got help from a man who gave her his coat and alerted police.

Paul evaded capture at first—no one knew his identity yet—but two weeks later, authorities arrested a male who trespassed in the same women's bathroom. Sandra Lott identified him as her attacker.

Despite the severity of his assault on Sandra, Paul got a sentence for only the "remainder of his juvenile life"—that is, until he turned 21. He spent the time at both the Louisiana Training Institute, now known as the Jetson Center for Youth, and the low-security Ponchatoula Police Jail.

But Judge Kathleen Stewart Richey let him out a few months early after psychologists said he had made "maximum progress" and recognized the seriousness of his crime. He had a job lined up, and Illinois officials had assured the judge that parole officers would supervise the young man on the outside.

After his release, he moved in with his mother two blocks from the future murder scene and began working at Hardee's.

The fast food restaurant used Fox's to clean employee uniforms.

Paul's manager at Hardee's told police that Paul actually had just quit and said he planned to return to Louisiana.

Investigators managed to find him before he left the area. "He was very polite and said he didn't do it," Brown recalled. "At some point, he said he wouldn't talk anymore until after the Van Halen concert" that he planned to attend with some friends.

"We followed him in," said Brown. "He saw us there in the bleachers. He started to go and get a soda and then said, 'Do you want to get me a soda so one of you can stay here and watch me?'"

That night would be the last time the troubled 20-year-old would ever see Sammy Hagar perform "There's Only One Way to Rock" in person again. After the concert's closing notes, Paul was arrested. "He confessed to the whole thing that night," Brown says. "At first, he told us about the murder but he didn't want to confess to the rape—that took a while."

The forensics strengthened the case. A partial pair of pantyhose Paul hid under his bed looked similar to a piece of hosiery found near the murder scene. His palm print matched an impression left on a plastic bag near Kathy's body.

Prosecutors alleged that Paul pulled pantyhose over his face, forced Kathy Woodhouse into the back room, and raped her.

When he heard the customer come in, he took off his stocking mask and greeted her to make sure she wouldn't come to the back room, they contended. Then, the six-foot, two-inch rapist killed Kathy because she could have identified him.

He robbed her purse of $3.

So why did he call police to report the murder and rape? "Sometimes you get people—especially the psychos—who think they're smarter than everyone else," Harry Spiller said. "They have a tendency to think, 'I did it. You can't catch me.' You've heard about serial killers who write letters to the police."

Despite Paul's confession, the case went to trial. In addition to Sandra Lott, the prosecution had Linda Schott, the accused's first cousin, as a witness.

Paul audibly grumbled the word "bitch" as Linda took the stand. She told the court that he propositioned her for sex and mailed her threatening letters after she declined. He signed his name to the letters and wrote his return address on the envelopes.

A prison employee testified that he overheard Paul bragging to another inmate about the murder. Paul reportedly said that he tried complimenting Kathy Woodhouse on her looks and said her jeans "were like a second skin." He also confessed to the other prisoner that he "had to have her." And once he had her, he "didn't want her anymore" so he murdered her, and his only regret was not wearing gloves, according to the witness.

Paul Taylor definitely had loose lips. Linda Schott testified that Paul told her that he considered Charles Manson his idol and wanted to gather himself a band of followers.

The criminal justice system doesn't particularly love hearing that kind of talk.

On the defense's side of the aisle, clinical psychologist David Warshauer testified that Paul Taylor suffered from alcohol abuse, depression, antisocial personality disorder, and schizotypal personality disorder.

Nonetheless, on cross-examination, Warshauer admitted that Paul probably knew right from wrong.

For Kathy Woodhouse's 77-year-old mother, Sybil East—who often held hands with older daughter Nancy Burlison during the trial—the proceedings were an exercise in terse self-control.

"In the courtroom I couldn't cry," Sybil told the *Southern Illinoisan* years later. "I was just so angry. I wanted to kill him."

The prosecution won a conviction, and for a while, it looked as though Kathy's loved ones might see Paul Taylor perish at the hands of the state. On October 15, 1992, a jury decided the case contained no mitigating factors that would preclude capital punishment. Paul "stared intently" as jurors individually confirmed the decision, according to a *Southern Illinoisan* account.

Paul Taylor, then 21, received a sentence of death by lethal injection.

But in 2003, Governor George Ryan gave a blanket commutation to all 167 convicts on death row in Illinois because of inequities in the legal system.

Paul ended up resentenced to life in prison without the possibility of parole. He declared that he would stop appealing and resign himself to life behind razor wire unless Illinois reinstates his death sentence.

He later said he had no remorse for the murder but didn't realize Kathy Woodhouse left three children, one of them just 13 years old, behind and felt sympathy for them.

Although Paul Taylor certainly didn't intend for it to happen, some good came out of his case for local law enforcement.

"We were all small communities and following the Woodhouse murder, we created a squad so we could work together on any homicide within the county," said Brown, who went on to serve as Herrin's police chief and has since retired. "Before that, none of the forces had the power to put resources in quickly."

Today, Paul Taylor resides at the Illinois River Correctional Center, a medium-security facility in Canton. He now sports a shaved head and long gray-and-brown beard.

The Illinois Department of Corrections' website states clearly that the 230-pound inmate, whose collection of tattoos includes a smiley face, a dog, and a rose, is ineligible for parole.

Sadly, for Kathy's mother, the case marked the second time she lost a child. A son named Randall died in 1967, according to her obituary. Still, she had plenty of family to turn to for support over the years. At the time of Sybil East's death at the age of 106 in 2021, she had accumulated numerous progeny including 13 great-great-grandchildren.

Sybil's obituary noted that she belonged to the First Baptist Church in Herrin. Kathy Woodhouse herself had experienced a religious awakening in early adulthood, according to Nancy Burlison.

"Everyday life is so mundane and boring," Kathy once said. "I want to live in the heavens."

CHAPTER 30

Reyna Marroquin's Story Unsealed

A PREGNANT WORKER, AN ENRAGED BOSS
Forensic Files *episode "A Voice from Beyond"*

With its blend of nostalgia and horror, "A Voice from Beyond" takes us back to a pre-internet world, when people kept handwritten address books with real paper.

It was exciting to see how investigators applied millennial-era forensic technology to evidence from the 1960s.

In fact, the story had everything a true-crime fan could hope for: an affluent businessman leading a double life, a desperate mother-to-be, a 95-year-old woman praying for word on her daughter, a crucial anonymous call to the police.

Oh, and a mummified body in a crawl space.

And for a little extra flavor, this Greek tragedy took place in Long Island, the same New York City commuter haven that gave rise to Amy Fisher, Joey Buttafuoco, and numerous others who can't quite pronounce the letter "r" in words that contain it but append it to words that don't.

Forensic Files, as usual, did a great job of telling the story in 22 minutes. But what about something absent from the narrative—the reaction of friends and neighbors when they learned a horrible secret about the respectable-seeming retiree in their midst?

So let's get started on the recap of "A Voice from Beyond," along with some extra information drawn from internet research

On September 2, 1999, as Ronald Cohen was preparing to vacate the Jericho, New York, house he had just sold for $455,000, he pried off the lid of a 55-gallon drum that had sat undisturbed beneath the bottom floor ever since he moved in. He smelled noxious chemicals and saw a hand poking out of a pile of plastic pellets.

Authorities found an intact, mummified body of a woman inside the barrel. She was fully dressed with a button-down sweater, a skirt, an imitation leopard-skin coat, and a gold locket, according to a *New York Times* article from September 5, 1999.

They determined the deceased was young, petite, dark-haired, and pregnant. She had died from blunt force trauma. She had some unusual dental work, likely performed in South America.

The fetus was a boy, 17 inches long.

The body had been preserved because the drum was airtight, but the pages of an address book (millennial readers: This is how folks kept track of friends before Outlook, iPhones, and Facebook) found in the barrel had decayed.

What really gave the episode armrest-grabbing suspense was the effort—via moisture extraction, magnification, and a video spectral comparator study—on the part of forensics experts to yield clues from the rotting paper.

They uncovered some names, addresses, and phone numbers, although the first batch yielded no leads because the people had long moved away or changed phone numbers. And this was 1999, post-internet but before social media enabled everyone to track down anyone.

By this time, police had traced the barrel to a chemical company in Linden, New Jersey, and dated its manufacture to 1965. It contained some plastic leaves in addition to the pellets.

Neighbors in Jericho remembered that an occupant around that time period, Howard Elkins, was part owner of the Melrose Plastic Company, a New York City maker of decorative artificial plants.

The neighbors didn't mention any gossip about him, but the aforementioned anonymous caller did, telling Nassau County police that, in the 1960s, Elkins had been having an affair with a Hispanic woman who worked in his factory.

The Elkinses had long since moved to Boca Raton, Florida. Howard was none-too-happy to find New York detectives on the other side of his door in his upscale retirement community.

Elkins explained that his house at 67 Forest Drive had acquired the crawl space when his family added a den with a fireplace off the kitchen, according to the *New York Times*. When asked whether he'd ever ventured into the crawl space, he answered, "What for?"

Presented with the evidence of the barrel and green dye inside, Elkins denied he'd ever seen such a thing. He admitted to having an affair but said he couldn't remember what the woman looked like or her name.

He refused to give a DNA sample to determine whether he was the father of the unborn baby. Before leaving, Nassau County detective Brian Parpan told Elkins the police would be getting an order for a blood sample.

Elkins, 70, promptly bought a shotgun and ammunition from Walmart and killed himself.

By this time, the lab had tapped the address book for the name of one more of the dead woman's friends, and this one answered when police dialed her 30-year-old phone number.

Kathy Andrade knew immediately the body belonged to a friend she met in an English class, Reyna Angelica Marroquin, who disappeared in 1969 at the age of 27. An alien registration number found in the address book substantiated the identification, according to *Cold Case Files Classic*'s "The Barrel" segment.

Marroquin came to the United States from El Salvador in 1966, went to fashion school, and got a job at the Melrose factory. Shortly before disappearing, she let on that she was pregnant and that the father told her he was going to marry her. But he already had a wife and three children, and Marroquin was worried he would never keep his promise.

(Something mentioned in more than one newspaper story that *Forensic Files* didn't bring up: Marroquin would sometimes bring a small child to the factory with her, and some of Elkins's workers suspected he was the father. Two readers of my blog, however, left comments explaining that the child didn't belong to Elkins or Marroquin—she was just babysitting.)

According to Kathy Andrade, after Marroquin called her boyfriend's house and told his wife she was pregnant, the man became enraged and threatened to kill Marroquin. She disappeared soon after.

Police theorized Elkins beat Marroquin about the head in a fit of anger, took the body to Long Island with the intention of dumping it in the ocean, put it in a steel drum, and weighted it with plastic pellets from his factory.

But at 350 pounds, it was too heavy to load onto his boat, so he pushed it into a crawl space, where it remained untouched for 30 years.

With the mystery solved and the perpetrator dead, the last loose end was finding Marroquin's family.

Newsday reporter Oscar Corral flew to El Salvador and tracked down Reyna Marroquin's mother in the town of San Martin. The 95-year-old, known as "Grandma Marroquin," nearly collapsed when told of the discovery, Corral recalled in his *Forensic Files* interview. She'd been heartbroken ever since Reyna stopped writing home with no explanation in 1969. She'd had dreams depicting Reyna in a barrel.

As for Elkins, it sounded as though he'd been able to mask any feelings of guilt about his role in the tragedy. The following are two excerpts, including neighbors' statements, from newspaper articles published after his suicide in 1999:

"Howard was very active in the community, very much in the social scene," said neighbor Robert Froment. Elkins's Florida neighbors yesterday were shocked that the big, bearded, jovial man could have been involved in such a crime.—New York Post

"He seemed like a very sociable fellow," Frank Lonano, a neighbor in Boca Raton, said of Mr. Elkins, whom he had known only casually around the walled and affluent community of townhouses overlooking a golf course. "He was just not the type." Judith Ebbin, who with her husband, Arthur, bought the Jericho house from Mr. Elkins and his wife, Ruth, in 1972, owned it for 12 years, never suspecting all that while that a woman's body lay in a drum in a crawl space under the

den. "They seemed like such a lovely family," she said of the former owners.—New York Times

(The 2,143-square-foot, 2.5-bathroom house that secreted the body still stands, and Zillow estimates its value in 2022 at $920,800.)

The one bright note to the story is the resolution brought to Reyna's mother. As CBS quoted her: "Now I know she's with me. She came flying like a dove back to her home."

CHAPTER 31

Sarah Johnson

A Killer at 16

A GIRL CRAVING FREEDOM ENDS UP IN CAPTIVITY
Forensic Files *episode "Disrobed"*

"Disrobed" tells the story of a small-town Idaho teenager who shot her mother and father after they forbade her to see a guy who sounded at best like a waste of time and at worst like a life ruiner.

Because a jury convicted Sarah Marie Johnson at age 18 and sent her to prison for life for a crime she committed at 16, an epilogue to her story seems in order. What's happened to her since *Forensic Files* debuted "Disrobed" in 2008? Has the justice system looked favorably upon the fair-haired middle-class youth?

Here's a recap of the episode plus extra information from internet research and an interview with retired sheriff Walt Femling.

Diane Johnson, a 52-year-old tax collector, and her husband, Alan, a 46-year-old landscaper, provided a lovely home for daughter Sarah and her older half brother, Matt, in Bellevue, a city on the outskirts of Sun Valley, Idaho.

By 2003, Sarah, 16, had taken up with 19-year-old Bruno Santos. He was a high school dropout suspected of gang membership and drug activity.

He also had a cocky personality. Sarah's parents found him none-too-endearing.

But Sarah had no intention of letting go of Santos. She tried the usual teenage tricks, like telling her mom and dad she was sleeping over at a girlfriend's when she was really with him.

When they found out about one such incident, her parents took away her car and threatened to file charges against Santos for statutory rape.

At some point, Sarah decided to quell the controversy by disposing of her parents.

That way, she and Santos could run off and set up their own affluent, love-filled household financed by her parents' $680,000 life insurance payout and the rest of their estate.

According to "Disrobed," Sarah was a fan of true-crime entertainment. Perhaps she felt she had picked up enough know-how to pull off a double homicide with impunity.

First, Sarah stole a .264-caliber rifle from the guesthouse on her family's property. The Johnsons rented out the structure to Mel Speegle, an electrician who was out of town at the time of the crime on September 2, 2003.

That morning, Sarah pulled a shower cap over her blonde hair, put a pink plush bathrobe on backward, crept into her sleeping mother's room, and shot her in the head at close range.

Her father ran out of the shower to see what happened. Sarah shot him in the chest.

To suggest gang activity, Sarah placed knives at the foot of her parents' bed and in her brother's room. (Matt Johnson was away at the University of Idaho in Moscow at the time.)

She put the rifle's scope on Speegle's bed and left the rest of it at the crime scene.

Then she made a beeline for a neighbor's house and said her parents had been shot by an unseen intruder.

Investigators were probably disappointed to rule out their first suspect, Bruno Santos. He was arrogant and disrespectful.

Sheriff Walt Femling thought Bruno had been an influence on Sarah in spurring the murder plot, but investigators couldn't connect any of the crime scene evidence to him or his DNA, Femling told me during an October 2021 interview.

Next up, there was Mel Speegle, but he gave police an alibi that checked out.

Meanwhile, the community was on edge. "You take a small town like Bellevue that hasn't had a murder for more than 40 years and then two people are murdered in their bedrooms," Femling said. "People worried that someone on the loose committed this crime."

By this time, Sarah's lack of sorrow over the tragedy had aroused suspicion.

Her aunt, Linda Vavold, who appeared on *Forensic Files*, noted that Sarah seemed more interested in having her fingernails painted than grieving her mother and father's demise.

And a lot more than innuendo was building up against Sarah. It turned out that she had pretty much left a trail of forensic breadcrumbs for the police to follow. First, the presence of her mother's blood and bone fragments on Sarah's bedroom wall contradicted her story that she was asleep with her door closed when she heard the first shot.

Police recovered the pink bathrobe from the trash—Femling spotted a garbage truck just one house away from the Johnsons' and stopped it from picking up the trash on the day of the murder—and it had high-velocity blood splatter from both Diane and Alan Johnson. Gloves found in the garbage had traces of gunpowder residue outside and Sarah's DNA inside.

Plumbers found the shower cap.

As crime scene investigator Rod Englert said during his *Forensic Files* interview, "The evidence was yelling and screaming."

Prosecutors charged Sarah with two counts of first-degree murder.

"I'm sure people were relieved that Bellevue was safe," Femling said. "But it was a sad day for all of us, for our community, that we arrested a 16-year-old for her parents' murder. It wasn't something where we high-fived each other."

A tidal wave of media attention followed the arrest. "Nationally, we were told that no other juvenile girl had ever acted alone to kill her parents," Femling said. The authorities moved Sarah's trial to Boise, 150 miles from Bellevue, and Court TV broadcast the proceedings live from the Ada County courthouse.

At this point, Sarah probably didn't need any more proof that her fairy tale had gone awry, but she got some anyway: Bruno Santos decided to testify against her in court.

He wanted to prove he had nothing to do with the murders.

Sarah's brother also took a turn in the witness chair in the 2005 trial as well, but he didn't seem to have an agenda. Matt Johnson said his sister was overdramatic and tended to stretch the truth when it suited her, but he loved her just the same.

Defense lawyer Bob Pangburn uncharitably pointed out that Matt would receive Sarah's portion of their parents' insurance money if the jury convicted her.

The prosecution brought in one of Sarah's cellmates, convicted drug trafficker Malinda Gonzalez, who testified that, during their jailhouse conversations, Sarah seemed to inadvertently confess.

As reported by Emanuella Grinberg for Court TV, Gonzalez testified: "One time, she said, 'When I killed . . .' Then she stopped herself and was like, 'When the killers . . .'"

Linda Vavold, Diane Johnson's elder sister, ended up on the prosecution's side as well. "When we would be discussing Alan and Diane and someone would be upset, [Sarah] would roll her eyes and act disgusted," Vavold testified.

Thanks to the bathrobe, shower cap, and DNA blood evidence, prosecutors had a strong forensic case against the teenager despite her strenuous attempts to cover all the bases.

"She was a smart girl," Femling told me. "She had the ability to set the stage and had a lot of books in her room about staging a crime scene. She made it look as though someone came in through the sliding back door, committed the crime, and then left through that door."

The jury didn't buy it. By the time of the sentencing hearing, Matt Johnson seemed willing to accept his sister's guilt, according to reporting from the Times-News on magicvalley.com on June 30, 2005.

Addressing her in court, he said: "One of the ugliest and most horrifying things I've ever had to do when we sold the house, is to go through and clean up blood, and tissue and hair so someone else could buy it and not be horrified."

Sarah received two sentences of life without parole.

As far as what's happening with her today, my initial guess was that Sarah had confessed to the crime, embraced religion, and was helping inmates in a prison literacy program—and asking the state for mercy since she was young and foolish and evil back in 2003 and regretted her crimes.

Or maybe she would take the Menendez brothers' route and admit to killing her parents but tell tales about why they deserved it.

Wrong on both counts.

Sarah, now 35 years old, still claims that someone else killed her parents.

"For her to just continue to deny it, it really hurt the family and hurt her chance of getting parole," Femling said.

She managed to draw help from the Idaho Innocence Project, which contended that she had ineffective counsel at the first trial.

Sarah's legal team also brought up the fact that the murder weapon carried someone else's prints (not Sarah's or Mel Speegle's).

But Speegle said that some prints probably came from a friend who had helped him move his things from his ranch to the Johnson guest-house in 2002.

And Sarah, who clearly had done her forensic homework, probably wiped her own prints off the gun.

In 2014, the U.S. Supreme Court denied a petition filed by Sarah's lawyers, and the Idaho Supreme Court denied an appeal in 2017.

Today, Sarah is prisoner number 77613 at the Pocatello Women's Correctional Center in Pocatello, Idaho.

Life has been no dream for the motivation for all this misery, either.

Bruno Santos, whom the Idaho Department of Corrections lists as "Bruno Santos-Dominguez," served some jail time related to drug charges around the time of Sarah's trial in 2005.

Then, in 2010, Blaine County brought him up on new substance-peddling charges, including the sale of a half-pound of meth-amphetamine to an undercover detective.

The following year, he received a 10-year sentence and earned himself a bunk at the Idaho State Correctional Facility.

Santos, who is allegedly in the United States illegally, received parole in May 2018. After 2024, which the Idaho Department of Corrections lists as his sentence satisfaction date, he could face deportation to Mexico.

Regardless of how bad of a guy Santos was and how he might have unduly influenced Sarah, her relatives seemed to place a lot of blame on her throughout the whole legal ordeal.

"I feel she has no remorse and feel she would do it again," Matt Johnson said at his sister's sentencing hearing, "except she would do better planning."

CHAPTER 32

Shannon Mohr

In the Path of a Con Man

DAVID DAVIS PREYS ON A NURSE ON THE REBOUND
Forensic Files *episode "Horse Play"*

Shannon Mohr's romance started out as a fairy tale and ended as a cautionary tale: If it sounds too good to be true, it probably is.

The "it" in this case was David Davis, a self-proclaimed millionaire.

As BellaMarley1, a viewer who watched the episode on YouTube, wrote in the comments section: "Never trust anyone who tells you he's a millionaire . . . nobody decent would do that."

Maybe it's not so much decency as wisdom. People with a lot of money usually know that announcing it can attract scammers and gold diggers or at least mean getting stuck with the check.

Of course, David Davis didn't need to worry about being victimized for his money—he didn't actually have any.

But he wanted a large cash infusion and tried his hand at the ever-popular murder and insurance fraud combo.

For this chapter, I looked around for more information about what David Davis did in the eight years between Shannon Mohr's homicide and his capture on a tropical island.

I also searched for biographical details on Shannon Mohr. *Forensic Files* mentioned only that she was a nurse who wanted a family.

So let's gallop into a recap of "Horse Play," along with extra information drawn from internet research.

Shannon Mohr was born on September 1, 1954, in Toledo, Ohio, to a devout Catholic family.

The sweet, caring child with light brown hair and pale skin was "daddy's girl and mommy's best friend," according to an episode of *Happily Never After*.

She fulfilled her dream of becoming a registered nurse but hadn't made progress on the marriage and children front.

One night in 1979, she reluctantly went to a friend's wedding without a date. She had recently broken up with a Toledo firefighter. "Go, maybe you'll meet somebody," her well-intentioned mother told her.

It worked.

At the nuptials, Shannon, 25, met David Davis. The 35-year-old had blond hair, blue eyes, and enough charm to make her forget about the age difference.

The handsome stranger with the healthy tan told her he owned farms all over the country and was worth seven figures.

He said that he was a veteran who had sustained an injury in the Vietnam War, then attended the University of Michigan, where he was on the football team—and played in the Rose Bowl—and graduated with a psychology degree.

Oh, and his fiancée died in a car wreck and he thought he'd never love again, he told Shannon, according to *Happily Never After*.

Shannon's parents, Lucille and Robert Mohr, liked the charismatic bachelor, too.

There were some negative indicators early on, nonetheless.

Shannon and David married in Las Vegas (bad sign) on September 24, 1979, after knowing each other for eight weeks (really bad sign), and they took out a $220,000 life insurance policy on her eight days after the wedding (worst possible sign). Shannon told her mother about the insurance when they got back from their honeymoon, according to *Unsolved Mysteries*.

But the warning signs probably got lost amid all the joy of a new relationship.

Shannon moved to David's 100-acre farm in Hillsdale County, Michigan. He grew corn and soybeans. She got a nursing job at Flower Hospital in Sylvania.

Shannon's pay was the only income the couple had, according to the *Chicago Tribune*, but David probably provided a typical con man story about his fortune being tied up. And the lovebirds weren't together long enough to start arguing about money.

On July 23, 1980, just 10 months after the wedding, the couple rode their Tennessee walking horses to visit neighbor Dick Britton. While at Britton's property, David helped him repair some machinery, and then he and Shannon trotted off toward home.

But David came rushing back to Britton's house, saying Shannon's mare bolted and Shannon fell, hitting her head on a rock.

Shannon was lying on her back with no shoes on and her blouse partly unbuttoned.

She was lifeless by the time the two men rushed her into the emergency room. Doctors attributed the death to head and spinal injuries.

Lucille and Robert Mohr arrived at the hospital to find David Davis crying.

In his grief, he managed to articulate that he wanted the body cremated, but he ultimately agreed to let the Mohrs bury Shannon back in Toledo.

David sheepishly told his in-laws that he couldn't afford to pay for a funeral because his money was wrapped up in the farm and he didn't have any life insurance on Shannon.

The Mohrs funded the funeral, which took a surprising turn when David Davis's mother and stepfather, Joyce and Theodore Powell, showed up.

David had told the Mohrs he was an orphan.

His father, David Ellsworth Davis, was still alive, too. The Mohrs also discovered that their daughter's husband wasn't a millionaire, didn't own multiple farms, hadn't really served in Vietnam or been in the military, never played college football, and hadn't graduated.

So who was he, really?

David Richard Davis was born in Flint, Michigan, on September 27, 1944, to parents who would split up when he was 12. His father described him as a good student at Southwestern High School who enjoyed archery and other outdoor activities.

He had two daughters from a previous marriage to a woman named Phyllis June Middleton (Shannon didn't know he had an ex-wife). Phyllis and David lived together on the Michigan farm. Alleging physical abuse, she filed for a court protection order, and the couple divorced in 1976, according to reporting from Gannett News Service.

Phyllis probably didn't realize how lucky she was to get out of that marriage alive—or maybe she didn't have enough life insurance to put her in danger.

Although David denied it at first, he had a total of $330,000 in life insurance—the original policy plus some subsequent smaller ones—on Shannon Mohr. The policies were due to expire at the beginning of August 1980, just days after Shannon's untimely death, according to a November 6, 1991, story in the *South Florida Sun-Sentinel*, a newspaper that does excellent, wide-ranging true-crime reporting.

David would later give various explanations for the existence of the policies, including that he didn't pay attention and never knew about them, that they each took out insurance on the other to help pay farm expenses in case one died, and that an insurance salesman sought them out and sold them on the idea of insurance.

The Mohrs also discovered that David had plans to go on a trip to Florida with a girlfriend shortly after Shannon's death, according to the *Toledo Blade*. David claimed he needed to get away and regroup—and his gal pal had invited herself.

While away, the grieving husband had neighbor Dick Britton forward him his mail. He needed multiple copies of Shannon's death certificate for six different insurance companies, according to *Unsolved Mysteries*.

To the police, however, Shannon's demise still looked like an accident, and they closed the case.

The Mohrs launched a letter-writing campaign to persuade the Michigan attorney general's office to continue investigating. Dick Britton also urged authorities to take a new look at the evidence against his former friend.

A month after Shannon's death, her body was exhumed, and an autopsy revealed a severe gash on her head and bruises on her face, hand, and arm.

Still, no forensic alarm bells sounded, and the case stayed closed.

Then, a *Detroit Free Press* reporter named Billy Bowles started poking around and discovered sketchy incidents from David's past. He had twice profited from fire insurance on his farm—he "insured everything," his father-in-law would later say—and collected workers' compensation from a suspicious injury he supposedly incurred while working for a car manufacturer.

Bowles also found out that David had taken some advanced courses in pharmacology at the University of Michigan. After speaking to local vets, investigators theorized that David used succinylcholine in the murder. Often used as a horse tranquilizer, succinylcholine paralyzes every muscle except the heart and makes it impossible to breathe without a ventilator. Detective Sergeant Don Brooks had learned that David once used the drug on the tips of arrows when he hunted deer.

Michigan reopened the case of Shannon Mohr's death.

Meanwhile, David had sold his Michigan property, collected five-figure payouts from Shannon's smaller policies, and taken up residence on a sailboat in the Bahamas with a girlfriend. He was awaiting the final results of Shannon's latest autopsy so he could get his hands on the bulk of the insurance money.

After a third autopsy, which uncovered injection marks on Shannon's shoulder and wrist, investigators farmed out lab work to Swedish scientists who had developed methods for detecting succinylcholine. They found high concentrations in two areas of Shannon's body, suggesting someone had given her two shots of the drug.

Investigators eventually concluded that the injections, not the head injury, killed Shannon. The drug probably left Shannon conscious as she slowly suffocated.

The authorities moved to arrest David Davis in December 1981, but he fled, leaving his sailboat behind. He eluded them for eight years.

Then, *Unsolved Mysteries* broadcast an episode about the case.

A Beverly Hills dentist named Cheri Lewis later said that the fugitive looked like a man with odd thumbs whom she had dated, according to the *Detroit Free Press*. Lewis later noted that David garnered sympathy by speaking of his wife Shannon, "who drowned."

And Hollywood stuntman Beau Gibson thought David Davis's picture resembled his best buddy, "Rip Bell," who had given him flying lessons, the *Detroit Free Press* reported.

But only one of David Davis's associates—who remained anonymous—actually called the toll-free number on *Unsolved Mysteries*. The tipster said the fugitive was living under the name David Myer Bell in American Samoa, where he and his 23-year-old wife resided in a tin-roofed shack.

Four FBI agents arrested David Davis in 1989 at Tafuna International Airport in Pago Pago, where he was working as a pilot for Pacific Island Airways. (He met his wife, Maria Koleti Sua, on the job. She also worked for the airline.)

He admitted his real identity and peacefully submitted to the arrest, according to the *Detroit Free Press*. News footage showed the suspect looking disheveled and wearing big aviator-style eyeglasses and handcuffs.

"Oh God, I don't know what to say," Lucille Mohr told the *Detroit Free Press* upon her ex-son-in-law's capture. "It has been eight years of hell . . . my heart's coming out of my chest."

At a stopover in Hawaii, David, 44, underwent FBI questioning while still wearing his blue and white Aloha shirt, according to the *Honolulu Star-Bulletin*.

In addition to identifying himself as a pilot, David had posed as a doctor, nurse, and "even as a harpsichord player" while on the run, according to an FBI spokesman quoted in an Associated Press account.

Only the pilot claim was genuine. He earned certification from the Federal Aviation Administration while on the lam.

The *Detroit Free Press* described David Davis as "overweight, slovenly," and "gray-bearded"—but he "nevertheless cut a dashing figure."

His trial kicked off in November 1989.

The prosecution would conclude that, on the day Shannon died, David Davis suggested they have sex outdoors. While Shannon was getting undressed, he sneaked up on her and gave her one or two shots of succinylcholine to immobilize and kill her, but she fought back before the drug took effect. She left scratch marks on his arm, which the Mohrs noticed at the hospital. (He said they came from tree branches he brushed by in his hurry to summon help for Shannon.)

He then staged the horse accident by hitting her head with the rock, the prosecution believed.

Early on, sheriff's deputies had noticed that the rock with the blood on it was the only rock anywhere near the scene of Shannon's death.

And evidence of David's con jobs and lies came spilling out.

David had asked a series of women to marry him after knowing them for just weeks, investigators discovered. Shannon was apparently the first one who said yes.

Jeanne Hohlman, one of David's gal pals, testified that David said he was a CIA agent assigned to protect Shannon. After Shannon died, he told her the mission was over and he could start dating again, according to *Happily Never After*.

David Davis chose not to take the stand.

The jury took two and a half hours to find him guilty of first-degree murder. Noting that Shannon's death by suffocation was "more despicable than a contract murder," Hillsdale Circuit Court judge Harvey Moes sentenced the wife killer to life without parole.

Lucille Mohr said she wished Michigan still had the death penalty, but her husband noted that "being locked up in a cage the rest of his life is probably 100 times worse," the Gannett News Service reported.

In captivity at Michigan's Marquette Branch Prison, David continued to profess his innocence.

"I could never have hurt her," he told the *Toledo Blade* in 2001, still maintaining that Mohr fell from her horse and hit her head.

David filed an appeal with a federal court that year. There was continuing controversy over the lab work purported to reveal the presence of succinylcholine—a number of industry professionals regarded the tests as junk science—but it didn't help David's case much.

The real smoking guns were the insurance policies, David's tall tales about his life, and the murder scene appearing staged.

He lost on appeal.

Ultimately, David got a taste of his own medicine. He acquired neuromuscular disease and died at the age of 70 in a prison health care facility in 2014.

Lucille and Robert Mohr, who ultimately received most of Shannon's life insurance payout, died in 2008 and 2012, respectively.

Investigator Billy Bowles, whom a colleague credited with spending seven years toiling over a "10,000-piece jigsaw puzzle" until a picture emerged in the Shannon Mohr murder case, died the same year David Davis did.

According to the *Chicago Tribune*, another hero of the whodunit challenge was "tenacious state police officer Detective Sergeant Don Brooks," who never bought the story that Shannon's death was an accident. Brooks went on to appear on *Forensic Files* and *Unsolved Mysteries*.

In addition to spawning episodes of many true-crime shows, Shannon's story also inspired a made-for-TV movie, *Victim of Love: The Shannon Mohr Story*, which the *Philadelphia Inquirer* called "great trash TV." It came out while David Davis was still alive, and, according to the *Toledo Blade*, he boycotted the television room when other inmates watched it.

CHAPTER 33

MaryAnn Clibbery and George Hansen

Unsalvageable

MURDER WRECKS A REMODELING BUSINESS

Forensic Files *episode "Frozen Assets"*

Local TV commercials starring small-business owners have their own special charm despite, or maybe because of, their low production values.

The folksy ads become part of a community's sense of place and security, particularly in the case of Al Zullo Remodeling Specialists, who for decades told homeowners that "one call does it all."

MaryAnn Clibbery and George Hansen were partners in the Loves Park, Illinois, company, named after the original owner, Anthony "Al" Zullo.

Before he died in 2000, Al decided to leave the business to Mary-Ann and George to reward their loyalty. MaryAnn had started there as a secretary in 1959, and George got on board at some point in the 1960s, according to reporting from the *Randolph County Herald Tribune*.

By 2004, MaryAnn, 69, was thinking about retiring from the business.

But she never got the chance. Her business partner bludgeoned her to death in a back hallway of Al Zullo Remodeling first.

For this chapter, I checked on George's whereabouts today (he's still alive) and looked for more information about the victim's life and what happened to the business after one owner died and the other traded his white button-down for an unfitted light-blue prison-issue shirt.

So let's get going on the recap of the 2008 episode "Frozen Assets," along with extra information from internet research.

At Al Zullo Remodeling, George Hansen handled sales, and Mary-Ann Clibbery did the finances. MaryAnn was known for her kindness to workers and sometimes fronted them their wages with her own money if they got in a jam, according to *Forensic Files*.

Born MaryAnn Romain, she had grown up in a family of five children who lived in the projects in Chicago, then moved to a house with no hot water in Rockford, Illinois, according to the *Beloit Daily News*. An obituary for MaryAnn's father notes he owned a Gulf station for 15 years, so perhaps things improved financially for the family.

MaryAnn went on to have five children of her own and two marriages. At least one of her husbands left her widowed, and it's not clear whether she divorced the other or he passed away. By 2004, she was single but had a long-term boyfriend.

Background information on business partner George Hansen is skimpy except for the fact that he was married with children. An employee named Raymond Beardsley told the *Beloit Daily News* that he had a temper and could become "unhinged."

Still, on the surface, everything looked great at the local institution until the early morning of December 22, 2004. When George and coworker Randy Baxter showed up for work, they discovered MaryAnn's body on the floor. Randy called 911 and reported MaryAnn wasn't breathing and rigor mortis had set in.

Investigators determined she sustained three blows to the back of the head plus other blunt force trauma inflicted during two separate attacks. "Her head was caved in," recalls defense counsel Frank Perri, who would go on to represent George Hansen. "The autopsy pictures were disturbing."

Harold "Gene" Sundeen, MaryAnn's boyfriend of 12 years, was heartbroken. "I remember the dress she wore for our first date," he told the Investigation Discovery Network's *Murder in the Heartland*.

"It was blue with white polka dots."

MaryAnn's son Robert Cleere, who also appeared on *Murder in the Heartland*, recalled that he was working on his mail route when his supervisor told him about his mother's murder.

Her well-attended funeral mass took place at St. Anthony's Catholic Church.

Police at first focused on Kevin Doyle, an employee MaryAnn had recently let go after he messed up on a job; he still had a set of keys to the business.

But there was also the matter of MaryAnn's relationship with George. In everyday business life, they didn't get along quite as well as they seemed to in the commercials. According to *Forensic Files*, George felt MaryAnn didn't deserve the partnership Al Zullo left her.

When questioned by police, George denied any conflict and gave an extensive alibi: The night of the homicide, he enjoyed several vodka-and-Squirts at the Backyard Bar and Grill with his wife, followed by some Brandy Old Fashioneds at Singapore Bar and Grill, where he bought a $50 gift card for MaryAnn. Later, he picked up his grand-daughter and, at her request, visited a tanning salon before heading home.

Witnesses confirmed George's alibis.

But things fell apart for George after a citizen notified police about a black garbage bag sitting on top of some ice on Rock River.

It contained a hammer, gloves, MaryAnn's tan suede purse, and a yellow sweater.

The sweater, which had originally belonged to founder Al Zullo—and was kept around the office for whoever caught a chill—had Mary-Ann's blood on the outside. Skin cells found inside the collar of the sweater matched George's DNA profile.

Likewise, the gloves contained MaryAnn's blood on the outside, George's DNA inside.

Forensic Files didn't mention it, but MaryAnn had already had at least two suspicious brushes with death before the murder.

According to *Fraud Magazine*, on one occasion, the brakes in her car failed right after George had borrowed it. Another time, someone set fire to a sofa MaryAnn was sleeping on.

But if MaryAnn was snoozing at the office, it didn't necessarily mean she was lazy. Police found the remains of the prescription sleep medication Zolpidem in her mug at the office. George used to deliver coffee to MaryAnn in the cup, and employees had seen her asleep at her desk.

He had good reason to keep MaryAnn a little woozy. She was investigating him.

That year, some of the Christmas cards received from vendors and subcontractors included notes saying that they hadn't been paid. Mary-Ann discovered George was pocketing the money owed to them. He falsified the books to hide his theft, which totaled around $100,000.

MaryAnn had told police and her doctor about her suspicions, according to *Fraud Magazine*.

The day she died, MaryAnn stayed late at the office to confront George about the embezzlement. It's not clear why she chose to meet with him alone after the frightening incidents. (Her friend Linda Cleveland recalled that over breakfast at Johnny Pamcakes in early December 2004, MaryAnn said that she feared something bad was on the horizon.)

Police believe George was wearing the yellow sweater while beating MaryAnn with a hammer during an argument over the missing money. After the initial attack, George opened some drawers to make the place look ransacked, then realized MaryAnn was still alive and beat her again, the authorities theorized.

He stuffed the evidence into the garbage bag and included her purse so the attack would look like a burglary that turned into a homicide. But police would find that nothing else was missing from the office.

George threw the murder bag off the Roscoe Road bridge into the Rock River, but it landed on the ice. A witness saw George's white truck with its "Zullo 51" vanity license plate driving back and forth on the bridge. Police believe he was trying to figure out how to retrieve the bag but gave up.

In addition to the desire to cover up his financial misdeeds, George harbored another motive to kill MaryAnn: The business had a $150,000 life insurance policy on her, which would have come in handy to pay off the vendors and subcontractors he cheated.

On December 27, 2004, Loves Park police entered Croc's Pub and interrupted George's game of video poker to arrest him. He reportedly didn't ask for a reason or make any comment. His pants pocket contained a single pink pill, which was identified as the same sleeping aid found in MaryAnn's mug. (George's sister would later admit to investigators that she had been illegally selling the prescription drug to him.)

The evolution of the quaint hometown business into a hub for murder and betrayal shook up the community. "These were people who had been in their homes, and it just gave everyone a horrible feeling," Jessica Olstad, a former WPTZ-TV Newschannel 5 reporter who covered the case, told me.

With so much evidence pointing his way, George changed his story.

He now said he stopped by the office to look for his gloves around 7 p.m. on December 21 and saw MaryAnn lying dead. Because the yellow sweater, hammer, and gloves that some anonymous evildoer used in the attack were associated with George, he was afraid he'd be blamed, so he panicked and covered it up by disposing of the evidence, he said. Then he retrieved his granddaughter from driving school and stopped off for a sandwich.

At the trial in 2005, prosecutor Margie O'Connor asked George why he didn't come to MaryAnn's aid when he saw her lying on the floor the evening before Randy Baxter notified authorities.

"It was the dumbest and worst thing I ever did," Hansen told the court.

George also claimed MaryAnn was in on the financial crimes and that he had no motive to kill her because they needed each other to keep the scam going.

"All I remember is wanting to go over the rail and strangle that guy," MaryAnn's brother Louis Romain—who was sitting just a few feet away from George at the trial—told *Murder in the Heartland*.

Randy Baxter also had trouble maintaining his composure. After testifying about finding MaryAnn "in a big scab" of dried blood, he became so rattled that he needed to take a break before looking at the crime scene photos, the *Beloit Daily News* reported.

Despite emotions running high, "it was the most civil trial I'd ever covered, eerily quiet," Jessica Olstad recalls. "MaryAnn's boyfriend sat there every day. He was incredibly friendly, but not boisterous and certainly didn't seek the limelight."

In her closing statement, Margie O'Connor warned the jury about George's guile: "He made his living as a salesman" and "is trying to make the sale of his life."

Frank Perri maintained that George was guilty only of "stupidity" and "selfishness" and that the contents of the garbage bag added up to nothing more than circumstantial evidence—there was no blood in his car.

According to the *Rockford Register Star*, after the guilty verdict, Hansen's family and friends filed out of the third-floor courtroom tight-lipped and headed straight for the elevators, trying to avoid TV cameras and other media. Clibbery's family and friends walked out looking somewhat haggard but relieved.

Outside the courthouse, George Hansen's 35-year-old daughter sobbed and told the media that her father had been convicted without evidence.

During the sentencing proceedings on October 13, 2005, MaryAnn's boyfriend as well as her brother Louis Romain and her daughter Charmaine Shelf addressed the court about the pain of losing MaryAnn.

Winnebago County judge Daniel Doyle gave George a 60-year sentence.

Meanwhile, what about the fate of Al Zullo Remodeling Specialists—whose friendly, low-budget commercials became part of Loves Park's identity?

Well, George's crime rendered it unsalvageable, leaving creditor Amcore Bank and vendors unpaid.

The bank sued in an effort to get the $92,000 Al Zullo Remodeling owed for a loan, according to the *Rockford Register Star*, which also noted that, just one month after the murder, phone calls to the business were greeted by an answering machine with no room for messages and no forwarding number.

The newspaper also reported that one homeowner who paid Al Zullo Remodeling in full for renovation services was "hounded" for money that the business owed to a lumber provider. Homeowners with half-finished construction work were out of luck. With MaryAnn gone and George about to begin a life of strip searches and Nutraloaf, the business ceased to exist.

Today, the man who brought about its demise is better known as inmate number R47647 at the Pontiac Correctional Center. The Illinois

Department of Corrections (DOC) notes that George has a projected parole date of December 23, 2064—when he's 123 years old.

In the meantime, he has kept his five-foot, seven-inch body free of tattoos and trim at 139 pounds, according to the state's DOC website.

Frank Perri, who went on to write the book *With Cold Ease: Inside the Fraud Offender Mind* (2021), points out that, since the trial started, George's story has remained consistent. "He says he didn't do it, he testified he didn't do it, and he still says he didn't do it," according to Perri.

As for MaryAnn's boyfriend Gene Sundeen, whom *Forensic Files* watchers will recall for his grief during his on-camera interview, he never remarried. He died a single man in 2019 at the age of 89.

CHAPTER 34

Mike Garvin

Camera-Friendly Killer

A Cheating Husband Is Oblivious to Electronics
Forensic Files episode "One for the Road"

Mike Garvin is memorable for something he forgot—or maybe was unaware of in the first place—a little piece of modern-day technology known as the security camera.

The video clips that contradicted the Florida real estate agent's account of his wife's disappearance helped authorities win a murder conviction against him. They also made it fun to watch "One for the Road," the *Forensic Files* episode about the case.

For this chapter, I checked into where the killer is today and looked for details about homicide victim Shirley Garvin's life.

So let's get started on the recap of "One for the Road," along with additional information drawn from internet research.

In January 2003, Michael Jay Garvin reported that his wife, Shirley, had vanished from their hotel room while they were on vacation in Key West, Florida.

Shirley Garvin, 55, was born in Washington, DC, the only child of Robert and Cecilia Fleming.

She met Michael Garvin when they both lived in Virginia Beach, and their 14-year marriage looked happy enough from the outside. Mike had no record of domestic violence or other prior criminal behavior, according to an Associated Press (AP) account.

None of the newspaper coverage about the murder mentioned an occupation for Shirley, but she was described as a socialite, and probably didn't have to worry too much about money. Her parents, who died in 2000 and 2001, had left her around $900,000, according to *Missing Persons Unit*, a Court TV series that produced an episode about her murder.

Shirley and Mike lived on the 9000 block of Whittington Drive in Jacksonville, Florida, and both enjoyed serving on the board of the Mandarin Community Club, where Shirley was the "driving force" behind organizing parties and other get-togethers, according to a *Florida Times-Union* account.

In Key West, Mike Garvin told police that he thought his wife went out for a walk, and he had gotten worried when she didn't return.

Shirley often wore a Rolex watch and other expensive jewelry that could have made her a target for thieves looking to prey on tourists. She also had high blood pressure and became disoriented without her medication, her concerned husband told police.

Local and state law enforcement sprang into action, searching every corner of the Quality Inn—where no one remembered seeing Shirley—and then mobilizing tracker dogs on the ground and a helicopter over the Atlantic Ocean in an effort to find her. On the beach a mile from the hotel, a citizen found a pair of sandals that looked like ones Shirley owned, so perhaps she'd accidentally drowned.

The authorities considered suicide as a possibility, too. Maybe she just walked into the sea. But friends said that Shirley hadn't lost enthusiasm for living—she was a lot of fun. It was Mike she'd grown tired of, and she was thinking about ending the marriage.

Detectives tracked down security footage from a rest-stop convenience store along the 500-mile route from Jacksonville to Key West. It showed Mike Garvin entering and exiting the Pilot Foodmart without Shirley in tow.

A woman who doesn't hit the restroom during a long road trip? Definitely suspicious.

Mike's account of stopping at a local eatery to pick up two meals for the couple to eat back at their hotel room fell apart, too. A bartender said Mike only bought one sandwich, and a receipt proved it. As YouTube commenters summed it up:

All that money and you stay at a Quality Inn?

What can you expect from a guy who's too cheap to buy a second meal for the sake of his alibi?

The authorities, who seized Mike's computer, found out that he not only had a girlfriend on the side but also was searching for other date mates on Match.com during the time police were searching for Shirley. (The tech-illiterate Mike didn't know homicide rule number one—destroy the hard drive.)

And the cameras implicated him again when authorities found toll-booth footage that showed him driving alone in a white Jaguar during the time he was supposed to be heading toward Key West with Shirley in the passenger seat.

In hopes of finding more evidence, the authorities did something that ultimately guaranteed Mike would be saying goodbye to romantic trysts with mysterious women and hello to uncomfortable encounters with male career criminals: They secretly attached a GPS device to his car.

The GPS—which at the time was relatively new technology, so we can't blame Mike, 62, for being blindsided by it—tracked him to a remote site on Jacksonville's Heckscher Drive, where authorities later found Shirley's body wrapped in plastic in a very shallow grave, according to the *Florida Times-Union*. She had died from two bullet wounds to the head from a .22-caliber pistol, probably fired while she was asleep.

Police found traces of her blood at the couple's home.

At that point, police already had a solid case that Mike Garvin had made the trip to Key West alone, as a cover story. But the incriminating evidence kept rolling in.

Shirley's close friends—the gals she met for ladies' night every week—told investigators that she hadn't mentioned anything to them about a trip to Key West. "She never went anywhere without calling," her cousin Nancy Fixx told the *Florida Times-Union*.

Mike's finances gave him a motive for the crime. He was $80,000 in debt and had bounced checks, according to *Forensic Files* and *Missing Persons Unit*.

Most of the couple's assets were in Shirley's name. And, as mentioned, she was thinking about divorce. What did the popular, fun-loving Shirley need with a promiscuous spendthrift of a husband?

Police arrested Mike and charged him with first-degree murder.

He took a long, hard look at the pile of evidence against him and did something rarely seen on *Forensic Files*.

Instead of changing his original story, he pleaded guilty.

Defense lawyer Mark Miller said his client wished to "spare his family" of a potentially "high profile trial," according to an AP account from August 27, 2004.

Before the sentencing, Judge Karen Cole listened to victim impact statements from Shirley's loved ones, some of whom had "traveled thousands of miles to be there," according to the *Florida Times-Union*.

"She tried and tried and he murdered her," said Shirley's cousin, Ellen Fleming. "Why could he not be man enough to just walk away?"

It also came out that Shirley had helped finance Mike's daughter's college education.

"Shirley was a good wife," said friend Wilma McLaren. "She created a beautiful home for her and Mike. She did not deserve this horrible ending."

Judge Cole gave him life without the possibility of parole on a charge of second-degree murder.

Up until recently, Garvin was better known as inmate number 126380 in the South Unit of the South Florida Reception Center (a rather friendly sounding name for a state prison) in Doral, about 10 miles from the Orlando International Airport.

He didn't have a chance to fly the coop—the Florida Department of Corrections kept him in "close custody," making him ineligible for work camps outside a secure perimeter.

As of March 2020, Florida no longer listed him as a prisoner, and one of my blog readers (thanks, M.S.) wrote in to say he died after serving 17 years.

Forensic Files mentioned that, before Shirley, Mike had a wife who had died by hanging herself.

Media accounts didn't reveal her name or any other information about her. Garvin had her body cremated, so police couldn't go back and look for forensic evidence of foul play.

It's lucky the Florida authorities did such a good job of building a case against him for Shirley's murder and put him in a place where security cameras—and bulked-up inmates with neck tattoos—discouraged him from harming anyone else.

CHAPTER 35

Paul Camiolo's Trial by Fire

A SURVIVOR NEEDS RESCUING
Forensic Files *episode "Up in Smoke"*

The story of the house fire that made Paul Camiolo into an adult orphan is a horrible tragedy, but it's free of evil or scandalous behavior.

"Up in Smoke" doesn't offer up a wife having an affair with a young janitor (chapter 21) or a funeral director who took out five life insurance policies on the kid who washes the limousines (chapter 13). The closest thing to a bad guy in this story is an anonymous flooring contractor who was probably just being a little bit cheap.

And the crucial forensics in the episode aren't your typical gruesome *Forensic Files* evidence—no bone fragments or blood splatter. You can watch the show while you're eating. It even has some fun facts.

For this chapter, I looked for an epilogue for Paul Camiolo, whom *Forensic Files* portrays as a devoted son transformed into the number one suspect for a double homicide that never happened.

Although I agree with the conclusion that he was innocent, online research yielded some information not mentioned in "Up in Smoke" that makes it easier to understand why the authorities mistakenly believed in his guilt.

So let's get started on the recap, along with additional facts drawn from the web as well as my interview with Richard Roby, PhD.

Software technician Paul Camiolo lived with his parents, Rosalie and Ed Camiolo, in a Colonial-style house in Upper Moreland, Pennsylvania.

Rosalie, 57, worked in the computer industry, and Ed, 81, was a retired government employee.

She had suffered a number of strokes along with other health woes, and he had one leg that was shorter than the other because of a childhood bout with polio, according to a *Philadelphia Inquirer* account. Ed had also recently battled cancer.

The couple's medical problems limited their mobility, so Paul, their only child, helped with tasks like shopping.

In the wee hours of September 30, 1996, Paul called emergency services to report a fire in the living room.

Willow Grove volunteer firefighters arrived to find Paul getting dressed on the front lawn. He told them that his parents escaped through the back door.

They discovered Rosalie severely burned on the back porch and Edward in cardiac arrest inside the bathroom.

Edward died that night. Rosalie succumbed to her injuries 11 weeks later.

Paul, who was around 30 years old at the time, explained that his mother was a chain-smoker and had probably set the couch on fire accidentally. He threw a pitcher of water on the flames, but instead of smothering them, it fed them, he said.

According to *Forensic Files*, Paul said that he told his parents to go out the back door, then phoned for help and left via the front door.

What the show didn't mention was that Paul allegedly gave shifting accounts about whether he was asleep or awake when the fire broke out and changed his story about the logistics of his attempts to save his parents, according to the *Philadelphia Inquirer*.

Former assistant district attorney Timothy Woodward, who appeared on *Forensic Files*, pointed out that Paul was the beneficiary of his parents' six-figure life insurance payouts. Woodward wondered whether Camiolo was tired of caring for his mom and dad.

Tests on the flooring near the couch showed traces of gasoline. The authorities built a case around their theory that Paul used the accelerant to start a fire while his parents were upstairs, then escaped and left them to die.

In January 1999, Paul was charged with first-degree murder, arson, and insurance fraud and held without bail in the Montgomery County jail.

Thus Paul Camiolo traveled from a literal burning hell to a figurative one of public infamy. According to a *Philadelphia Inquirer* story published on January 21, 1999, "Paul Camiolo wanted money, Montgomery County authorities say, and he didn't want to pay the health-care costs of his sick parents. . . . Camiolo took care of both problems. . . . [He] inherited more than $400,000 and moved to Bucks County."

The article noted that he purchased a house for $77,000 in the town of Holland, Pennsylvania, after his parents died.

Fortunately for Paul, his extended family—including nephew Vince Camiolo, who appeared on *Forensic Files*—believed in his innocence. More than a dozen of his relatives showed up to support him at his preliminary hearing, according to the *Philadelphia Inquirer*.

Vince Camiolo noted that his uncle Paul was "unusual," but that didn't make him guilty. Relatives attested to the fact that Paul was happy to transport his parents to family picnics and the annual Polenta Night at the Sons of Italy, according to a *Philadelphia Inquirer* story from March 30, 1999.

Bill Burns, who was Paul's boss at Shopman Inc., a software business in Ivyland, Pennsylvania, called the charges against him "outrageous" and spoke of Paul's patient, empathetic approach to helping customers. He said that Paul had never once complained about his parents.

Burns continued to pay Paul his salary while he was in jail and vowed to keep his job open for him until his release, according to the *Philadelphia Inquirer* piece.

Paul had another supporter in Steve Avato, one of the volunteer firefighters who had responded to the blaze. Avato also worked as a special agent for the Bureau of Alcohol, Tobacco, and Firearms—and he doubted that the traces of gasoline found on the floor added up to arson.

During his *Forensic Files* appearance, Avato also noted he didn't find it suspicious that Paul escaped via the front door—instead of the back door, with his parents—because people tend to flee fires through the door they normally use to exit.

Plus, by the time Paul had directed his parents through the back door and then called 911 from the dining room, the fire near the back door had spread, making it logical for Paul to exit out the front door, said Roby, who is president and technical director of Combustion Science & Energy in Columbia, Maryland.

As part of the investigation, Roby built a replica of the house. After some testing, he determined that an intentionally set fire would have spread faster than the one in the Camiolos' house that night in 1996.

Here's where the interesting trivia comes in. John Lentini, one of the fire investigators hired by the defense, said that in the 1970s—when the house was built—some flooring contractors thinned out varnish with gasoline because it cost less than higher-quality agents.

"Guys who put in wood floors would combine wood dust and gasoline to make a paste to fill in gaps," Roby says.

That explained why the lab found traces of gasoline on the floor but not the rug.

Also, tests had pegged the gasoline as leaded, a type of fuel not sold in Pennsylvania in more than a decade at the time of the fire. How could Paul have used leaded gasoline as an accelerant when there was no place to buy it?

And the most useful fact: Polyurethane, a material used in the Camiolos' couch, burns more fiercely when it comes into contact with water. (One more reason to keep a fire extinguisher handy—actually, I need to go to the hardware store.)

That and other gaps in the knowledge of Camiolo's accusers hindered the investigation. In the *Forensic Files* episode, Lentini called arson investigation a "profession largely controlled and dominated by hacks. They make complicated decisions about chemistry and physics and they never took chemistry and physics."

In other words, they weren't bad guys—just wrong guys, whose overconfidence ended up saddling an innocent fire survivor's life with an awful stigma.

The defense theorized that Rosalie accidentally dropped a match on the polyurethane sofa. Like a grease fire, the flames on the polyurethane responded to water by getting bigger, lending credence to Paul Camiolo's statement to investigators.

The prosecution did its own test with polyurethane and got similar results.

Also, as Roby points out, when a policewoman first reached Rosalie after her escape out the back door, she was conscious and lucid—yet she didn't implicate Paul.

Furthermore, the fact that Ed died in the bathroom instead of exiting the back door didn't necessarily indicate foul play. "The cyanide in smoke disorients you, which explains how the father ended up taking a wrong turn in the bathroom," Roby says. "It's typical for people to get into a dead end when there's disorientation."

The Montgomery County attorney general's office—which had announced in March 1999 that it was seeking the death penalty—reversed its decision, dropped the charges against Paul Camiolo, and set him free in the fall of that year after 11 months of confinement.

He returned to his software job at Shopman Inc.

In July 2000, Camiolo filed a lawsuit against the Upper Moreland police, fire investigators, and State Farm insurance for false imprisonment, intentional infliction of emotional distress, bad faith, and even some RICO (Racketeer Influenced and Corrupt Organizations) Act offenses. He asked for $150,000 in damages.

Three years later, a federal appeals court ruled that Camiolo couldn't sue the authorities or the insurance company (which had settled with him for $240,000).

The decision, dated June 30, 2003, noted that there was no scheme "to defraud or to deprive Camiolo of something by trick or deceit."

Although he didn't win any money as a result of his legal ordeal, on January 14, 2007, Paul got the satisfaction of having the *Philadelphia Inquirer*—the same newspaper that ran numerous articles about him as a murder suspect—include him in a feature story about the havoc that shaky arson investigations can wreak.

"Where do you go to get your name back?" Paul told the paper. "The mere accusation is so disgusting."

He also got to vent in a *Tribune-Review* story that questioned the practice of insurance companies paying law enforcement to conduct arson investigations.

"It's sad," Paul told the *Tribune-Review*, "that there are cases all throughout this country where insurance companies function as police in a district attorney's case."

He got additional support from John Lentini, who dedicated the reference book *Scientific Protocols for Fire Investigation* (2019) to Paul Camiolo and others "for whom a second look at their fire made all the difference."

And the court of public opinion appears to have migrated over to Paul's corner, as numerous online comments indicate.

So where is Paul today?

According to an internet posting dated 2016, he has moved to Argentina.

It's not clear why he relocated to South America, but his presence on social media affirms that he still has the support of the large extended family of Camiolos, who know firsthand of his kindness to his parents and always believed in his innocence.

CHAPTER 36

What Happened to Tim Boczkowski's Children?

TWO WIVES DIE UNDER THE SAME CIRCUMSTANCES
Forensic Files *episode "All Wet"*

On November 7, 2018, media outlets all over the country ran an Associated Press (AP) story reporting that Tim Boczkowski was up for parole in North Carolina.

The prospect of the Tar Heel State releasing a man found guilty of drowning both of his wives—one in a bathtub in Greensboro in 1990 and the other in a hot tub in Pittsburgh in 1994—made for scintillating headlines.

Boczkowski's prison record reflected good behavior, no infractions to hinder his chances with the board.

But the fact is that Boczkowski, whom the press has called an American Bluebeard, had almost no chance of winning freedom and snagging a new spouse on PlentyofFish.com.

The onetime owner of a dental-supply business did ultimately get parole—but North Carolina immediately turned him over to authorities in Pennsylvania, where he is now serving a separate life sentence.

That's what happened with Tim, but the story leaves a big question: What happened to his daughter and two sons, who lost their loving biological mother and then their kindhearted stepmother?

At the time of the second murder, of Maryann Fullerton Boczkowski, in 1994, Todd was 9 years old, Sandy was 10, and Randy was 13.

For this chapter, I looked for some answers, but first here's a recap of the episode along with extra information from internet research.

Tim Boczkowski was tall and still had a fair amount of blond hair left in 1979, when he married Mary Elaine Pegher, called Elaine. She worked as a secretary. The couple had three children and ran an ice cream parlor, King Kones, in Greensboro, North Carolina. But it all fell apart in 1990. The store failed, and they sold it as well as a miniature golf complex, according to a *Pittsburgh Post-Gazette* story.

Later that same year, a horrible tragedy struck when Elaine accidentally drowned in a bathtub.

"There are things in life that only your mom can teach you," her daughter later said during an interview with *Forensic Files*, "and I'll never have a chance to find those things out."

The Boczkowskis moved to Pittsburgh, and Tim started his dental company. He met Maryann Fullerton at a Catholic singles dance. An AP account would later note that their 1993 wedding took place at the Nativity Catholic Church, where she "sang solo in the choir and taught school."

Maryann loved Tim's children so much that during the ceremony she read vows pledging her devotion to them.

The kids loved her too.

But the Boczkowskis' second chance at a two-parent nuclear family abruptly ended when Maryann, 35, died on November 7, 1994.

Tim, then 39, said that Maryann drowned in a hot tub after she consumed more than a dozen beers. Her alcohol level was 0.22 percent, twice the legal limit.

Todd told *Forensic Files* that her death was "probably the worst feeling in the world."

The police in North Carolina had some feelings of their own—namely, suspicion. They noticed scratch marks on Tim and bruising on Maryann's neck as well as dozens of smaller marks on her torso. Prosecutors made a case that she died by strangulation; she and Tim both had injuries suggesting that she had fought back.

Now, investigators looked further back and pressed for the full story on Elaine's death in 1990.

Tim had said he heard a thud in the bathroom and forced open the door only to find Elaine, 34, unconscious in the bathtub, on her back. He lifted her out and tried to revive her, he claimed. Elaine died of drowning anyway.

But responders found the tub and the bathroom floor dry. And she didn't have water in her lungs.

At the time, police officer Brenda Vance, who was about the same size as Elaine, did some tests at home in her own tub. She found it impossible to submerge her head under the same circumstances that Boczkowski described.

And Elaine had no alcohol in her system despite Tim's assertion that she had been drinking.

Tim was charged with murder in two states. A North Carolina jury convicted him of Elaine's death in his first trial.

In Pittsburgh, there was some drama to the proceedings. At a hearing, Maryann's supporters wore buttons with her picture, and Tim's lawyer later complained that one of them tried to take a swing at the handcuffed Tim, the *Pittsburgh Post-Gazette* reported on September 26, 1995.

The Pennsylvania jury didn't feel terribly sympathetic toward Tim and found him guilty.

At the sentencing for Maryann's murder, the kids asked the court to spare their dad's life, but he got a death sentence anyway. (Judge Donna Jo McDaniel later reduced it to life.)

Despite reports that Elaine Pegher Boczkowski and Maryann Fullerton Boczkowski were preparing to divorce Tim shortly before they died—and he had six-figure life insurance policies on each one—the children were all saying that they believed the deaths were accidental when the *Forensic Files* episode about the case came out in 2003.

SO WHAT EXACTLY HAPPENED TO THE KIDS AFTER TIM BOCZKOWSKI TRADED HIS DOCKERS FOR PRISON SCRUBS?

Although they were shuffled around a lot, the Boczkowskis managed to stay together. They first lived with their aunt and then their grandparents, but for whatever reason they couldn't care for them permanently.

The kids landed in a happy foster home; however, it was overcrowded, and its location made it impossible for all of them to continue school in the North Hills School District of Allegheny County, Pennsylvania.

In 1996, the AP reported that the Boczkowski kids were searching for a new foster home where they could stay together and in the same school district.

Here's the best part of the story: 100 people applied to adopt them.

County authorities narrowed down the list to 20. The kids, who were ages 12 to 15 by then, decided on a couple whose own children had grown up and moved out, according to an AP story from January 17, 1997.

But they hadn't forgotten about their original dad. According to another AP account: "They write him and are allowed one phone call a year. They've mailed him photos and sent him tins of cookies for Christmas."

In the meantime, the new foster family must have done a good job.

The kids participated in sports in school, finished college, and went on to have successful careers.

And the youngest Boczkowski, Todd, trained with the Civil Air Patrol when he was 16. He joined the U.S. Air Force and became a military police officer. In 2006, a *Virginia Daily Press* story mentioned Todd after he came to the aid of a child at the scene of a shooting in Hampton.

After his military service, Todd worked in online marketing for several years before he and a business partner established their own digital consulting firm in Pittsburgh.

But at some point during his teen years and his dive into entrepreneurship, Todd began to feel his bond with Tim loosening. Traveling 90 minutes to visit him in maximum security grew taxing.

"I distinctly remember going through high school when all my friends were out doing fun things—they didn't have to jump through hoops to see their parents," Todd told me during an interview. "I started to see how the relationship changed."

Like the legal system that convicted his father, Todd began to doubt the likelihood of an individual having two spouses accidentally drown in tubs. "Maryann's autopsy showed signs of strangulation," Todd says. "It's hard to argue with that."

Todd also uncovered some oddball plans Tim was brewing up shortly before Elaine's death in 1990. "He had written to a congressman to ask about opening a business in Kuwait," Todd recalls. "As the father of three kids going through a divorce, why a move to Kuwait? He probably figured it would be a great way to make a lot of money to go to a country where they don't have a lot of dental treatment. I have a good sense of how my father thinks and operates."

As of 2021, Todd was working on *My Two Angels*, a book about both the mothers he lost. "I'm sharing my story and talking about it in the way that I want to share," Todd says. "It's taken a long time for me to do that. It's something that has gnawed at me over the years."

Meanwhile, his father, Tim Boczkowski, lives in the maximum-security State Correctional Institution at Greene in Waynesburg, Pennsylvania.

As for his older sister and brother, Todd tells me they have soured on the press and have zero interest in speaking to the media today—but they respect any differences of opinion among one another and the three of them are still close.

CHAPTER 37
Ron Gillette

An Air Force Man Who Didn't Exactly Aim High

Q&A WITH DEFENSE LAWYER MARK F. RENNER
Forensic Files *episode "Strong Impressions"*

To those tasked with repairing aerospace equipment at George Air Force Base, Ron Gillette was a competent, accommodating supervisor.

Ron was friendly and open. He let on that he was having problems at home.

"He had a girlfriend and wanted a divorce, but his wife didn't," said Barbara, who worked for Ron at the Victorville, California, hangar (and spoke to me on the condition that her last name not be used). "I was having marital problems, too, and we talked a lot. He said, 'Maybe I should just kill her' a few times, but I thought he was joking."

On August 28, 1984, he left early for lunch, telling his coworkers he "had to take care of something," and then returned at the normal time. "He was his regular self, didn't show any nervousness," according to Barbara.

Little did his colleagues know that Ron was in all likelihood preparing to stage the scene of Juana "Vicki" Gillette's death that very night.

Ron first tried to kill her with sleeping pills dissolved in an alcoholic drink. When that failed, he suffocated her by pressing her face onto a plastic bag.

To make it look as though Vicki, just 26, died when she accidentally rolled onto a laundry bag in her sleep in her sedated state, he put some clothing in the bag and placed his sleeping three-year-old son in bed with her body.

At first, the authorities bought his story that is was an accident. The coroner found more than 11 doses of sleeping pills in her blood—Ron later admitted to putting the medication in Vicki's beverage but claimed he only used four pills and that she had asked him to do so—but not enough to make it a fatal dose.

A coroner ruled her cause of death as undetermined but not suspicious.

Ron's colleagues never suspected anything. "Everyone from the shop went to the funeral," Barbara recalls.

Meanwhile, however, a neighbor told investigators something intriguing. On the day Vicki died, he saw Ron sitting outside looking untroubled, but as soon as an ambulance showed up, he started crying.

Next up, a car rental employee tipped off police that when Ron had returned a rented vehicle, it was decorated for a wedding. When questioned about the hasty marriage, just 11 days after Vicki died, Ron said that his children needed a mother.

In another sign that Ron was no husband of the year, after an exam revealed that Vicki's kneecaps had been severed, Ron admitted it happened when he knocked Vicki to the floor because she dropped some pretzels.

Police also found out that shortly before his wife died, Ron had started calling his girlfriend from the Gillettes' home phone. Vicki was the one who handled the finances in the household, so he must have known she would be dead by the time the bill arrived.

The circumstantial evidence got a partner in the forensics, when tests on the bag found in bed with Vicki suggested someone had intentionally pressed her face into it.

Investigators eventually built a solid case that Ron had killed Vicki to get his hands on her $27,000 life insurance payout. He used it to finance a wedding to his Nicaraguan girlfriend 11 days after Vicki's death—he'd sent out the invitations while she was still alive. A jury convicted Ron of first-degree murder, and he received a sentence of life in prison without parole, according to *Forensic Files*.

I imagine that anyone who's seen the *Forensic Files* episode "Strong Impressions" would be happy to let loose all manner of name-calling and cursing to Hades in the general direction of the former air force mechanic, who is now a free man.

But we already know Ron Gillette's actions were awful. To offer insight into some of the related issues—like how an individual convicted of murder managed to exit prison for good behavior after just 15 years—I turned to Mark F. Renner, who was tasked with defending the ex-military man in 1985. A former Judge Advocate General attorney who left the military and became a magistrate of Marion Superior Court in Indianapolis, Renner agreed to answer a few questions:

Rebecca Reisner: Were you surprised Gillette got out of prison so soon?

Mark Renner: Yes. I got a Christmas card from him and the return address wasn't Leavenworth, and that's how I found out. I thought he would have to serve at least another five years before being considered for parole.

RR: How did this happen? The show [*Forensic Files*] said he got life in prison without the possibility of parole?

MR: When he was sentenced, it was simply life, not life without parole. Then the Uniform Code of Military Justice—the bible of discipline for all military branches, not just the air force—changed some of the rules, which ultimately applied positively to Ron's case.

RR: As one of his defense lawyers, did you really believe he was innocent?

MR: I never thought he was innocent. No lawyer approaches a defense having to believe someone's innocent. What you're doing is compelling the government to establish its case beyond a reasonable doubt. The death penalty was on the table, so our real focus was defending him from that.

RR: What about the brutal assault that injured Vicki Gillette's legs? At least one web commenter felt he deserved 15 years for that crime alone.

MR: He was never charged with anything in respect to the battery. He was charged with murder and faced a possible death penalty.

RR: Did it surprise you when Gillette married another woman 11 days after Vicki Gillette died?

MR: Yes, and it's unlikely the government would have ever investigated the case as a murder if he had not remarried and brought his new wife back to George Air Force Base. The original cause of death was linked to possible alcohol and accidental drug intake. At first, they had not determined the suffocation and homicide.

RR: I'm a big fan of *Forensic Files*. Did working on the episode about Vicki Gillette's murder leave you with a favorable impression of the way *Forensic Files* creates its stories?

MR: I found the part I had very appropriate, and I thought their efforts to be thorough were great. They wanted facts and information, and I appreciated that they didn't try to dramatize or minimize anything.

CHAPTER 38

Thomas Druce

Pennsylvania's Not Proud

WORLDS COLLIDE, TRAGEDY ENSUES
Forensic Files *episode "Capitol Crimes"*

Thomas Druce panicked and made a bad decision that ultimately meant trading his job as a Pennsylvania lawmaker for a 42-cent-an-hour gig on the grounds crew of Laurel Highlands State Prison.

On his way home, Druce, who for four terms represented the 44th District in Central Bucks County—and enjoyed a $57,367 annual base salary, per diem expenses, and a government-paid car—struck a pedestrian and then sped off without reporting the accident.

The deadly meeting of two men worlds apart in socioeconomic status (both of whom drank inadvisably) was a real-life *Bonfire of the Vanities*. But what really makes "Capitol Crimes" compelling is the way it unfolded predictably, confirming what viewers would pretty much suspect all along. We can all relate to the way desperation dissolves morality—and wonder how far we'd go to escape responsibility for a mistake.

So what really happened that night, and where are the cast of characters today? Let's get going on the recap of the episode, along with additional information from internet research and an interview with a journalist who covered the case from its beginning.

The story starts on July 27, 1999, when Thomas Druce, a 38-year-old member of the Pennsylvania House of Representatives, was driving home after having drinks with coworkers in Harrisburg, the state capital.

Druce hit and mortally wounded pedestrian Kenneth Cains, a former Marine who worked as a day laborer. Cains, 42, was a Vietnam veteran with a severe drinking problem. He lived in a rooming house in a dodgy section of Harrisburg and had no spouse or children.

Investigators determined that Cains had a blood-alcohol level of 0.17 percent, twice what's considered impaired, which possibly contributed to his stepping into traffic on Cameron Street.

Whether or not Cains was walking in a careless fashion didn't matter once Druce fled the scene without checking on the injured man or calling 911. The politician instantly turned himself into a criminal.

Another driver witnessed the accident and summoned the authorities. He had seen the brake lights go on right before the vehicle zipped away but couldn't determine its make or model.

Paramedics pronounced Kenneth Cains dead at the scene.

By taping together fragments left on the road, police officer Raymond Lyda uncovered a Chrysler logo and concluded that the car was a 1996 or 1997 Jeep Cherokee.

The leads stopped there until the police received an anonymous Christmas card a few months later. It suggested they investigate Rep. Thomas Druce because he had taken in his state-provided black Jeep Cherokee for repairs and traded in the vehicle shortly after Kenneth Cains's killing.

"Very quickly, every news organization in the state was chasing this story," recalls Glen Justice, one of the three reporters who covered the case out of the Harrisburg bureau of the *Philadelphia Inquirer*. "Druce was an up-and-comer. People had whispered his name as a prospective governor."

The story speedily unspooled once investigators had his name. He told them what just about any criminal trying to cover up a deadly hit and run would—that he didn't stop because he thought he struck an object (a traffic barrel), not a person.

He also lied by asserting the accident took place on the Pennsylvania Turnpike.

Then, he explained, he got the cracked windshield fixed and traded in the car because he wanted a vehicle with lower mileage.

Druce claimed that a stop he made at the state capitol building happened before the accident and that he did so to pick up some files.

Once investigators obtained the identification of the Jeep, they traced it to an unsuspecting consumer who had purchased it from a car dealership.

Despite the repairs and many washings, the car held a cache of evidence. Glass lodged in Cains's elbow and paint on his clothing matched those of the Jeep. Investigators recovered a hair in the seam of the side-view mirror and determined it had come from Cains's arm.

The police suspected Druce stopped at the capitol building to assess the damage. The video camera at his entry gate that night had mysteriously stopped working, and the "capitol cop"—the complex has its own police force—who witnessed the car enter the parking lot retired shortly after the incident.

Investigators discovered that, on his insurance claim, Druce had said he hit a sign, not a traffic barrel.

On March 16, 2000, Druce was arrested and charged with homicide by vehicle, a third-degree felony with a mandatory minimum of three years, in addition to lesser charges such as tampering with evidence and insurance fraud.

"Druce, in a wrinkled blue suit, chewed gum and appeared nervous at his arraignment, where he also was charged with leaving the scene of an accident—which carries a mandatory jail sentence," the *Inquirer* reported. "The eyes of Druce's wife, Amy, filled with tears as District Justice Joseph S. Solomon rejected the 38-year-old lawmaker's attempt to pay 10 percent of his $20,000 bail with a personal check."

Glen Justice, who spent some time with Druce amid the scandal, told me that he didn't seem like an evil person or even a bad one. "But I did get the impression he didn't quite understand the weight of what he'd done," Justice said.

Maybe Druce felt protected. He had the top Pennsylvania government official in his corner. "This story is a tragedy," then-governor Tom Ridge said. "I have known Tom Druce to be a man of honor, integrity, kindness, and compassion. Like others who know him, I have been shocked by this news, and I have hoped that it is untrue."

In September 2000, Druce got the homicide charge set aside and pleaded guilty to leaving the scene of an accident, evidence tampering, and insurance fraud. While Druce awaited sentencing, his family and friends paid $600,000 to bail him out of jail.

Along with a tongue-lashing about how Druce "lacked character" and "betrayed the public trust," Judge Joseph H. Kleinfelter handed him a two-to four-year sentence in 2000. Druce resigned from office and paid a civil fine of $100,000 to Cains's brother and two sisters.

Delores Williams, one of Cains's sisters, said Kenneth was a beloved uncle to her daughters.

Once sentenced, Druce filed various motions that delayed his imprisonment for four years, during which time he went "on vacation at the Jersey Shore, visited New York and Washington, attended parties and sporting events, and traveled to Harrisburg, where he worked as a political consultant," a *Philadelphia Inquirer* editorial noted.

Druce finally went to jail in 2004. (His attorneys argued unsuccessfully that the time Druce spent with an electronic monitoring device on his ankle and an evening curfew should be subtracted from his jail sentence.)

Kenneth Cains's brother felt some relief, according to a 2004 *Pocono Record* story:

> *Louis Cains Jr. has criticized the courts for giving Druce what he viewed as special treatment during his drawn-out appeal but said at a news conference Thursday that he was satisfied with the outcome. "I knew in my heart he was going to have to do that time,'" the 51-year-old manufacturing worker said.*

Louis and his sisters also got to hear Druce come close to admitting to what he'd done. "Although the state police ruled the accident was 'unavoidable' since Mr. Cains stepped onto the roadway and into the path of my car," Druce said, "I have no excuse for not stopping near the scene and reporting the accident to the police."

Indeed, calling 911 after the accident and giving an honest account might have gotten Druce off with a DUI plea—or nothing if his blood-alcohol level tested below 0.10 percent, Pennsylvania's generous legal limit before Act 24 in 2003.

Druce "might well have fled the scene of his innocence," as then-columnist Dennis Roddy put it in a *Pittsburgh Post-Gazette* piece.

More important, reporting the accident would have spared Kenneth Cains's family the anguish of knowing the driver of the car that killed their brother didn't care enough to stop.

Druce was paroled on March 13, 2006, after serving two years of his sentence. He exited Pennsylvania's Laurel Highlands prison.

His wife, Amy Schreiber-Druce, a former ballet teacher, had already filed for divorce and found a job working for a political caucus, according to a *Philadelphia Inquirer* story, which also noted that the house in Chalfont that the couple and their three sons had shared still belonged to the family at the time of his release. Hence, it's unlikely Schreiber-Druce ended up moving into the boarding house room vacated by Kenneth Cains when her husband went to prison.

"It's a tragedy all the way around," Druce's mentor, former Bucks County commissioner Andrew Warren, was quoted as saying in a *Morning Call* story. "And now it's probably best everyone start anew."

So what did ever happen to Druce's career? Well, it might have stalled but it didn't flat-line.

Druce actually had already begun something of a new chapter even before he reported to jail in 2004, according to his LinkedIn profile. He launched PoliticsPA.com in 2001.

Although he's no longer associated with the website, PoliticsPA.com still exists, under new ownership, as a "one-stop shop for political junkies in every part of the state" and has attracted ads from the likes of Uber and the University of Pennsylvania.

He also founded a public-policy consulting business, Phoenix Strategy Group, worked in business development for Grace Electronics, and, since January 2020, has held a position as a quality assurance manager at Vision Manufacturing Technologies, his LinkedIn page says.

Meanwhile, there was more heartbreak for the Cains family. Louis died at the age of just 60 in 2013. His obituary mentioned that, in addition to Kenneth, two other siblings predeceased him.

CHAPTER 39

Tina Biggar

Escort and Scholar

CON MAN KEN TRANCHIDA MURDERS A COLLEGE STUDENT
Forensic Files *episode "Deadly Knowledge"*
Tina Biggar turned an academic research project about prostitution into a personal foray into sex work.

The Michigan college student quietly went to work for escort services and made a tidy sum to use toward the costs of school and housing. Sadly, one of her clients, a sleazy little ex-con named Ken Tranchida, murdered her after the two argued about a car loan.

Ken, who would ultimately give the court quite an original excuse for ending Tina's life, pleaded guilty just weeks after the 1995 murder.

But the *Forensic Files* episode about the case leaves some questions not completely answered.

Why did someone like Tina take a chance on a wild card like prostitution? She was studious and came from a stable home with a caring father. She had a nice boyfriend and close girlfriends.

And she already made good tips serving up the likes of James Beard New England clam chowder and 22-ounce rib eyes at a local restaurant.

Plus, once she took on high-paying escort work, why did Tina still need to borrow cash for a car? And how did the slimy Ken charm the intelligent Tina into believing he could be her personal hero?

Finally, what was the Biggars' reaction when they found out that the tragedy of losing their daughter came wrapped in a salacious secret?

For this chapter, I looked for some answers and checked on Ken's incarceration status. So let's get going on the recap of "Deadly Knowledge," along with extra information drawn from internet research.

Tina Suzanne Biggar was born in South Dakota on December 31, 1971, the daughter of a Coast Guard commander and a registered nurse.

The Biggars moved around a lot, to Florida, Alaska, and Michigan. They educated their kids at Catholic schools and participated in church activities and community goings-on.

Friends would later describe Tina as a hard worker who was friendly and fun to be with.

Tina started college at South Dakota State University, then transferred to Oakland University in Rochester, Michigan, to be closer to Traverse City, Michigan, where her father was stationed.

By summer 1995, the psychology major was getting ready to start her senior year in college and had plans to attend graduate school.

Forensic Files didn't bring it up, but before Tina began her independent study about sex work, she was one of eight Oakland students who worked on a larger project funded by the Centers for Disease Control and Prevention (CDC) to educate prostitutes about HIV and AIDS, then follow up to gauge their retention.

Tina interviewed prostitutes both on the streets and in jail. A friend told the *Oakland Post* that Tina "put her all in this study."

Her own separate project, "A Survey of Sexual History and Health Practices among Women Employed as Escorts," involved higher-priced prostitutes, the ones who don't work on street corners. Tina reportedly sought financing for the project, but the university declined.

While doing research, Tina lived in an apartment in Farmington with her boyfriend, Todd Nurnberger, who attended the University of Michigan and worked as a chemical engineer.

On August 23, 1995, Todd returned home to find Tina gone even though the two had plans together that night. "Since we'd lived together, that never happened," Todd would later testify. He called the Rochester Chop House and found out that Tina had quit her waitress job four months ago. She'd been play-acting by ironing her uniform at home.

By September 13, 1995, Tina was still missing. Her parents offered a $5,000 reward for help.

Back at Tina's apartment, boyfriend Todd had discovered a full-on "my girlfriend's moonlighting as a call girl" bag. The red duffle contained thigh-highs, KY Jelly, condoms, and correspondence with the LA Dreams escort service.

LA Dreams didn't know anything about a Tina Biggar, but the service did have a popular escort named Crystal who matched her description—five feet seven with blonde hair and perfect white teeth.

Narrator Peter Thomas gently explains what an escort service is, and, because even a tasteful show like *Forensic Files* can't resist the myth that prostitution is sexy, the episode features visuals of women wriggling out of front-zipped miniskirts while anonymous customers watch.

It turned out that Tina also worked for two other escort services, Elite Desires and Calendar Girls, and had dozens of clients. She'd been in the biz for about a year. According to the *City Confidential* episode "Detroit: A Coed's Secret," she sometimes freelanced by cutting out the agencies.

So what kind of wages did Tina snag as an escort?

LA Dreams charged its clients around $250 of which Tina got $150, according to author Fannie Weinstein, who appeared on *Forensic Files*. Max Haines, a columnist for the *Times Colonist*, reported that Tina netted just $100 per date but sometimes did three a night.

Phone records revealed she'd talked frequently to a 42-year-old named Ken Tranchida. He would later say that he met Tina by chance at a restaurant and she gave him the number of her escort service.

Ken, born in Detroit in 1953 and brought up in Southfield, Michigan, was a drifter and con man who held a series of menial jobs. He'd served time for passing bad checks, embezzlement, and breaking and entering. After a gig working the front desk at an E-Z Rest Hotel, Ken helped himself to its cash and fled, the *Detroit Free Press* reported. In 1987, he received a sentence for escaping from prison, according to the Michigan Department of Corrections.

Among Tina's belongings, investigators found a love letter with a poem from Ken.

Ken told police he last saw Tina when he dropped her off at the airport. She had a business trip to Ohio planned and left her car at his place. Oh, and Tina liked him so much that she had started dating him free of charge, he said.

As for the car loan that played a role in the story, a Honda dealership told investigators that Ken and Tina together signed a contract for a $15,000 car. She put up her share of the money, $5,000, but Ken failed to produce his $10,000. He said the remainder was coming via his "ex-mother-in-law who was flying in from England."

Neither she nor the money materialized. Tina and Ken had a loud argument at the car lot.

But lacking forensic evidence against Ken—a tracker dog that searched the woods around his house came up with nothing—police released him.

Meanwhile, Tina Biggar's father, Bill, launched into action in hopes of finding his daughter alive.

He put together a team of amateur sleuths consisting of escort-service co-owners identified as Donna and Debbie, tow-truck driver Jerry Holbert (who was friends with Ken but sympathetic to the Biggars), and Todd. They stayed close to Ken Tranchida in an effort to get information.

When Ken landed in jail for skipping meetings with his parole officer, Bill and company paid $250 to bail him out. They shadowed Ken while he was staying at the Pink Flamingo Trailer Park.

Bill even took Ken out to dinner at a local Ram's Horn. According to the *Detroit Free Press*, Ken offered various stories about Tina's whereabouts: She was at a Hilton Hotel in Dayton, or his friend knew where she was but he lost his number and would page him later.

But police soon made a grim discovery. During a second search of Tina's Honda Accord, they found a pool of her blood under the carpeting in the trunk—it's not clear how it had been missed on the first pass on the vehicle. It indicated too much bleeding for Tina to have survived.

On September 21, Southfield police located the badly decomposed body of Tina Biggar behind a house once owned by Ken's aunt.

Sadly, the Biggars first learned about the positive identification of Tina's body from a TV report.

The family buried Tina in a light blue and silver casket in Elkton, South Dakota. About 100 students attended a service for Tina at Oakland University and raised $500 for the Biggars.

Meanwhile, Ken Tranchida went on the lam. When investigators tracked him down in a rundown Detroit neighborhood, he made a pretense of committing suicide by slitting his wrists and drinking chemicals.

His arrest came as a relief to law enforcement, but Tina's grieving mother, Connie, told the media it brought her no comfort.

Ken, who said he was in love with Tina, broke down and told police that Tina died accidentally when she fell and hit her head during a scuffle in his rented room. After placing her on the bed, he blacked out and couldn't remember what happened next, he said.

But a forensic examination didn't find a fatal head injury, so Ken came up with a revision to his story: He purposely mercy-killed Tina because she was unhappy and worried about financial problems. Ken also said he would "switch places with Tina in a heartbeat."

Prosecutors alleged that Ken beat and strangled Tina to death on his bed and then hid the bloody mattress in the attic. (He had told his landlady that he got rid of the mattress because he threw up on it.) Ken put Tina in the trunk of her car, dumped her body in the woods, and drove the vehicle back to his place.

Ken ended up pleading guilty to second-degree murder in a deal that the Biggars agreed to in order to avoid publicity. Judge Rudy Nichols handed Ken Tranchida two life sentences, one for homicide, the other for habitually offending.

The family felt the court handled the case well but had no warm words for the media. Bill Biggar said journalists profit by others' pain. "Put your name in the headlines," he said to reporters. "Put your daughter's and son's names in the headlines. The sustaining hurt is right here."

Getting back to the question of why Tina needed money so badly, some insight surfaced. First off, although Oakland is a public school, it's expensive. Today, tuition costs as much as $27,000 a year.

Second, Tina needed to replace her old Honda Accord—it would have required a huge cash outlay to fix it after a recent accident—and her credit cards were maxed out, said Fannie Weinstein, who cowrote the mass market paperback *The Coed Call Girl Murder*. According to the *Already Gone Podcast*, Tina's 25-mile commute to school also strained her budget.

Third, Tina and Todd enjoyed wining and dining themselves at nice restaurants, and the apartment the two shared in Farmington was in a high-rent, gated community. *Forensic Files* asserts that Tina was thinking about leaving Todd and getting her own place, another big expense.

And fourth, Tina was the oldest of six kids and probably wanted to minimize any financial burden she put upon her parents.

But why did she choose work as a call girl? As part of the CDC study, she no doubt heard harrowing tales from drug-addicted prostitutes working for abusive pimps on the streets. Perhaps employment for an escort service looked like a safer, easier way to earn better money.

Tina was probably just young enough to believe at least a little bit in fairy tales, and maybe Ken was the closest thing to a Prince Charming/ Richard Gere she could find among the escort-patronizing population. Ken could make a good impression when it suited him. Former employers described him as well liked and conscientious. Although he was working as a laborer at the Classic Touch Auto Wash when he met Tina, it's a good bet that he told her he owned the place and had a string of other businesses as well.

As far as how the Biggars reacted to revelations about Tina's work, at first Bill denied it. He said that "people of good heart can see through much of what's printed" and that "escorts make more money than she had," according to accounts from the Associated Press (AP) and *Detroit Free Press*. Likewise, coworkers from the Rochester Chop House believed that Tina worked for the service for research only, the *Detroit Free Press* reported.

Once it looked certain that Tina had indeed been a call girl, Bill said he loved his daughter regardless.

When some women from the escort service attended a funeral for Tina in Traverse City, the Biggars offered them a place to stay and gave them homemade food, the *Detroit Free Press* reported.

According to an AP account, the funeral eulogy delivered at Christ the King Catholic Church was also kindhearted. "Rev. Edwin A. Thome noted that Jesus had spent time with prostitutes and sinners. 'And he, too, suffered the consequences,' the minister said. 'The self-righteous did not understand. Eventually, they put him to death. Tina had that spirit of adventure, which took her into uncharted waters. And she died for something she believed in.'"

The client who ended Tina's sabbatical into sex work was placed in the Muskegon Correctional Facility. Although one media source reported Ken wouldn't be eligible for parole until 2030, sure enough, news broke in 2021 that the Michigan Parole Board had scheduled a public hearing to decide whether he deserved early release.

Under questioning from Assistant Attorney General Alicia Lane and Michigan Parole Board member Jerome Warfield on May 18, Tranchida acknowledged that Tina had found out that he lied about having money and connections.

"I was mad 'cause I got discovered," he said, according to the *Detroit News*, which described him as having shoulder-length gray hair and wearing a dark-blue uniform. "I was not who I said I was."

That part sounded credible enough, but even for the purpose of a one-day hearing, Ken couldn't get his story straight about Tina's death. He tried the accidental injury ploy again—she hit her head on a safe—but also testified, "I smothered her with my hand. I put my hand over her face. She couldn't breathe."

His reason? He didn't want her to leave his room or his life.

He also contended that he had a sad life history during which he'd been raped twice. And no one ever told him that he was adopted; he discovered that fact only by accident as an adult.

The 10-member board didn't find his narrative compelling in the way he hoped. He was denied parole.

He remains in prison today—and, in all likelihood, the rest of his life—and any more of his lamenting, conning, or thieving will play out behind razor wire.

CHAPTER 40

Tracey Frame's Murder of David Nixon

A CHARISMATIC REAL ESTATE AGENT MEETS HIS END
Forensic Files *episode "Separation Anxiety"*

When it came to brokering deals on houses, David Nixon had great instincts. He "could sell a screen door to a submarine," according to one friend.

In the 1990s, the personable six-foot, four-inch Texan's name dotted the *Fort Worth Star-Telegram*'s real estate ads, where he advertised homes with "commercial grade appliances" and "pool & cabana."

By the millennium, he was collecting commissions on million-dollar spreads.

But he didn't always make the right decisions when managing his money or his personal relationships, and it ultimately cost him his life at age 40.

For this chapter, I looked for additional information on the case and whether Tracey Frame—the younger woman who cut down David Nixon in the early years of his midlife crisis—is still in prison. So let's get going on the recap for "Separation Anxiety," the 2010 episode of *Forensic Files*, along with extra information drawn from internet research and an interview with prosecuting attorney Sean Colston.

In 1990, David Nixon married Donna Lella, and they had a son the following year.

They enjoyed a happy union until David began an affair with a big-haired flight attendant referred to as Lisa Hill on TV and Lisa Hemby in court papers.

After divorcing Donna, he married Lisa. That relationship lasted for just a couple of years, and things had turned so stormy toward the end that David obtained a temporary protective order against Lisa.

Soon after, he met Tracey Frame at a party. A number of sources give her occupation as accountant, but she was really a bookkeeper who had taken some accounting classes and liked to tell people she was a certified professional accountant, according to Detective Larry Hallmark's interview on the "Tracey Frame" episode of *Snapped*.

Whatever the case, David found her crystal-green eyes and confident personality irresistible, and they settled into a house on Pecan Hollow Court in Grapevine, Texas, an upscale lakeside community known for socializing, boating, and general high living.

Tracey and David were a popular, fun-loving couple, but they began arguing about money a lot, according to acquaintances.

Even though he bought Tracey a Lexus and took her on ocean cruises, she reportedly resented the child support he paid Donna for their son, Nicholas.

The finances behind Tracey and David's shared home aren't completely clear, but one report said that she had contributed about $80,000 of her own money toward the four-bedroom, three-bathroom abode and he paid for the rest. (Not sure of the purchase price in 2002, but the house is worth $488,000 as of this writing, according to Zillow.)

At the same time, the Internal Revenue Service was nipping at David's heels for around $100,000. As all true-crime followers know, things tend to go badly for folks who refuse to suck it up and find a legal way to pay off their taxes.

In David Nixon's case, he attempted to shield his house by putting it in Tracey's name. On April 9, 2002, he called 911 for help after he came home to find she had changed the locks. "Basically, it's my house," he told the operator. "I was dumb enough to put it in my girlfriend's name."

Tracey eventually allowed him in the house that night, and the visit from the police ended in no arrests.

Little did David Nixon know that Tracey had far more insidious plans to ensure she could stay ensconced at the 2,647-square-foot residence. On April 20, 2002, Donna Lella called police after David skipped a dinner date with Nicholas, then age 10, and didn't answer his phone.

No one remembered seeing David Nixon after April 18, 2002, when he showed a property in Southlake to a prospective buyer, according to the *Fort Worth Star-Telegram*.

Four days later, a motorist alerted emergency services of a fire in the parking lot of an abandoned building in Grand Prairie, Texas. Police found a burning body wrapped in a blue camping tarp and a blanket with fibers characteristic of electric blankets; gasoline had been used as an accelerant.

It looked as though someone tried to stuff the body into a drainpipe at the scene, failed, and then left him there to burn beyond recognition.

An investigator would later tell *48 Hours Mystery*'s "Secrets and Lies on Grapevine Lake" that the blaze consumed the body to such a degree that he couldn't tell whether it was male or female. Dental records identified the remains as those of David Nixon.

In the investigation, early leads centered on second wife Lisa as well as Donna—whose son would be receiving David's $500,000 insurance payout—but it was Tracey Frame whom police would arrest just a few days after the body turned up.

"Once everybody heard that David was missing, I don't think there was a soul who didn't say, 'Tracey did something,'" his friend Karl Ekonomy later told *Snapped*.

Donna Lella told *48 Hours Mystery* that David had a premonition Tracey would kill him.

Investigators would ultimately conclude that Tracey—who got out of jail thanks to $100,000 in bail and an electric ankle monitor—shot David in his sleep, then wrapped him in the electric blanket and tarp. In the house, police had found electric blanket controls without the blanket.

She used a hand truck to move his body—he weighed nearly 100 pounds more than she did—into a rented Penske moving vehicle, and she abandoned his white Lexus in a Tom Thumb supermarket parking lot, investigators alleged. The driver's seat had been moved forward, as though someone shorter than six feet four had driven it; Tracey is five feet seven.

Employees from H&H Janitorial Supply told police that a woman matching Tracey's description came into their store to buy cleansers and asked how to get blood out of her carpet. They suggested trying muriatic acid.

Next, investigators found video footage of a woman who looked like Tracey buying muriatic acid at the Tom Thumb supermarket. She used her customer loyalty card when she paid. (*Forensic Files*, *Snapped*, and *48 Hours Mystery* all made a big deal of how cheap Tracey was to risk getting caught to save less than 50 cents on her purchase, but to be fair, getting out your plastic discount card is pretty much an automatic reflex these days.)

Additional security footage caught Tracey parking David's Lexus in the lot and also leaving the Penske truck there, presumably because it would have raised suspicions to have it parked in front of her house for a long period of time.

An unregistered small-caliber gun that David kept in the house was missing, and Tracey had recently bought (yikes) a new mattress.

Plus, she seemed to know, before anyone told her, that David's body suffered trauma. When authorities informed Tracey about the murder, her first words were, "How did they identify him?" according to trial reporting from the *Fort Worth Star-Telegram*.

It also came out that Tracey had given varying explanations for David's disappearance. She informed Donna Lella that he had gone on vacation but told an investigator that he had moved and was working out of state. When Gary Yarbrough, the managing director of David's real estate office, asked about his whereabouts, Tracey said she had no idea.

Despite the factors pointing to Tracey, the case had its challenges. "There were so many moving parts," prosecuting attorney Sean Colston told me in an interview. "Of all the cases I've handled, it probably had the highest number of witnesses. Fortunately, the detectives had done a great job of painting a clear picture."

The defense strenuously tried to muddy that portrait at the 2005 trial.

Tracey's lawyers claimed the woman in the security footage wasn't Tracey and that someone else had used her customer loyalty card. Her side also tried some typical smear-the-victim tactics, alleging that David was involved with prostitutes and had gambling debts that might have prompted someone to kill him.

Team Tracey contended that Jerry Vowell, a used car salesman who owed money to David, might have killed him to cancel the debt. (Vowell said on TV that he had repaid David.) Or maybe an anonymous robber killed David, who often walked around with large amounts of cash on his person, according to Tracey.

Tracey's new fiancé, a British dentist named Roland Taylor, maintained she was nothing like the intimidating shrew the prosecution portrayed. He would later tell *48 Hours Mystery* that Tracey had a strong motive to keep David alive because he owed her money. He also said Tracey was a sweet person who just wanted to "love and be loved."

"To me, Tracey was somewhat of a con artist," says Colston. "A lot of people consider her attractive and that kind of sucks people in."

Members of the jury didn't find her all that enchanting. In March 2005, it took them four hours to convict Tracey, then 35, of first-degree murder. She got 40 years and will be eligible for parole after 20 years.

She lost an appeal in 2006.

Today, Tracey Ann Frame resides at the medium-security Murray Unit in Gatesville, Texas. She has a shot at parole in September 2024.

If she ends up serving her full sentence, she'll get out of prison in September 2044 at age 74.

In the meantime, Tracey can rub elbows with hundreds of other women at Murray, which has a capacity of 1,341. The population includes Chante Mallard, a nursing assistant who made headlines in 2001 after she struck a homeless man with her Chevrolet Cavalier and left him lodged in the windshield inside her garage until he died of his injuries.

If she and Traccy ever bump into each other in the cafeteria line, they'll probably have a lot to talk about.

Q&A with *Forensic Files* Producer Paul Dowling

What You've Been Dying to Know about the Show

How did *Forensic Files* become the *I Love Lucy* of true-crime shows—with reruns on every day, everywhere from Montreal to Melbourne? The half-hour series has been compelling fans to procrastinate on their housework and homework and gym schedules for two decades.

Since starting my blog, I've used it to answer lingering questions about specific *Forensic Files* episodes. With this Q&A, I hope to solve some mysteries about the series as a whole.

Executive producer Paul Dowling, whose Medstar Television made all 400 episodes, allowed me to interrogate him:

Rebecca Reisner: *Forensic Files* is shown in 142 countries—why are overseas viewers so interested in U.S. crimes?

Paul Dowling: In many countries, cases aren't covered in the media the way they are here. Often the laws are different from American laws. In Great Britain, there is confidentiality until the case is decided. The crime files aren't open the way they can be in the U.S. Same thing in Canada—you don't learn about someone being arrested for rape or murder before the case is decided. And if he's exonerated, you never know about it. That can give people in other countries the wrong idea about the U.S. Brazil has a murder rate three times higher than ours. Everyone has guns except for innocent law-abiding people, and when bad guys come to the door, they can't defend themselves. And then they see American television and think the crime rate is much higher in the U.S. There was a rape and murder in Brazil in front of 12 people and no one testified. People in Brazil asked me whether I'm afraid to walk the streets in the U.S. I said no, I'm afraid here. When I was in Paris, I was told to dress like a bum [to prevent robbery].

RR: Some of the *Forensic Files* cases are so complicated. How do you pack the whole story into 30-minute episodes?

PD: We have 22 minutes. It's like a Broadway musical: Every line of that song has to move the story along. As you are creating the story, you don't think, "How will I write this?" You think, "How will I say this?" You can tell a lot with the pictures you use. If we show a girl holding a fish [that she caught], it says something about who she was. For every story we did, all 400, before the show aired, I sat down with three people and told them the story. It enabled me to see how the story worked. If their eyes glazed over, I knew the story was going too slowly. It's like campfire storytelling—if you want to keep boys and girls awake, you have to tell a good story.

RR: How is it contending with the pressure for Nielsen ratings?

PD: Imagine you're doing a Broadway musical, and at any moment, the audience can stay right in their same seats and have their choice of switching to 500 other musicals. That's TV. TV producers are not evaluated on the value of their show—or how many people watch it. They are evaluated on how many viewers watch the ads during breaks. You have to have a show that people are emotionally tied to so that they are afraid to get up.

RR: How do you keep viewers in their seats?

PD: When I started the show on TLC in 1996, they wanted us to use teasers. I said no: The show should provide the incentive for viewers to come back. Toward the end of *Jeopardy*, when they come back from the break, the host goes right into the Final Jeopardy question—there's no recap. People don't want to miss that question. Viewers of *Forensic Files* want to know who killed that guy. That's why you can't open the show with any hint of who did it. When we interviewed a killer on camera, we would go to the prison with our own [street] clothes for him to wear. That way, viewers don't know yet that he did it. We also use the passive tense in scripts, even though writers are taught not to in school. The passive tense lets you put information out there without saying who did it.

RR: Why do you interview the murder victims' mothers and fathers separately—even if they're still married?

PD: If you have two dogs in the house, there's always one dominant one. Likewise, sometimes people say things in front of you they wouldn't say in front of their spouse. There are interview tricks that work with one person but not two at the same time. People are often uncomfortable with silences, so sometimes they'll blurt out something they wouldn't [with a spouse present].

RR: A lot of true-crime series show victims' family members in tears. Why doesn't *Forensic Files*?

PD: Because it's manipulative. There are techniques TV producers use to make a person cry. And the viewer feels sorry for the person and gets mad at the TV show for subjecting that person to heartache. And oftentimes it's a year or more after the crime, so people are more composed. We give murder victims' families a cleaned-up version of the episode they're in.

RR: You mean a version without graphic footage of wounds, autopsies, etc.?

PD: Yes, we tell them that this is the version they'll want to watch and show their friends.

RR: You've tweeted about your dog Chloe who passed away at age 15. How was she involved in the show?

PD: She used to come in the editing room with us, next to the editor. I was working so hard that I wasn't home a lot, and my kids would come in with sleeping bags and pizza and the dog would eat pizza behind our backs. Chloe was here when we did reenactments with German shepherd–style attack dogs. She started running in circles and getting bent out of shape.

RR: So you used real dogs and cats in the reenactments?

PD: Yes, and we had a trained squirrel and homing pigeons and a kangaroo once.

RR: What about reenactments of vehicular accidents—did you use stock footage?

PD: No. Every crash you see on *Forensic Files* is something we created. We did a show about boat crashes, and we bought boats. We use cars that are the same model and color [as those in the real accidents]. Some movies edit crashes and fast-forward to a stock shot of the outcome. *Forensic Files* shows crashes without an edit. With crashes, you can't have gasoline in the cars—you don't want explosions. So sometimes you have motorized pushers. But you have to be fair as far as the speeds used, so a defense attorney doesn't come back and say to you, "Hey, the real crash was 30 mph, but the show's was 70 mph."

RR: Doesn't all that make accident reenactments awfully expensive?

PD: Yes, but there was never a budget limit for re-creations. I never wanted anyone to be hurt in an accident re-creation and to have the director say afterward, "Well, I only had $50,000."

RR: Were there any episodes that chilled you to the bone, that you couldn't forget after you went home?

PD: Yes, if we hadn't done one particular episode, three people would be in prison for something they didn't do. It was for the Norfolk rape and killing of Michelle Moore-Bosko in 1997, and these three people didn't do it. Someone else confessed to the crime, and the prosecutor wouldn't act. Tim Kaine was governor of Virginia then, and he saw the episode ["Eight Men Out," 2001] and had the state police reinvestigate.

RR: I read that "Bad Blood"—the story of a woman raped by a doctor (John Schneeberger) while she was unconscious—was your favorite episode of *Forensic Files*. Why?

PD: If a forensic hall of fame existed, that victim would belong in it. The doctor's DNA didn't match the rapist's. The victim was sure the hospital was being paid off to throw the tests or something. So she broke into the doctor's things and got his ChapStick. She paid for a DNA test with her own money, and it matched the DNA from the rape. It turned out the doctor had implanted a plastic tube into his arm with somebody else's blood and was having that blood tested. The doctor's wife had been saying on TV that this woman was a slut. And then the wife's daughter from another marriage who lived with them told her mother that the stepdad [Schneeberger] had been drugging and raping her.

RR: After talking to various people who watch Forensic Files, I haven't really been able to identify a demographic pattern. Have you?

PD: One thing we know is that a lot of women watch the show for safety reasons—knowledge of safety they can pass along to their daughters.

RR: Can you share any safety tips?

PD: We don't get into victim shaming, but we do show things that the victims shouldn't have done regarding situational awareness. Some girls and women don't know that there are predators at bars and clubs casing them out. A predator will watch for things like two women walking in together late. He knows that later in the evening they will have parked farther away. So when they're ready to leave, if one stays and the other goes out to get the car and drive it around, the predator will follow her out to the car. I tell my daughter and her friends what the FBI says: When you go to your car, have your keys in your hand. If someone with a gun comes up and says to get in the car, throw your keys and purse in one direction and run in the other. The bad guy isn't expecting this, so he thinks, "I can get the money and car instead of going after her."

The Life and Times of *Forensic Files* Narrator Peter Thomas

The Voiceover Artist Who Left His Prints Everywhere

Peter Thomas's voice has lured me away from all kinds of good intentions: organizing tax documents, cleaning between the sofa cushions with the Dirt Devil crevice tool, going to bed early.

It's not easy to describe his voice, although I've listened to it for a minimum of 600 collective hours. Thomas was the narrator for *Forensic Files*, and he's part of the reason fans like me can't stop rewatching all 400 episodes of the true-crime series's 1996 to 2011 run.

I guess what's so inviting about his narration is that his assuring voice is devoid of affectation. He speaks smoothly, although not in an "absolutely free with your BeDazzler" manner. Like all voice artists, he has great diction. But his speech isn't so crisp as to make it alienating.

"Peter Thomas is the same guy who narrated school documentaries," says Paul Dowling, creator of *Forensic Files*. "He's not some sleazy guy from AM radio. He makes it okay to watch."

Indeed, something about Peter Thomas's narration enables me to see an episode about a college student who hacked his father to death with an ax—and sleep like a baby afterward.

Randy Thomas, a voiceover artist who narrates the Oscars and Tony Awards, also admires his work on *Forensic Files*.

"There are some voiceover actors who think they're doing a good job just because they pronounce the words correctly," she says. "Peter was different. He had an inquisitive nature about so much of life, and that transferred to whatever he narrated."

My own dream of interviewing Peter Thomas someday—and having that voice all to myself for a little while—expired when he passed away in 2016, but I had fun researching a bit about his life.

Thomas was born in Pensacola, Florida, in 1924, to two people who enjoyed speaking aloud and enunciating well: an English teacher and a minister.

"His father told him to paint pictures with words," says Randy Thomas (no relation, but the two were close friends).

Peter Thomas started acting in school plays as a child and, at age 13, picked up some voice work at a local radio station. A sponsor gave him flying lessons for free because he was too young to receive a real salary legally.

At 18, he took a detour, enlisting in the army and then fighting German gunfire in Normandy, France, in 1944. He earned a Purple Heart after suffering a shrapnel wound during the Battle of the Bulge.

After returning to the United States and marrying longtime girlfriend Stella Ford Barrineau, he worked at Memphis radio station WMC at night and went to college during the day.

His big break came when a Hamilton Watch Company executive heard Thomas's voice on a Florida poetry program and invited him to New York City for an audition. He won the gig, and soon nationwide audiences got to hear his voice say: "The passage of time is beyond our control, but it passes beautifully when Hamilton marks the hour."

A tidal wave of offers followed. CBS hired Thomas as the New York City anchor of *The Morning Show* with Jack Parr. Thomas narrated medical shows and educational documentaries and did commercials for Estée Lauder, Coca-Cola, American Express ("Don't leave home without it"), Visine, Listerine ("The taste you hate twice a day"), and Hewlett-Packard.

A 2004 Broadcast Pioneers documentary from Florida station METV recalled how—in the days long before TV assaulted viewers with Preparation H and Cialis commercials—Stella rebuked her husband for narrating a Vicks Mentholatum ad. She didn't appreciate having to watch ointment rubbed onto an actor's chest.

Plenty of more serious work came his way. He snagged narration gigs for the PBS series *Nova* as well as for the History Channel—the holy grail for voice performers.

His association with *Forensic Files* began when the 30-minute docu-series was still in development. "I fell asleep on the couch one night and there was a World War II documentary on," says Paul Dowling, "and I heard this voice, and he was carrying the whole thing. It was mesmerizing."

Thomas turned down Medstar Television's offer for the *Forensic Files* job at first because he was still earning a fortune from TV commercials and other one-offs. But after some persuading, he agreed.

His approach to the gig reaffirms one of my favorite truisms about life: No matter how talented the worker, there's no such thing as an easy job. Thomas would spend six hours rehearsing each script at home. Stella would give him feedback.

"*Forensic Files* is on somewhere in the world at any given time," says Randy Thomas. "There's always the consistency of Peter Thomas's voice behind the microphone, and he's become the show's brand."

He also occasionally contributed to the show editorially.

"If he didn't like something I wrote, he'd say, 'I don't want to offend you, but can I change this?'" recalls Dowling. "And I said, 'I can take all the help you can give.' We never told him to just shut up and do the script, which is how most producers treat talent, and I didn't find out until his funeral that we were the only ones who didn't treat him that way."

Thomas remained in demand for his work through age 90. He died at 91, but his voice lives on—and not just on recordings. His sons, Peter Jr. and Douglas, followed him into the profession.

ACKNOWLEDGMENTS

Thanks to Paul Dowling for making a captivating true-crime series way before the genre became trendy. And to the late Peter Thomas, whose voice still entices and soothes listeners and will for decades.

Next up, thanks to Jake Bonar at Prometheus Books for taking a chance on this project and making edit suggestions I agree with 95 percent of the time. And Priya Doraswamy at Lotus Lane Literary for cheerfully studying contractual documents that made me dizzy to read. And Richard Hofstetter at Frankfurt Kurnit for his help laying the legal foundation for this book.

Speaking of dizziness, thank you to my older brothers and sister, Bruce Reisner, Andy Reisner, and Susan Reisner, who were nice about it when I got car sick. And thanks also to newer family, Debbie Reisner, Paul Schneider, Aurora Schneider, Alyssa Reisner, Sophie Mendez, and David Reisner.

Old friends who have suffered me gladly—Terrie Piell, Sandy Pickup Thomas, Diane Galbo, and Miriam Sandgren. And Melissa Abernathy, who doesn't like true crime but reads my blog anyway.

The Tudor City crew—Gloria Kass, Elaine Furst, Vicky Kriete, Deborah Berk, and Susan Zelman.

Ex-colleagues Susan Demark, Larry O'Connor, Kirk Nicewonger, Tom Gilbert, Mike "Coach" Tully, and Paola Morrongiello.

Mark Graham at Decider.com, John Byrne at Poetsandquants.com, Patricia O'Connell, and Steve Petranek, who encouraged me to write more.

IT consultant Jovan Hernandez, who handled everything so well when my blog's name changed (it started out as Truecrimetruant.com).

Gary Lico for the opportunity to work on *Forensic Files: A Special Tribute*, the TV show that celebrated the 25th anniversary of the series.

Finally, many thanks to the people who read ForensicFilesNow.com and write in with insights and opinions and supportive messages—and assure me I'm not the only person up at 2 a.m. wondering whether the wood chipper guy ever got paroled. You make the work more fun and the stories more compelling.